MEMORY WORK

Davis W. Houck, Series Editor

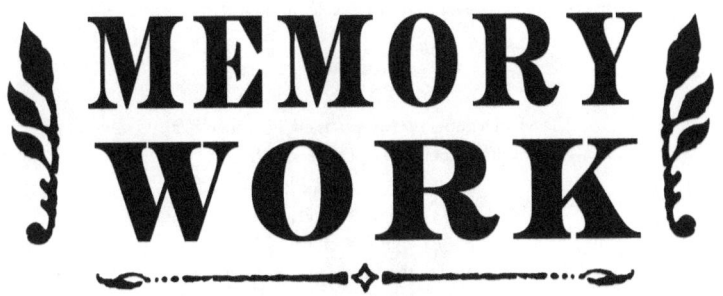

MEMORY WORK

White Ignorance and Black Resistance in Popular Magazines, 1900–1910

MARY E. TRIECE

University Press of Mississippi / Jackson

The University Press of Mississippi is the scholarly publishing agency of the Mississippi Institutions of Higher Learning: Alcorn State University, Delta State University, Jackson State University, Mississippi State University, Mississippi University for Women, Mississippi Valley State University, University of Mississippi, and University of Southern Mississippi.

www.upress.state.ms.us

The University Press of Mississippi is a member of the Association of University Presses.

Copyright © 2024 by University Press of Mississippi
All rights reserved
Manufactured in the United States of America
∞

Library of Congress Cataloging-in-Publication Data

Names: Triece, Mary Eleanor, 1967– author.
Title: Memory work : white ignorance and Black resistance in popular magazines, 1900–1910 / Mary E. Triece.
Other titles: Race, rhetoric, and media series.
Description: Jackson : University Press of Mississippi, [2024] | Series: Race, rhetoric, and media series | Includes bibliographical references and index.
Identifiers: LCCN 2024034596 (print) | LCCN 2024034597 (ebook) | ISBN 9781496854155 (hardback) | ISBN 9781496854162 (trade paperback) | ISBN 9781496854179 (epub) | ISBN 9781496854186 (epub) | ISBN 9781496854193 (pdf) | ISBN 9781496854209 (pdf)
Subjects: LCSH: Mass media and race relations—United States—History. | Mass media and minorities—United States. | American periodicals. | African American periodicals. | African Americans—Periodicals. | African Americans and mass media—United States. | Racism—United States—History. | Racism in the press—United States—History. | United States—Race relations.
Classification: LCC P94.5.A372 U577 2024 (print) | LCC P94.5.A372 (ebook) | DDC 302.23/2408996073—dc23/eng/20240827
LC record available at https://lccn.loc.gov/2024034596
LC ebook record available at https://lccn.loc.gov/2024034597

British Library Cataloging-in-Publication Data available

CONTENTS

3   **INTRODUCTION.** Communication, Race, and Popular Magazines

13   **CHAPTER 1.** Popular Magazines, Race, and the Construction of Cultural Knowledge

40   **CHAPTER 2.** Memory Work and White Violence

66   **CHAPTER 3.** Memory Work and a Cult of White Purity

88   **CHAPTER 4.** Countermemory Work: Reconsidering Black History and White Racism

124 **CHAPTER 5.** Countermemory Work and Narrative Inversion

147 **CONCLUSION.** Persistent White Ignorance and the Optimism of Resistant Cultural Memory

175 **ACKNOWLEDGMENTS**

177 **NOTES**

187 **REFERENCES**

215 **INDEX**

MEMORY WORK

INTRODUCTION

Communication, Race, and Popular Magazines

> History . . . does not refer merely, or even principally, to the past. On the contrary, the great force of history comes from the fact that we carry it within us, are unconsciously controlled by it in many ways, and history is literally present in all we do.
> —James Baldwin, quoted in Grossman (2016)

In August 2019, sixty-four years after the brutal murder of Black teenager Emmett Till, John Whitten, a white former prosecutor in Sumner, Mississippi, framed the Till murder this way: "Fella who came down here and got into trouble, overstepped his bounds to a degree some folks thought, and they cured him of his problems." Regarding local efforts to commemorate Till, Whitten asserted, "Every day, somebody's dragging up the race card. Somebody's saying we have racial disparity here. If nobody would stir that damn pile of stuff up, it wouldn't stink" ("'Why Don't Y'all Let That Die?,'" 2019).

Whitten's comments are appalling for a number of reasons, not least of which is the overt racism in his notion that Black people like Emmett Till occupy an inferior position, that they have a white-designated place or "bounds" they dare not "overstep," and that infringing on white spaces is deserving of white terrorism inflicted on the Black body.[1] But there is also something unsettling in Whitten's frustration with efforts to recall, remember, witness, and testify through commemoration to Emmett Till's life and senseless murder. Somehow, for Whitten and doubtless many other white people, if we just didn't continue to remember (to "stir that damn pile of stuff up"), it would go away. Or more to the point, white people would not have to confront the ways their present-day privilege is threaded to the US history of white terrorism against Black people. Whitten's comment is a form of "whitesplaining," a response on the part of some white people that Black people are being too emotional, too controversial, or pulling the race card when they attempt to call out race or, in the case of Till, remember a history of white violence against Black people (Blake, 2019).

In more academic terms, whitesplaining is an epistemological device, a way to confront and form an interpretation of the world and to communicate that view by exercising "willful white ignorance" (Alcoff, 2007; Medina, 2011; Mills, 1997; Pohlhaus, 2012). Willful white ignorance is a willing misinterpretation (Mills, 1997, p. 18), the "active use of faulty epistemic resources" (Pohlhaus, 2012, p. 730). The present-day phrase "All Lives Matter," evoked by some white people as a response to "Black Lives Matter," embodies a willful white ignorance: it is a statement conveying a refusal to acknowledge the relevance of history and the persistence of systemic racism (as borne out repeatedly in evidence-based research) that impact the lives of Black Americans every day and that have prompted Black people to assert that their lives matter.

The epistemological frame of willful white ignorance gains traction in discourses that employ "memory work," the communicative processes—the narratives, tropes, and images—that suggest what a culture should remember and forget. Gillis (1994) reminds us that memories are not fixed or objective, nor are they accurate reflections of past events; rather, they are "selective, inscriptive rather than descriptive, [and] serve interests and ideological positions" (p. 4). Importantly, memories create and maintain subject positions and identities and, by extension, power differentials. We see memory work in public discussions about pressing social issues, in public commemorations and monuments, in museum displays, and in debates over school curricula. Unlike history, which is understood as fixed and static, cultural memory is rhetorical, meaning it is contested, constitutive of identities, and publicly debated in media outlets (K. R. Phillips, 2004). Ongoing discussions of the "race question" in the early 1900s were, at heart, about remembering/forgetting slavery and the continued role of white terrorist violence in sustaining the nation's economy and shaping race and gender relations.

Memory Work explores the social constructions of memory advanced in popular magazine discussions of the "race question" or what the white press sometimes called the "race problem." Popular debates—whether appearing in early 1900s magazines or on twenty-first-century social media sites—shape a culture's collective knowledge of what counts as true, important, or worthy of attention. The following chapters call attention to the intimate connection between public communication and how we as individuals and as a culture come to know, as well as how a culture decides what "counts" as either knowledge worth remembering or a "pile of stuff" that shouldn't be "stirred up."

In 1892, the African American philosopher Anna Julia Cooper wrote eloquently about a chief problem facing the United States: "The colored man's inheritance and apportionment is still the sombre crux, the perplexing *cul de sac* of the nation,—the dumb skeleton in the closet provoking ceaseless harangues, indeed, but little understood and seldom consulted" (1892/1988, p. i). Cooper entered the larger national debate over the "race question," calling to light the absence—and the acumen—of Black women's voices within this ongoing discussion. "The 'other side,'" she pointed out, "has not been represented by one who 'lives there.' And not many can more sensibly realize and more accurately tell the weight and the fret of the 'long dull pain' than the open-eyed but hitherto voiceless Black Woman of America" (p. ii). Predating her contemporary W. E. B. Du Bois, whose book *The Souls of Black Folk* likewise considered the dimensions of racism in America, Cooper—and many other African American women—shaped the contours of the race debate by insisting on their own visibility.

Journalists, academics, scientists, and religious leaders—both Black and white—fervently debated what was termed the "race question" in the years following Reconstruction as freed Black men and women were attaining education, starting businesses, settling communities, and moving northward. Popular magazines provided a platform for circulating these discussions and shaping the larger social imaginary. In an article in *The Outlook*, the daughter of a former slaveholder expressed alarm over the "dangers of political life" that come from Black enfranchisement and the lack of moral and mental development of Black people (Hammond, 1903, p. 14). An article in *The Independent* was likewise infused with anxiety as the writer lamented the "total depravity" of Black women who were "lacking in virtue." The author wrote with alarm that Black women were the "greatest menace possible to the moral life of any community . . . they are . . . the chief instruments of the degradation of the men of their own race" ("Experiences of the Race Problem," 1904, p. 593). Indeed, she concluded, "I cannot imagine such a creation as a virtuous black woman."

A vast difference in perceptions of Black people and the Black experience in America appears when we turn to writings on racial justice in Black-owned and -edited magazines such as *The Colored American Magazine* and *The Voice of the Negro*. Black writers often turned the race debate on its head, reclassifying the so-called "problem" as a white one. Writing in *The Voice of the Negro*, Sylvanie Francoz Williams (1904) directly referenced and responded to *The Independent* article noted above. Her reaction was "righteous indignation," and she wrote, "I am sorry for one whose version of purity is so limited" (p. 299). She continued by implicitly referring to the often-hidden issue of white men's rape of Black women: "Colored women . . . are trying to lift their race away from temptation that allures them through immorality of the superior race" (p. 299). Furthermore, she noted that Black women are "doing more to preserve the purity of white people than any laws against miscegenation." Prominent Black club woman and activist Mary Church Terrell similarly turned the tables on the white racist narrative of Black women's sexuality, writing in the March 1905 issue of *The Voice of the Negro*, "no one who has studied the conditions in the South as they exist today can doubt that the average white man dwells in a state of mental and moral darkness" (1905, p. 182).

Taking up the call of the rhetorical scholar Lisa A. Flores (2016) to recognize the imperative of race in communication studies, *Memory Work* explores early 1900s popular magazines as spaces that engaged the dynamics of race, gender, and power through *memory work*, the rhetorical processes used to remember, forget, and strategically frame America's racist past. How did white and Black magazines—often in dialogue with one another over issues of race—differently engage memory work to either reinforce or upend white supremacy in a post-Reconstruction context of both Black advancement and white backlash?

The exercise of willful white ignorance—seen in silences and strategic narrative gaps—shapes how a culture remembers its violent, racist past (see Alcoff, 2007; Medina, 2011; Mills, 1997; Pohlhaus, 2012). Countermemories work in opposition through strategies that bring to light, bear witness, and call for racial justice. In the early 1900s, white-controlled magazines carried stories of southern nostalgia, union reconciliation, and white purity that relied on willful white ignorance to mis-remember past experiences of suffering by way of silence or by severing violent histories from present-day policies and worldviews. In Black magazines, women writers leveraged countermemory to document, and thus bring into focus, Black women's accomplishments and to invert popular white narratives that obscured Black women's experiences of sexual exploitation during slavery.

The following chapters suggest the insights that emerge through interdisciplinary efforts bridging rhetorical criticism, epistemology, and Black Feminist studies. Studies of race and rhetoric may fruitfully draw on concepts from Black feminism and philosophy to shed light on the ways understandings of Blackness and whiteness become seamless parts of the social imaginary and, in turn, how Black writers seek to both rupture and reimagine what counts as cultural memory. Studying magazines, with their in-depth coverage, expanded editorials and essays, and popular fiction, sheds light on the relationship between public discussion, such as what appears in media outlets, and cultural knowledge about a common past. Whether in early 1900s magazines or twenty-first-century media platforms like X (formerly known as Twitter), cultural content—in the forms of entertainment and discussion of social issues—shapes bodies of knowledge. And the lived experience of writers and content creators plays an incisive role. Then as now, Black writers, specifically Black women, marshal new cultural resources—tropes, narratives, and imagery directed at making sense of the world—for shaping and resetting public understandings of race and gender.[2] Then as now, this push for recalibration comes in the wake of a massive contradiction between lived experiences and the prevailing framings and narratives of Black Americans proffered by white journalists, academics, politicians, and religious leaders.[3] And then as now, Black writers struggle against an "epistemology of ignorance," a willful refusal to know, what the Black philosopher Charles Mills (1997) calls "an agreement [on the part of white people] to misinterpret the world" (p. 18).

The time period of this book's rhetorical analyses—1900–1910—holds material and rhetorical significance. Almost twenty years after Reconstruction and the passage of the Thirteenth, Fourteenth, and Fifteenth Amendments, white America had disenfranchised Black males (having never franchised Black females), imposed segregation through Jim Crow policies, and carried out physical violence and terrorism against Black people and their communities.[4] Lynching reached a peak in 1892, and four years later the US Supreme Court legalized the "separate but equal" doctrine in *Plessy v. Ferguson*. The popular press—both magazines and newspapers—became a locus of public discussions over Black education, employment, threats to white economic and political control, and of course, the widespread practice of lynching. In the 1890s, narratives perpetuating the myth of Black bestiality, rape, and white purity "reveal an alarmingly vituperative strain of racism, a monstrous incarnation of proslavery thought" (Hodes, 1997, p. 177).

In this context, magazines played an important cultural role in the engagement of contested issues around race and white violence. Popular periodicals served as "intertextual networks," connecting Black and white readers, writers, and their viewpoints. Particularly in the first few decades of the twentieth century, Black literary and periodical writing emerged from "Jim Crow networks" and prompted readers and writers alike to participate in the cultural negotiation of and resistance to popularized white racist narratives (Dahn, 2021). With extended space for lengthy discussion and an array of both fiction and nonfiction, and, as Dahn notes, "affordances of proliferation, ... connectivity, and interactivity," magazines created public spaces for exercising memory work and engaging the dynamics of race and gender in a historical moment of heightened racial tensions, Black advancement, and increasing white violence (p. 166).

Both white- and Black-controlled magazines deemed the "race question" a pressing social issue facing the nation. In 1903, editors of the popular magazine *The Outlook* described the "Race Problem" as "one of the two most important National problems which the people of the United States have to meet and solve" ("Editor's Note," 1903).[5] In this and other white-owned and self-identified socially conscious magazines like *The Arena*, *The Independent*, and *McClure's*, writers took on issues of race and gender through efforts to shape public memory of slavery in ways that assuaged white guilt and anxiety.

Black-owned magazines like *The Colored American Magazine* and *The Voice of the Negro* joined the swell of early 1900s magazine production and can arguably be said to fall into the wider "period of Black intellectual Reconstruction" in the first two decades of the 1900s (Gates, 1988b, p. 131). Black writers identified the "problem of the color line" (Du Bois, 1903/1982, p. 54) or race question as the definitive issue facing the nation or, as *The Voice of the Negro* contributor Kelly Miller noted, the "disturbing element in American politics from the founding of the Constitution to the present hour" that "will persist as a political factor" (1904, p. 18). As part of the burgeoning literary endeavors of Black women, magazines offered a space for these writers to assert countermemories that recalled their experiences of both suffering and resilience.

Chapter 1 introduces concepts from philosophy and Black Feminism that contribute to understandings of the rhetorical influence of memory work. This chapter also establishes the cultural role magazines played in the early 1900s. Chapters 2 and 3 examine articles in *The Arena, The Independent, McClure's,* and *The Outlook* that recalled slavery and the Civil War and discussed lynching—issues that fell within what writers called the "race question." Chapter 2 looks at the ways writers used memory work as a way to assuage white guilt and address white anxiety in the early 1900s context of Black economic growth and advancement. First, through leveling, contributors drew on "Lost Cause" ideology to argue there were good and bad people on both sides of the Civil War. Next, writers tapped a fictive white past to suggest that lynchings were aberrations as opposed to contemporary manifestations of a long history of white violence against Black bodies. And finally, white magazines used "Black abstraction" to erase historical subjectivity in articles on Black men and women. Chapter 3 looks more pointedly at white writers' portrayals of Black and white women and the ways they drew on a cult of white purity as a way to excise memories of the systematic white sexual assault against Black women and girls in recollections of America's past.

Chapters 4 and 5 turn to Black women's contributions in *The Colored American Magazine* and *The Voice of the Negro* for the ways they used countermemory work to set the record straight, as it were, when it came to how magazine readers were encouraged to view slavery and white violence. Black women writers exercised a "liberation historiography" to intervene in and invert widely accepted narratives of America's past (Ernest, 2002, p. 415). They used documentation (chapter 4) to reconstitute the public image of Black women and to rewrite histories that had omitted their roles and accomplishments. And writers engaged a historical "haunting" (chapter 5) to call to light the culturally repressed memory of white male violence against Black women and girls. The observations provided in the conclusion are twofold, exploring the uses of both memory and countermemory work in the twenty-first century. Political debates over how history is taught, the alarm around academic and corporate efforts to include diversity, equity, and inclusion (DEI), and nostalgic efforts to bring back a fictive past (as in "Make America Great Again") tap a willful ignorance that operates rhetorically to expunge histories of white violence and thus render Black trauma and suffering unimaginable. On a more optimistic note, digital media have opened spaces for "black critical memory" (Reyes, 2010) to push back, to reset cultural narratives, and to bring to the fore the relevance of American histories of racist violence.

The rhetorical framings of race and racism in Black and white popular magazines were not static or monolithic. White-controlled periodicals like *McClure's* and *The Independent* published articles supporting the ideas of scientific racism. However, some white magazines, like *The Independent*, *The Arena*, and *The Outlook*, featured Black writers such as Ida B. Wells, Booker T. Washington, Margaret Murray Washington (wife of Booker T. Washington), and W. E. B. Du Bois, pointing to a willingness to provide space for Black voices. The views expressed by African American writers in Black magazines were those of a literate and educated cadre of activists, those who saw their mission as "uplifting the race" (Gaines, 1996). And importantly, Black writers shifted narrative responses to the race question and to white violence as the context changed over the decades (Hill, 2016). Further, it is essential to note that Black writers throughout history have gone beyond reaction or response to white discourses. They have created identities, spaces, and narratives in their own right that served numerous ends (Dahn, 2021; Fagan, 2016). A comparison of widely circulating writings on the race question undercovers which rhetorical strategies were employed to differently remember the past, how American history becomes sanitized and severed from white terrorism, and looking to the future, how we may differently conceptualize that past so that we may be able to fruitfully and truthfully participate in present-day debates over race and racism.

CHAPTER 1

Popular Magazines, Race, and the Construction of Cultural Knowledge

Bell hooks (1984) explains of Black women, "we looked both from the outside in and from the inside out.... This sense of wholeness, impressed upon our consciousness by the structure of our daily lives, provided us an oppositional world view" (p. ii). Hooks is describing Black women's "outsider within" standpoint, a social location shaped by the experience of living within but also marginalized by a white world, a daily reality that may push a critical view of power disparities to the fore. Standpoint, or one's locatedness in the social world, shapes worldview and, in turn, the rhetorical strategies one may utilize to describe or frame an array of social issues. This chapter sets the stage for the following magazine analyses by elaborating on the relevance of standpoint to the study of memory work and magazine writings of the early 1900s.

Standpoint and Communication Studies

Standpoint theory suggests that knowing is situated and shaped by one's social position vis-à-vis a host of social relations, structures, and power dynamics (Alcoff, 2006, 2007; Collins, 1986; Harding, 1993;

Hartsock, 1983). One's location within various hierarchies of power shapes how one views the world, remembers the past, and envisions the future. Because knowers are situated, their understandings and worldviews are partial. A "knower's social position" draws "attention to particular aspects of the world" and may either enable or "set limits on what one can know" (Pohlhaus, 2012, p. 715; see also Harding, 1993). In other words, social position directs what parts of the world stand out to us as relevant and/or meaningful (Dotson, 2014, p. 120; Pohlhaus, 2012). People in positions of power occupy "critically unexamined" spaces of privilege that are "more limiting," have an interest in maintaining the status quo, are less likely to "generate the most critical questions about received belief," and remain resistant to fomenting critical thought around economic, political, and cultural arrangements (Harding, 1993, pp. 54, 55). Whether a magazine writer, social advocate, or politician, one's position within the matrix of power disparities (e.g., as a Black female reformer or as a white male academic) shapes what one knows and how one views and describes the world.

Knowledge is perspectival, but not all perspectives are equally valid—that is, not all knowers stand on equal epistemological footing. The perspectives derived through firsthand experience with oppression lend greater critical insight or "epistemic advantage" (Alcoff, 2006, p. 96) regarding social relations and systems that perpetuate oppression. A "reality gap" or space between prevailing, widely accepted ideologies and the physical experiences of day-to-day existence often creates paradoxes that provide an opening for social critique and change, as in the Black feminist's "outsider within" (Collins, 1986).[1] The insights of African American mill worker Annie Adams illustrate the way experiences of discrimination create fertile ground for developing insight on power or a "more revealing" understanding of social relations (Bar On, 1993, p. 83). Adams explained:

> When I first went into the mill we had segregated water fountains. . . . Same thing about the toilets. I had to clean the toilets for the inspection room and then, when I got ready to go to the

bathroom, I had to go all the way to the bottom of the stairs to the cellar. So I asked my boss man, "what's the difference? If I can go in there and clean them toilets, why can't I use them?" Finally, I started to use that toilet. I decided I wasn't going to walk a mile to go to the bathroom. (quoted in Collins, 1991, p. 28)

Adams's physical practice of cleaning the bathroom gave rise to contradiction that arose from the presence of the Black body in a space marked white. The experience of being both denied and allowed created an "aha" moment for Adams and gave rise to a critical perspective on her position as a Black woman. Such moments—in conjunction with a host of communication processes from conversations and consciousness-raising groups to speeches, songs, websites, and publications such as magazines and newspapers—raise awareness, confirm one's perspectives, or challenge one to think in a more critical manner. Adams's experience prompted her to "recalibrate" how she understood her job responsibilities and how she resisted workplace discrimination.

Oppressed people have less of a vested interest in maintaining ignorance or remaining silent; indeed, they hold a stake in encouraging vigorous critique and debate over systems of oppression and patterns of discrimination. Black women's experiences along the lines of race, sex, and oftentimes class highlight the intersectionality of oppressions—the ways they overlap and intertwine—and situate them to criticize how race is gendered male and woman is rendered white, in both cases erasing the knowledge generated by and from the position of Black women. Adopting a critical view of the world is not automatic but rather a politicized process, developed out of a combination of interpersonal conversations, exposure to the writings and speeches of other justice advocates, and not least of all, one's daily experiences with deprivation and discrimination.

Epistemic oppression results when the worldviews of those in power hold greater sway "in 'structuring' our *understandings* of the social world" (Fricker, 1999, p. 191) and when these widely accepted views prevent or exclude others from contributing to knowledge production (Dotson, 2014). The process of interpretation—and deciding which interpretation will "stick" or hold as "true"—is imbued with power and, often, exclusion. Powerful people are situated such that their experiences "count more in the development and circulation of epistemic resources" (Pohlhaus, 2012, p. 718) and lead to epistemic exclusion, or an "unwarranted infringement on the epistemic agency of knowers" (Dotson, 2014, p. 115). For Black women, exclusion comes in the form of a paradoxical position called "Jane Crow" wherein they are both hypervisible, an object of scrutiny and surveillance, and invisible, or routinely omitted or disappeared in broader cultural narratives about gender and race (Dotson, 2017, p. 417). Dominant ways of knowing—conveyed through culturally shared narratives, attitudes, and beliefs—relegate Black women to a "negative, socio-epistemic space," submerging their experiences and denying them plausibility as a knower (p. 418).

The cultural maintenance of hierarchy and exclusion often comes through a "willful ignorance," a position of *unknowing* that is not innocent or unintentional, but rather is a "*substantive* epistemic practice in itself" (Alcoff, 2007, p. 39) that results in a "systematic and coordinated misinterpretation of the world" (Pohlhaus, 2012, p. 731).[2] Willful ignorance is a form of "active social production," a "constant cultural pressure to accept" irrational or spurious beliefs in the name of preserving white dominance and justifying white violence (Bailey, 2007, pp. 77, 80). The production of ignorance is systematic, institutionalized, and generational and sits at the "intersection between cognitive norms, structural privilege, and situated identities" (Alcoff, 2007, p. 39). Through a host of discourses from popular television, film, music, periodicals, and literature to political and religious texts and speeches, a culture creates a "collective" social understanding or "social imaginary," which "provides the representational background against which people tend to share their thoughts and listen to each other in a culture" (Medina, 2011, p. 33). Dominant—that is, widely available and long-standing—narratives, images, and collective memories contribute to a social imaginary that is "resilient" or difficult to alter/challenge (Dotson, 2014).

A culture's social imaginary is deeply entrenched, but not fixed or static. Prevailing images and narratives evolve through processes of hegemonic struggle, whereby competing groups vie to get their interpretations accepted as the dominant ones. Consider how the myth of the violent Black male has resonated but also been challenged over the past one hundred-plus years. A staple in early 1900s popular, academic, and political discourses, the rape myth posited a dangerous Black male brute who preyed on virtuous white women. The narrative reinforced white male control over white women's and Black men and women's sexuality and functioned to misremember the dynamics of race and gender violence during and after slavery, a time period of white sexual assault on Black women and girls so widespread it "compelled thousands of women to leave the South, or to urge their daughters to do so" (Giddings, 1985, p. 86). The rape myth continued to provide a subtext for the brutal murder of Emmett Till in 1955 and haunted the racist media frenzy surrounding the conviction of the Central Park Five in 1985. In that case, five young men of color were eventually exonerated after spending years in prison for a rape they did not commit. Their wrongful convictions have since sparked a national debate that has raised awareness of racial profiling and discrimination in the legal system, illustrating how culturally shared long-standing myths may be dispelled through rhetorical efforts on the part of racial justice advocates.

At key historical moments, whiteness serves as the "invisible hand of official public memory" (Reyes, 2010, p. 2). During a time period that saw expanding education and wealth for many Black families and communities, early 1900s white magazine writers exercised willful ignorance to rhetorically misremember a racist past and, in turn, obscure the systemic dimensions of racism that thread past and present-day policies and structures. Likewise, twenty-first-century debates over how to teach American history—and the conservative scapegoating of critical race theory—tap a willful white ignorance as backlash during a period that witnessed the first Black American president and increasingly vocal and physically visible calls for racial justice, evidenced in the more than ten thousand protests—at times numbering in the tens of thousands—in cities across America between May and August 2020 ("Demonstrations and Political Violence," 2023).

In contrast, Black-controlled magazines provided spaces for Black women writers to "recalibrate" resources so that they more clearly embody their experiences of oppression. Pohlhaus (2012) explains, "when there is a tension between the world of experience and the resources that we use to make sense of our experiences..., when the proper language for describing an experience appears to be missing, or when our current concepts fail to track recurring patterns, we recalibrate our epistemic resources and/or create new ones until the tension between our resources and the experienced world is alleviated" (p. 719). Black women who wrote for *The Colored American Magazine* and *The Voice of the Negro* engaged memory work to "voice against" white silences by demanding visibility in recollections of slavery and in struggles for racial justice.

Popular Magazines and Cultural Understandings of Race and Gender

Much like present-day social media platforms like Facebook, X (formerly known as Twitter), and Reddit, early twentieth-century magazines provided a public space to debate—and, in some cases, dialogue about—the status of race and gender in America. Understanding popular magazines as "dialogic" points to the roles they played in cultural meaning-making as "key sites where readers and writers worked toward bottom-up sociopolitical changes" (Dahn, 2021, p. 3). Further, cultural artifacts—whether magazines, books, film, or television—sit in a dynamic relationship to the broader socioeconomic and political contexts in which they circulate. Popular magazines embodied and reflected and, in turn, shaped community views, local and national political debates, and perhaps to a lesser degree public policy. The first decade of the twentieth century—marked by expanding Jim Crow policies, disenfranchisement of Black men, and heightened white violence—provides a window into the ways magazines, growing in both popularity and influence, debated what was termed the "race question" through *the cultural construction of memory*. Even as newspapers were providing information to American homes on a daily/weekly basis, magazines played a unique role as a space to debate social issues. First, the magazine format featured an array of contributions, from editorials and essays to monthly columns and serialized fiction, that both energized and responded to broader cultural debates over race equality, Black male enfranchisement, and interracial intimacy. Magazines had a "something for everyone" quality: they provided a "dynamic environment, in which a range of generic contents and contributing readers engaged in dialogue" (Aronson, 2000, p. 197). Further, Aronson notes that magazines acted as public forums providing spaces for debate and discussion "through which new language, new images, new stories can . . . emerge," even as hegemonic cultural constructs were reinforced. Black-controlled magazines such as *The Voice of the Negro* interacted textually with white-controlled magazines like *The Independent*, rebuking racist content and countering with narratives of racial uplift. Recurring columns, essays, and serialized fiction shaped readers' identities and views on an array of issues, thus establishing a community of readers (Okker, 2003). And finally, for both Black and white women, magazine writing provided an "opportunity to break through a gender-imposed silence in the public sphere" (Aronson, 2002, p. 12).

Magazine Expansion in the Early 1900s

It would be challenging, and beyond the scope of this project, to ascertain the precise impact the periodicals studied here had on their readers. On the whole, their circulation was limited, particularly in the case of Black periodicals, which often suffered from lack of funding, hostility from the white community, and an unwillingness of white companies to purchase advertising (Bullock, 1981, p. 70). Interestingly, some editors renounced high circulation as indicative of appealing to the lowest common denominator, reflective of lower quality and literary standards. *The Independent*'s editor stated in 1895, "The fit audience in an educated country like ours is not few, but it is not yet unlimited"; the audience "worth addressing" is comprised of the "thinking people" (quoted in T. Peterson, 1964, p. 402).

The magazines studied here merit attention for at least two reasons. First, popular periodicals participated in a larger cultural production of discourses on race that included the writings and speeches of academics, politicians, journalists, and fiction and nonfiction authors (see Carey, 1992). Magazines provided spaces where the dynamics of race, gender, power, and resistance could play out, creating a social community for readers, writers, and editors (see Dahn, 2021) while variously drawing upon or subverting culturally constructed memories of race relations in America. This matrix of discourses, if you will, becomes apparent in magazines that carried the writings of academics and politicians, published forums and "conversations" on race from multiple viewpoints, and printed articles that directly responded to those of fellow writers in other magazines.

Secondly, Black magazines and newspapers provided an essential—often the only—outlet for Black writers and racial justice advocates and, at times, the only place where Black families could find information untouched by white racist frames. The readers of Black magazines included secondary readers—people who picked up the magazine while visiting friends or family—as well as college-educated African Americans and members of the "artisan" class, which enveloped a host of factory workers, miners, seamstresses, and domestic workers (Carby, 1987, p. 127). Black writers and editors clearly expressed their optimism that a vibrant Black press would enlighten and motivate their communities, with W. E. B.

Du Bois stating eloquently and unequivocally that he published *The Horizon: A Journal of the Color Line* "not as a matter of business but as a matter of spiritual life and death" (quoted in Bullock, 1981, p. 65; see also "Editorial and Publishers' Announcements," 1900; "Editorials," 1904; Wells, 1893). In her 1893 article appearing in the *A.M.E. Zion Church Quarterly*, the anti-lynching crusader Ida B. Wells proclaimed to her fellow journalists, the "time has come as never before that the wielders of the pen belonging to the race which is so tortured and outraged, should take serious thought and purposeful action.... Blood, tears and groans of hundreds of the murdered *cry to you for redress;* the lamentations, distress and want, of numberless widows and orphans appeal to you to do the only thing which can be done—and which is the first step toward revolution of every kind—the creation of a healthy public sentiment" (1893, p. 89, emphasis mine). For Black women, specifically, magazine writing figured into their burgeoning literary movement of the late nineteenth and early twentieth centuries.

In the late 1800s–early 1900s, magazines became America's public podium (Sumner, 2010). During this period, magazines experienced a "spectacular enlargement and increase in effectiveness" (Mott, 1957, p. 2). Hand in glove with developments in printing and transportation, the evolution of corporate capitalism, and a new consumer culture, magazines emerged as a predominant form of entertainment and information dissemination at the turn of the twentieth century (Ohmann, 1996, p. 24; Mott, 1957; Pendergast, 2000; Tebbel & Zuckerman, 1991). By the last decade of the nineteenth century, there were nearly ten thousand different magazines, many with circulation numbers in the hundreds of thousands (Okker, 2003, p. 11; Tebbel & Zuckerman, 1991, p. 58). The owners of magazines like *McClure's* and *Munsey's* developed a new formula whereby they made their magazines affordable to the middle classes—ten cents per issue—and relied primarily on advertising for income (Ohmann, 1996, p. 25). The ten cent monthlies widened magazine readership and became ground zero for the development of a consuming public. By 1900, half-tone technology that facilitated the printing of photographs in periodicals made illustrated magazines more affordable, an important advancement for Black periodicals that could now reach readers who may not have been textually literate (Zackodnik, 2015, p. 148).

Journalistic Norms and Practices

Magazines like *The Arena*, *The Independent*, *McClure's*, and *The Outlook* relied on the journalistic ethic of objectivity, the notion that news writers could transcend the peculiarities and contingencies of place, time, and body and write from the "view from nowhere." Influenced by the Enlightenment belief in scientific advancement through the uncovering and analysis of facts, news outlets situated themselves as the "chronicler of the important events of the day, relying on a (putatively) neutral and experientially grounded method for gathering and reporting on those events" (Meyers, 2020, p. 183). Abiding by the practice of objectivity, journalists believed social issues could be grasped with clarity through reason, application of facts, and verification on the part of writers capable of transcending bias (Schudson, 1978). The stance of objectivity, along with professionalization, played a role in expanding periodicals' readership and enhancing their credibility in the early twentieth century (Meyers, 2020, pp. 183–185). In this vein, reform-oriented white journalists published essays on corporate greed, political graft, industrial exploitation, and race-related issues like enfranchisement and lynching, distancing themselves from moralizing and, instead, viewing their own work as based on fact and rooted in a profession with routines and norms (Barnard, 2018, p. 28; Schudson, 1978, p. 87). Muckrakers like Ida Tarbell and Lincoln Steffens of *McClure's* "believed that by researching fraud and corruption, descriptively assembling the facts, and intelligently and critically analyzing the issues to offer solutions," they would identify "shared concerns" and create fertile ground for discussions of public welfare (Fordham, 2016, p. 427).

Scholars like Meyers (2020), Schudson (2003), and Wallace (2019) have shown the stance of objectivity to be a myth, what Tuchman (1972) called a "strategic ritual." Barnard (2018) describes the "journalistic value of objectivity" as a "powerful smokescreen that has been most successful at masking the latent political ideologies of journalistic acts and accounts" (p. 42). In the case of white writers covering issues about race, objectivity veiled white racial frames (Feagin, 2020) that relied on deeply entrenched stereotypes of Black men and women. These writers' position as (largely) white men writing for white readers shaped what stories were deemed newsworthy and how they would be covered. Popular early 1900s magazines such as *The Atlantic Monthly, The Century, Harper's Magazine,* and *North American Review* used cartoons, articles, fiction, and poetry to promote demeaning racist stereotypes of African American men and women throughout the first two decades of the 1900s (Logan, 1965). Black women were portrayed as hypersexual and Black men as untrustworthy (Logan, 1965, p. 250). Logan concludes the "magazines contributed not only to the fixing of stereotypes" but also the more widely embraced "Lost Cause" ideology of the time period (p. 254). Socially conscious weeklies/monthlies like *The Arena, The Outlook, The Independent,* and *McClure's*—whose combined circulation was well over 100,000—similarly invoked white nostalgia as they debated the race question in hundreds of articles published between 1892 and 1910. From the partial and limiting perspective of race privilege underwritten by racist cultural narratives, white editors and writers believed they "could be trusted to write objectively" about events with which they had no firsthand experience. Simultaneously, they believed Black writers "could not be depended upon to take an objective view of their own status" (Shapiro, 1970, p. 77).

News coverage is always necessarily subjective insofar as our cognitive, linguistic, and moral apparatuses for understanding events are socially constructed and historically situated, thus making standpoint—discussed earlier—an important consideration in studies of magazine writing. The concept of magazine frames exposes the fault lines in claims to objectivity and highlights the rhetorical elements in magazine coverage. Media frames rely on repetition, association, reinforcement, selection, and deflection to suggest a particular view of the world, one that is partial and incomplete, but may masquerade as truth (Entman, 1991, 1993; Gitlin, 1980). Journalism's doctrine of objectivity is itself a frame that prompts us to see the language of news reporting as a mirror on reality.

Black writers did not claim a stance of objectivity, but neither did they back down when asserting their views represented a truer version of race in America.[3] In their own words, Black magazine writers and editors situated their journalistic endeavors as key to racial uplift, with *The Colored American Magazine* editors proclaiming the magazine "aspires to develop and intensify the bonds of that racial brotherhood, which alone can enable a people, to assert their racial rights as men, and demand their privileges as citizens" ("Editorial and Publishers' Announcements," 1900, p. 60). Their journalistic practices may be seen as forerunners to what has been termed "participatory journalism," "alternative journalism," "native reporting," "radical embodied advocacy," and "engaged journalism" insofar as they viewed themselves as change agents not unlike those covering racial justice protests during the summer of 2020 (Harlow, 2022).[4]

Magazines as Public Forums

The decade from 1900 to 1910 is a significant time for exploring race debates. During this period, Black men and women established successful businesses and schools and created vibrant communities. In a backlash, white terrorism expanded to include hundreds of lynchings and collective white violence against Black communities such as those in Springfield, Ohio, East St. Louis, Missouri, and Tulsa, Oklahoma. Supreme Court decisions such as *Plessy v. Ferguson* (1896) and Jim Crow policies codified segregation and race hierarchy. More so than books or newspapers, magazines acted as public forums: they represented spaces for dialogue and discussion even as they filtered viewpoints through specific lenses (Roessner, 2011, p. 88). Noting the difficulty of "pinpoint[ing]" the "effects" of magazine discussions of race, Roessner makes a clear case for the role late 1800s magazines played in "reflecting, contesting, and perpetuating dominant racial ideologies" (p. 100).

Unlike newspapers, magazines provided space where "competing discourses played off each other, . . . provoked revision, rebuttal, continuation, and other forms of response" both within and between magazines (Aronson, 2002, p. 11). Still, to suggest that magazines "reflect" or "record" social life (Tebbel & Zuckerman, 1991, p. 73) or that they are "polyvocal" texts with an unlimited capacity for meaning-generation (Aronson, 2002, p. 11) overlooks the racialization of magazine publishing and the influence of willful white ignorance on widely embraced social frames that shaped popular magazine content. Although white-controlled magazines included the viewpoints of Black thinkers like Booker T. Washington and, on occasion, Ida B. Wells, overall what we see when viewing white-controlled magazine content on the race question is a savvy use of memory work through rhetorical referencing to "Lost Cause" and "civilization," which act to quell white anxieties and assuage white guilt. Looking at Black-controlled magazines alongside them calls attention to the ways magazines provided a space for public dialogue over issues of race rights as when Sylvanie Francoz Williams responded with outrage to the racist commentary on Black women in *The Independent*. We also see how Black-controlled magazines deployed memory work in resistant ways, rendering slavery salient and giving a name to Black women's experiences of trauma and assault while celebrating their roles in Black community survival.

The Black- and white-owned magazines engaged dialogically, publishing articles that at times responded to or addressed pieces in other magazines. For instance, when it came to discussions of racial hierarchy, civil rights organizations, or interracial relations (often referred to as "amalgamation"), articles in *The Voice of the Negro* did not hesitate to reference and in some cases take on articles in other popular magazines such as *The Independent, The Arena,* and *The Outlook* (Barber, 1906; Du Bois, 1905; F. G. Lewis, 1906; Miller, 1905; M. M. Washington, 1905). Writing in *The Voice of the Negro*, W. E. B. Du Bois (1905) and Jesse Max Barber (1906) excoriated articles in *The Outlook* for their racist portrayals of Black advancement and coverage of the Atlanta massacre, which killed or injured more than a hundred Black citizens on a September evening of white terrorism in Atlanta. Writers in both *The Voice of the Negro* and *The Colored American Magazine* took on *The Independent* writer who, in 1904, noted that she could not fathom that Black women could be "virtuous" (M. M. Washington, 1905; S. F. Williams, 1904). Writing in the white-owned muckraking magazine *McClure's*, the well-known racist author Thomas Nelson Page (1904c) referenced the "discussion that takes place in the periodical press and conventions relating to the progress of the colored race." Later, Page (1907) directly addressed an article by Carrie Clifford, an organizer of the Ohio Federation of Colored Women's Clubs, which *The Outlook* had published in 1906. Page (1907) derided Clifford's support of interracial marriage, noting the "great white race in its entirety and in its integrity means to preserve itself as a white race unadulterated and unmongrelized."

Reading both white- and Black-owned magazines across a span of a decade highlights the ways popular periodicals differently engaged in the race debate and at times engaged with each other. Since the publications of early Black newspapers in the early 1800s, Black editors and writers have expressed concern for the need for a public platform that would counter or disrupt the white racist narratives dominating widely circulating white periodicals (Wolseley, 1971). In the early nineteenth century, white publications demonstrated an awareness of the growing Black press (Detweiler, 1922, p. 60) and variously quoted from Black periodicals or redoubled efforts to enforce prevailing ideologies of white supremacy. At a time of suffrage agitation on the part of Black and white women and broader pushes for gender equality, popular magazines like *The Colored American Magazine* and *The Voice of the Negro* provided an outlet for Black women's writing, both nonfiction and fiction, contributing to an ever-growing body of Black women's writing and public speaking. By the early 1900s, it was not unusual for white magazines like *The Independent*, *The Outlook*, and *The Arena* to publish pieces by Margaret Murray Washington (wife of Booker T. Washington) and anti-lynching activist Ida B. Wells. Black writers were most certainly aware of how white writers portrayed them in popular magazines; and there is evidence to suggest that white readers were exposed to writings in Black-controlled magazines as they occasionally wrote letters to the editors of Black magazines. African American women speakers and writers such as Maria Stewart addressed their messages directly to fellow members of the Black community as well as indirectly to "overhearers" or "people that [they] wished to have listen but who are probably not paying attention" (Royster, 2000, p. 171). Pauline Hopkins targeted both Black and white readers with her novels, with the intent of raising the consciousness of a white audience (Matter-Seibel, 2003, p. 77). Upon publication of Hopkins's *Contending Forces* in 1900, the Colored Co-operative Publishing Company asserted, "The book will certainly create a sensation among a certain class of 'whites' at the South" (quoted in Matter-Seibel, 2003, p. 77).

Magazines and Reader Identity

Magazines, much like social media in the twenty-first century, shaped readers' identities and self-concepts (Brake et al., 2000). They were and remain a part of a "media culture" that "provides the materials out of which many people construct their sense of class, of ethnicity and race, of nationality, of sexuality, of 'us' and 'them'" (Kellner, 1995, p. 1). Magazine writers and editors of the early 1900s recognized their growing role in shaping "public opinion" (Ewen, 1996) and used the race question as an entrance into discussions of race and gender and wider cultural meanings attached to concepts of whiteness and Blackness.

White writers often relied on strategic forgetting to frame the race question in terms of white normativity. Whiteness, as an epistemic viewpoint, encourages an understanding of white as universal. Anything "not white" becomes marked as "other," deviant. Whiteness otherizes and simultaneously elevates itself above; white supremacy is part and parcel of whiteness (McClendon, 2004). Thus, ideologies of whiteness go hand in hand with economic and political oppression and violence. Popular white-controlled magazines played a key role in the making and remaking of whiteness and white supremacy in ways that rendered these concepts invisible and thus inscrutable. Through reliance on specific narratives, tropes, and rhetorical strategies discussed in the following chapters, white magazines created a space of "epistemic impossibility and unimaginability" (Medina, 2011, p. 33) for understanding Black Americans.

In early 1800s white periodicals, slave advertisements provided a primary means of funding and a vehicle for wide distribution of racist imagery that implicated white readers in the slave system by offering rewards for capture of enslaved humans. Through ad content, form, and placement, slave ads "scripted whiteness as individualized from blackness as type" (Zackodnik, 2015, p. 141). Popular magazines, both white- and Black-controlled, also figured into and drew upon larger cultural discourses of both race and gender—for instance, casting both white and Black men in roles of traditional masculinity (Pendergast, 2000). Importantly, white masculinity gained meaning vis-à-vis white depictions of Black men that relied on dualities—for example, child/beast, docile/dangerous—to caricature and control Black men.

African American writers and magazine editors frequently expressed concern over the role of the white-owned media in shaping and perpetuating racist public opinions that often acted as a rhetorical springboard for white violence against Black communities and businesses (see Adams, 1904; Burroughs, 1905; Clifford, 1907; P. Hopkins, 1903a; A. B. Jackson, 1901; Queen, 1906; Yates, 1907; Terrell, 1905; Todd, 1902b; F. B. Williams, 1906). Articles and editorials in *The Voice of the Negro* and *The Colored American Magazine* castigated the "medieval padlock on free speech" enforced by the "daily newspapers" ("Editorials," 1904, p. 36). In 1902, a writer in *The Colored American Magazine* bemoaned that, "If one believes the squibs constantly put in circulation by the press, the Negro is a thief, an adulterer, a murderer; is shiftless, lazy, and altogether a bad lot" ("Mrs. William Scott," 1902, p. 228). The writer further noted how these widely circulating misrepresentations, common in the South, begin to affect northerners' perceptions: "All these slogans of the clans the Northerner has heard, until wearied of the never-ending bickering he gravitates naturally towards the side of his own class, and the Negro has become the under dog in the racial fight" (p. 228). Writing in the July 1905 issue of *The Voice of the Negro*, Emma F. G. Merritt pointed to the hypocrisy of the white press, noting that "entire columns, sparkling with ridicule and contempt" focused on the bad deeds of Black people while the "cold-blooded, diabolical acts of the members of 'some of the most respectable white families in the community' are so minimized that dastardly fiends are frequently transformed into objects of charity" (1905, p. 468).

Black writers sought to reset, or recalibrate, prevailing notions of Blackness. Black "journalism was meant to educate, missionize, inspire and stir people to action" (Matter-Seibel, 2003, p. 80). In its inaugural issue in January 1904, editors of *The Voice of the Negro* noted the important role of their magazine in contributing to the race debate: "It will be our purpose to tell the truth through our columns, not offensively, either in language, spirit or time, but plainly for the sake of the truth and for the good of the public" ("Editorials," 1904, p. 34). W. E. B. Du Bois, who would go on to co-found the NAACP's widely circulating magazine, *The Crisis* (1910–present), emphasized the need for a Black magazine that would "interpret the news of the world [to Black readers] and inspire them toward definite ideals" (quoted in Bullock, 1981, p. 146). Magazines like *The Colored American Magazine* created "the boundaries of a black magazine-reading public" (Carby, 1987, p. 125) that spoke to a larger Black community and collective efforts for survival and growth. The figure of the African American New Woman (also called the New Negro Woman) featured in these magazines positioned Black women as central to community uplift.

Through serialized fiction, Black women writers told stories of racial passing and hidden race identities, thus casting the idea of fixed identity into doubt. Black magazines also seized on technological developments by using photographs and portraits such as those appearing in *The Colored American Magazine* to "wage a war of the image" that might "dismantle racist stereotypes" (Gallon, 2015, p. 14). In addition, Black magazines used images to "manage external and self-perceptions of 'the Negro'" (Zackodnik, 2015, p. 152). *The Colored American Magazine*'s cover portraits countered the demeaning narratives of Black women proffered by writers in *The Independent* by depicting the African American New Woman. Pauline Hopkins, co-editor of and contributor to *The Colored American Magazine*, put memory work to resistant ends through profiles and portraits that recast Black women's roles during slavery and into the twentieth century (Zackodnik, 2015, p. 152).

Magazines and Black Women's Writing

For African American women in particular, the late 1800s was a period of significant organizational and literary activity as they formed their own clubs (C. L. Peterson, 1995) and published a flurry of influential nonfiction and fiction books that addressed issues of race and sex, including Anna Julia Cooper's *A Voice from the South* (1892), Frances Ellen Watkins Harper's *Iola Leroy* (1892), and Pauline

Hopkins's *Contending Forces* (1900) and her three novels serialized in *The Colored American Magazine* between 1900 and 1903.[5]

Both newspapers and magazines engendered a women's literary tradition that provides a window into a rich history of Black women's fiction and nonfiction writings that have yet to be fully appreciated. Magazines like *The Colored American Magazine* and *The Voice of the Negro* served as a space to "subvert and redress the problem of women's silence in the public realm," a social wrong heightened by the double jeopardy of both racism and sexism so eloquently described by Anna Julia Cooper in the opening of this book (Aronson, 2002, p. 12). The fiction and nonfiction writings of Gertrude Dorsey Brown, Carrie Clifford, Pauline E. Hopkins, Addie Waites Hunton, Maybelle McAdoo, Emma F. G. Merritt, M. Cravatt Simpson, Albreta Moore Smith, Mary Church Terrell, Ruth D. Todd, Louise Burgess-Ware, Fannie Barrier Williams, Sylvanie Francoz Williams, and Josephine Silone Yates challenge the masculinist bent of W. E. B. Du Bois's "talented tenth" and demonstrate that Black women have been key to framing race attitudes for over a century. Their intersectional approach to race uplift provided a foundation for women who wrote in Black magazines like *The Liberator* in the 1860s. Women contributors to *The Liberator* addressed the "body politics facing women" as well as issues of "self-definition, protest politics, aesthetics, and education," all issues initially brought to the fore by early magazine writers like Pauline Hopkins and Albreta Moore Smith (see Tinson, 2017, p. 84). Chapters 4 and 5 call to light Black women's magazine writing within a broader context of magazine writing, exploring how they used countermemory to challenge popular white narratives that rendered them simultaneously hypervisible as sexual threat and invisible, a nonbeing.[6]

Cooper (2017) argues that shaping public opinion was a central project of early twentieth-century Black women writers such as Fannie Barrier Williams and Mary Church Terrell. For Terrell, according to Cooper, "dignified agitation took as its goal the shifting of public opinion by unapologetically calling attention to the violation of rights and the preponderance of wrongs" (p. 64). Josephine Silone Yates[7] (1907), a president of the National Association of Colored Women, viewed Black women as playing a crucial role in rhetorical efforts to reset the public narrative about race (see also A. M. Smith, 1902a, 1902b; Mossell, 1901; Routledge, 1902; Terrell, 1904b). Yates pointed out the "Negro . . . understands the Anglo-Saxon far better than the latter comprehends the Negro" because white people get their information about Black people from the "daily press" that depicts the "race in general as a degenerate type better left uncultivated" (p. 45). She continued, writing that Black women "show themselves a strong factor in the solution of this part of the problem" through their club work (p. 45).

Black-Controlled Magazines, 1900-1909

The Colored American Magazine and *The Voice of the Negro* were two of the most popular magazines of the early 1900s targeted to a Black readership (Bullock, 1981, p. 68), and both were situated within the larger growth in popularity of affordable monthly magazines.[8] *The Colored American Magazine*'s circulation was around seventeen thousand (Carby, 1987, p. 193) and *The Voice of the Negro* was about fifteen thousand (Gaines, 1996, p. 60). Both magazines relied on advertising dollars, sought subscriptions from readers, and were distributed by agents.[9] Although short-lived, they "lasted as long as did numerous magazines controlled by white" editors, and they laid a foundation for Black journalism into the twentieth century (Johnson & Johnson, 1977, p. 335). Their circulation numbers were impressive given these periodicals often had little in the way of financial resources and faced opposition from white communities. For instance, a Black reader in Greenwood, Mississippi, wrote to *The Voice of the Negro* saying white people in the community threatened their Black neighbors if they were seen reading the paper ("Monthly

Review," 1906, p. 466). Reading Black magazines, then, was viewed as a threat to white supremacy.

The Voice of the Negro, a "leading Black periodical in the United States" (Bullock, 1981, p. 118), ran from 1904 to 1907 with Jesse Max Barber and John Wesley Edward Bowen as co-editors. In 1906, Barber was a key voice condemning the Atlanta riots in which white residents violently assaulted Black residents, noting especially the white press's role in stoking white rage against the Black population in the city. With threats of white "retaliation" and a criminal trial for publicly articulating his views, Barber moved the publication from Atlanta to Chicago, again underscoring the extent to which white supremacists viewed published Black voices as a threat (Bullock, 1981, p. 123; Gaines, 1996, p. 65).

The Colored American Magazine, proving more financially stable with assistance from Booker T. Washington, circulated from 1900 to 1909. Hazel Carby (1987) describes it as a "pioneer of the contemporary Black magazine market" that reached a "significant proportion of the potential Black readership" (pp. 125, 126). The magazine sold for $1.50 a year, and its masthead indicated the breadth of subject matter covered in its pages: "An Illustrated Monthly, Devoted to Literature, Science, Music, Art, Religion, Facts, Fiction and Traditions of the Negro Race." Founded in Boston, *The Colored American Magazine* was run by the Colored Co-operative Publishing Company. In 1904, when it was unable to maintain solvency, Washington stepped in with financial assistance, but when he withdrew support in 1909, the magazine ended publication.

African American women figured prominently as editors and writers in both *The Colored American Magazine* and *The Voice of the Negro*. More well-known women include Pauline Hopkins, the "most prolific Black woman writer of her time" (Knight, 2007, p. 41), Mary Church Terrell, Josephine Silone Yates, and Fannie Barrier Williams. Numerous other women, including Gertrude Dorsey Brown, Addie Waites Hunton, Maybelle McAdoo, Emma F. G. Merritt, M. Cravatt

Simpson, Albreta Moore Smith, Ruth D. Todd, Louise Burgess-Ware, and Sylvanie Francoz Williams, had perhaps shorter, more obscure literary careers but were no less important in efforts to establish resistant memories.

Pauline Hopkins—who also wrote under the names Sarah A. Allen and J. Shirley Shadrach (Cordell, 2006)—held positions first at *The Colored American Magazine* and then at *The Voice of the Negro*. A founding member of the staff at *The Colored American Magazine* in 1900, she edited a Women's Department in the magazine and published serialized fiction stories, a biographical series, and three serialized novels there between 1901 and 1903: *Hagar's Daughter*, *Winona*, and *Of One Blood*. Hopkins's influence on *The Colored American Magazine* cannot be overstated. As editor, "Hopkins virtually made [the magazine] an organ of African-American New Womanhood and maternal racial uplift" (Bergman, 2003, p. 89). Her writing represented a "radical" position (Knight, 2007, p. 43) that was "unconciliatory to all forms of white oppression" (Cordell, 2006, p. 60). According to Hopkins, the Women's Department had an "enthusiastic desire to do good and pleasing work for our lady patrons" (P. Hopkins, 1900, p. 118) and encouraged an active female readership. She continued, "we would be glad to correspond with all women's clubs in relation to club matters, to insert club notices, etc." Hopkins's two biographical series—"Famous Women of the Negro Race" and "Famous Men of the Negro Race"—covered figures such as Harriet Tubman, Sojourner Truth, Frederick Douglass, and Booker T. Washington and "constituted a significant model for public history narratives and inspired contemporaries, most notably W. E. B. Du Bois, editor of *The Crisis* magazine, who would imitate her to great benefit" (L. Brown, 2008, p. 285).[10]

In 1904, Hopkins joined the staff at *The Voice of the Negro* after losing her position at *The Colored American Magazine* due to philosophical conflicts with Booker T. Washington, who assumed leadership of the magazine that year (Bergman, 2003, p. 99; Kassanoff, 1996, p. 159; Knight, 2007, p. 43). Hopkins's "anti-accommodationist" perspective on racial uplift (compared to Washington's assimilationist stance) "subverted Washington's sociopolitical agenda" (Knight, 2007, p. 43). Bergman (2003) suggests Hopkins's departure was due to her unwillingness to comply with Washington's outlook coupled with Washington's desire for a magazine with a more masculine voice (p. 100). *The Voice of the Negro* published a "woman's number" in July 1904, which carried articles such as "Negro Womanhood Defended," "The Social Status of the Negro Woman," and "What Has Education Done for Colored Women." Contributors included Mary Church Terrell, Nannie Helen Burroughs, Addie Waites Hunton, and Josephine B. Bruce.

White-Controlled Magazines, 1900-1909

As *The Colored American Magazine* and *The Voice of the Negro* sought an expanding Black readership, popular white-owned magazines experienced their own growth in circulation. The widely read *McClure's* magazine described earlier was not the only socially conscious monthly circulating in the early 1900s. B. O. Flower, described as "zealous for the reform of all abuses," founded *The Arena* in 1889 and maintained editorial control until its demise in 1909 (Mott, 1957, p. 402). Not unlike *McClure's*, *The Arena*, which reached a circulation of around thirty thousand (p. 414), covered hot button social issues of the period such as child labor, poverty, and poor working conditions (p. 404). The magazine historian Frank Luther Mott points to *The Arena*'s open-mindedness when it came to issues facing women, including contraception, prostitution, and age of consent (p. 405). Yet, *The Arena*'s coverage of the race question suggests the magazine's idea of gender progressivism was focused almost singularly on white women.

The Outlook, which ran from 1893 to 1928, positioned itself as a politically minded magazine regularly featuring articles by and about Theodore Roosevelt in the early 1900s. With a circulation of 100,000 (Mott, 1938, p. 430), it was more competitive with the popular *McClure's* and *Cosmopolitan*. The Outlook Company, led by Lawrence Abbott, published the periodical, which ran weekly until it merged with *The Independent*, becoming a monthly, *The Outlook and Independent* (Mott, 1938, p. 422). Between 1897 and 1904, *The Outlook* and *The Arena* carried symposia and forums with multiple contributors who proffered their ideas on the race problem.

The *Independent*, which ran from 1848 to 1928 primarily as a weekly, was originally formed as a publication of the Congregationalists. In the early 1900s, it was published out of New York by Clarence W. Bowen and edited by William Hayes Ward. Early in its tenure, the paper positioned itself as antislavery, encouraged noncompliance with the Fugitive Slave Law of 1850 (Mott, 1958, p. 369), and celebrated the publication of Harriet Beecher Stowe's *Uncle Tom's Cabin*. But by the turn of the twentieth century, the magazine showed ambivalence toward issues of race and racism, as the following chapters illustrate. By the early 1900s, *The Independent* had turned away from religious matters, focusing instead on politics and social issues (Mott, 1958, p. 377).

S. S. McClure launched the monthly magazine *McClure's* in 1893. With a circulation topping 370,000 by the early 1900s, *McClure's* is widely considered one of the most popular magazines of the period, having "set the pattern for the golden age of the ten-cent illustrated magazines" (Mott, 1957, pp. 596, 607). The exposé journalism of *McClure's* writers Ida Tarbell, Ray Stannard Baker, and Lincoln Steffens made the magazine "synonymous with muckraking" (J. P. Wood, 1971, p. 130). Tarbell's 1902 series, "Standard Oil," revealed fraud, violence, and bribery; and Steffens's succession of articles on "The Shame of the Cities" disclosed corruption in Minneapolis, St. Louis, Pittsburgh, and Philadelphia. In *McClure's*, matters surrounding economic and political rights for African Americans rarely fell under the reform banner as this magazine did not address the race problem to the extent the others did. Between 1900 and 1910, *McClure's* carried a four-part series written by the racist lawyer

Thomas Nelson Page, whose fiction and nonfiction drew on scientific racism and Lost Cause ideology, and a two-part series on lynching by Ray Stannard Baker.

The Relevance of History

Racism in the United States "has received fresh impetus" at the "dawn of the twentieth century," wrote Pauline Hopkins in the January 1903 issue of *The Colored American Magazine* (1903a, p. 211). Hopkins may just as well have been observing the first two decades of the twenty-first century. We are currently in a period of widespread normalization of white supremacy. The political slogan "Make America Great Again" represents a tacit nostalgic nod to a time when white supremacy was du jour. Travel bans from Muslim-majority countries, fabricated crises around migrants and transgender rights, alarmist narratives of teaching critical race theory, and conspiracy theories like the Great Replacement stoke white racist anxiety. A 2020 report from the Center for American Progress revealed how white supremacy has made its way into mainstream politics, legitimating racist narratives, tapping into long-standing and ongoing racist attitudes, and giving justification for racist discrimination.

We can draw a line from these discourses to those found in popular white-controlled magazines of the early 1900s. These connections are explored more fully in the conclusion. Early twentieth-century white racist frameworks continue to provide a foundation, a rhetorical storehouse, from which contemporary racisms may draw. Donald Trump's statement that "there were good people on both sides" of the 2017 white supremacist rally in Charlottesville, Virginia, is rhetorical shorthand for Lost Cause ideology, which asserts that antebellum southerners were decent persons, benevolent toward those they enslaved, and that the South's actions in the Civil War were noble. Federal law that justifies the use of deadly force on the part of police "'if the officer honestly and reasonably believes' they are in danger of death or injury" provides a white racist pretext for the ways white people regularly, implicitly or explicitly, draw on slave-era stereotypes of Black male bestiality and criminality.[11] And statements from politicians like Marjorie Taylor Greene and Donald Trump that US Representatives Ilhan Omar and Rashida Tlaib represent an "Islamic invasion" (Mutnick, 2020) and they should "go back" to where they came from ("'Our Squad Is Big,'" 2019) provide a near-mirror reflection of early 1900s white anxiety over threats to white purity expressed through fears of the "peril of contamination" and "constant association" with nonwhite people.[12] Each of these twenty-first-century examples demonstrates how willful white ignorance is reliant on and continues to amplify centuries-old racist epistemic resources. Each underscores James Baldwin's observation in 1965 that "it is to history that we owe our frames of reference, our identities, and our aspirations" (quoted in Grossman, 2016).

African American writers' responses to white racism provide a more optimistic repository of rhetorical strategies for widening epistemic resources, an issue taken up again in the conclusion. When Black women writers and activists of the 1970s-early 2000s call attention to the interlocking, intertwining experiences of race, gender, and class oppression, they are hearkening back to the writings of their foremothers who labored to document Black women's double oppression and their efforts to overcome it. And when activists like Kimberlé Crenshaw, Patrisse Cullors, Alicia Garza, and Opal Tometi declare "Black lives matter" and "Say her name," they are calling up, answering to, and demanding a rethinking of a deeply entrenched white social imaginary that has suggested, implicitly and explicitly, for centuries that Black lives do not matter and that Black women are to remain invisible.

Both claims ("Black lives matter" and "Say her name") recalibrate and recenter the being-ness of Black men and women. The emphasis on lives and names calls out an existence in a space and location, what Terrance Nance has called an "ontological integrity" (quoted in Ugwu, 2018, p. 12). The remaining chapters set in dialogue the journalistic writings of Black and white men and women as they debated race in America. My hope is to highlight the ways memory work remains relevant to our present-day struggles against racism and willful white ignorance.

CHAPTER 2

Memory Work and White Violence

> Whatever evils slavery may have entailed upon the Negro, this much may unquestionably be predicted of it; it left him a trained laborer and in good physical condition . . . [and] with a large share of friendliness on the part of the South.
> —Thomas Nelson Page, 1904c

> Ignorance . . . is at least sometimes an appalling achievement; managing to create and preserve it can take grotesquely prodigious effort.
> —Elizabeth V. Spelman, 2007, p. 120

Widely circulating collective understandings of race in the United States are negotiated and maintained, in part, through memory work. Evidenced in the writings of academics, politicians, and popular pundits, willful white ignorance has been and continues to be leveraged to secure a misremembering of America's racist past. Spelman's observation is a reminder that ignorance requires rhetorical labor for its maintenance. The opening quote by the *McClure's* writer Thomas Nelson Page illustrates the "grotesquely prodigious effort" deployed to rewrite the brutal terrorism endured by enslaved Black people, which also positioned the white speaker as authorized to recall, and thus undermined the notion of those individuals as fully human subjects. A twenty-first-century version of Page's appalling sentiments has found a home in Florida's K-12 curricula. In July 2023, the Florida Board of Education developed new requirements—given a thumbs-up by Florida governor and former 2024 Republican presidential candidate Ron DeSantis—which state that when teaching social studies, instructors must cover how "slaves developed skills, which, in some instances, could be applied for their personal benefit"—in essence, suggesting there were upsides to slavery ("Florida's Academic State Standards—Social Studies," 2023, p. 71).

This chapter examines how white-controlled magazines repainted America's past in discussions of crime and lynching. Articles in *The Arena*, *The Independent*, *McClure's*, and *The Outlook* engaged three rhetorical strategies that severed early 1900s racialized violence from its historical roots in slavery. First, through leveling, magazines often suggested there were good and bad people on both sides of the Civil War. Second, appeals to law and order summoned a white fiction of "civilization" that suggested white violence was an aberration, as opposed to a continuation of over two centuries of violence against non-European peoples in the country. And third, through "Black abstraction," articles about lynching amplified the brutalized Black body, which denied a history of Black subjectivity (Ross, 1997a, p. 90).

These three strategies found a suitable home in politically conscious magazines targeted to white middle-class readers. Strategies like leveling and appeals to "civilization" provided a framework for recognizing white violence as a societal evil and a threat to law and order while shirking white accountability and eliding the historically rooted and systemic nature of white violence (see Goldberg, 2009). Suggesting there were good and bad people on both sides was—and continues to be—a conciliatory strategy fitting for white readers who experience what Kelly (2020) refers to as "white ambivalence," or the white desire to embrace ideals of racial equality without letting go of white superiority. The format of the popular magazine, with its efforts at broad appeal through a variety of content (e.g., editorials, regular columns, essays, fiction), provided the flexibility to include a range of voices, including those of Booker T. Washington and W. E. B. Du Bois, suggesting white readers listened to and/or understood the Black experience, while selectively forgetting the systemic nature of white violence. Muckraking magazines did not engage or question "deep social structures" (Ohmann, 1996, p. 282) such as racism and white violence, nor did magazines similarly cued to political issues, such as *The Independent*, *The Arena*, and *The Outlook*.

Scientific Racism and the Cultural Context for Misremembering

"Memory work" or a rhetorically constructed amnesia masks a sense of apprehension—a white anxiety—over the presence and perceived threat of a freed Black population. For a few years, a period historians call Radical Reconstruction (roughly the end of the Civil War until the early 1870s), thousands of Black men held political office and served as police and on juries and school boards (E. Foner, 2005, pp. 129, 159), and southern states adopted new constitutions that "built upon and extended the language of the Fourteenth Amendment" (E. Foner, 2019, p. 90). Racial segregation emerged in the 1880s–90s as a backlash to Black gains, a way to codify racist discrimination that had been challenged by the Thirteenth, Fourteenth, and Fifteenth Amendments, and a way to reassert white superiority in visible ways. The Supreme Court decision in *Plessy v. Ferguson* (1896) legalized "separate but equal" facilities for Black and white citizens and cemented Jim Crow policies that would remain in effect well into the twentieth century. White supremacy as well as imperialist efforts at home and abroad—including immigration policies and removal of indigenous peoples from their land—depended upon clearly defined race differences (Carby, 1987, p. 134). Without the institution of slavery to physically reinforce race difference and hierarchy, states passed Black Codes, and political and popular discourses ramped up racist stereotypes to invoke white anxiety over threats to white hegemony. Between 1892 and 1900, white people killed nearly two thousand Black people and terrorized Black people for exercising political rights like voting and for having successful farms and businesses (Hodes, 1997; de la Roche, 2008; Shapiro, 1988; J. D. Smith, 1993). White rioters, well into the twentieth century, attacked and burned many Black communities (Shapiro, 1988).[1] These acts of white terrorism were rationalized by the circulation of images and narratives that suggested Black men and women posed a threat to white purity and thus civic and domestic stability.

White anxiety imbued popular magazine articles in the early 1900s. This rhetorical unease found solace in a broader pseudo-knowledge called scientific racism, which purported Black people from African nations were naturally lazy, untamed, and inferior to those of European descent (Farr, 2004; Haller, 1971; Mills, 1998; Muhammad, 2011; Omi & Winant, 1994; Parris, 2015). The ideology of racial hierarchy represented a response to a specific historical moment when the notion of race as biologically situated and racial difference as fixed and immutable, granted white people a "sense of superiority when social reality might suggest otherwise" (Malik, 1996, p. 105). In the wake of the Fourteenth Amendment that granted equal rights to formerly enslaved persons and all Black Americans, white journalists, academics, and political leaders characterized, and managed, this situation as a threat by (re)invoking race hierarchy to anchor race to predefined notions rooted in slave-era stereotypes.

Scientific racism, of course, was not scientific at all; rather, it was a set of discourses that utilized a *language of science* to justify a host of inequalities (Gould, 1981; Myrdal, 1944). Reflected in the Enlightenment thought of David Hume and G. W. F. Hegel and preserved in the writings of Thomas Jefferson, the idea of a hierarchy of races performed important racist ideological work to justify enslavement and colonization of non-European persons; historically, it becomes a "vehicle for overt and active hostility" when subordinate people are perceived as out of line in the constructed hierarchy (Fredrickson, 1997, p. 41). Scientific racism relied on categorization and classification to place races into hierarchies and to script the Black body as dangerous "other," criminal, or hypersexual (Gould, 1981; Haller, 1971; R. L. Jackson, 2006; M. M. Smith, 2006).

Stereotypes that categorize are often contradictory and shapeshift over time as the ideological needs of groups in control change. So, we see, for instance, in the magazines studied in this chapter, people of African descent were variously categorized as a "child race," immature and imitative of whiteness, and also as criminal and hypersexual, a threat to white civilization. Despite variation, most often articles relied on the images of Black male criminality and Black female immorality, supporting Fredrickson's (1997) observation that during periods of Black advancement or political/economic gains, such as the early 1900s, stereotypes of threat reemerge. These categories helped preserve white supremacist policies and practices during and after Reconstruction when the institution of slavery no longer served to maintain a rigid racial hierarchy.

Communication scholarship has explored the symbolic construction of public memory (Dickinson et al., 2010), highlighting rhetorical processes of "selective amnesia" (Hoerl, 2012), "strategic forgetting" (Sturken, 1997), "omission" (Zelizer, 1992), and "countermemory" (Dunn, 2011), which, like memory work, underscores the culturally negotiated, partial, and politicized nature of collective public memory. In order to be convincing, scientific racism had to excise or erase the histories and contributions of people of African descent, accomplishing this through categorization, which rendered Black people "subhuman ahistorical beings whose four centuries of slave labor were *deemed negligible* to modern capitalist development" (Parris, 2015, p. 8, emphasis mine; see also Webster, 1992). The strategies used to frame issues of crime and lynching were part of a project of lapsed memory wherein white constructions of Black people ignored the history of Black labor in and outside of the white home and the centuries-long chronicle of white terrorism against Black people, what Ida B. Wells (1895) referred to as the "red record."[2]

Race is, in part, a "worldview, structured by historical narratives" that recur over time (D. M. Jones, 1997, p. 68) and that, particularly in the twenty-first century, often hide in plain sight. When police officers and civilians charged with killing an unarmed Black man, woman, or in the case of Tamir Rice, a twelve-year-old boy, cite fear of attack or are acquitted based on "stand your ground" or "reasonable use of force," we are witnessing the reinvocation of the mythic narrative of the dangerous Black brute. To assert otherwise is to use willful ignorance in the form of strategic forgetting to social and political white advantage. Reference to Eric Garner's "lumbering" body, which a *New York Times* article made a point to say "was hard to miss" at 6 feet 2 inches and 395 pounds (A. Baker et al., 2015), reveals how the Black body is deployed in cultural representations to "jog . . . memories" and tap historical renderings of the racialized Black body (R. L. Jackson, 2006, p. 1). In these cases, a racist historical narrative reinforces a "mythical structure with cognitive and cosmological distortions as the result" (D. M. Jones, 1997, p. 75).

During the first decade of the 1900s, popular magazines like *The Arena*, *The Outlook*, *The Independent*, and *McClure's* became vehicles for exercising memory work that constructed a social imaginary around Black violence and white purity. Within the context of the "race problem," narratives of violence and morality rendered the Black body at once hypervisible for white analysis and invisible as Black speaking subjects.

White Violence and Selective Memory

From the end of the Civil War until well into the twentieth century, white people inflicted torture and violence on Black individuals and communities in the form of lynching and group violence. I use the term "group" as opposed to "mob" to avoid the suggestion that the violence was spontaneous and/or at the hands of ruffians or rabble-rousers. On the contrary, much of the violence was carefully planned, organized, and supported by white businessmen, law enforcement, local politicians, housewives, and the local press. The 1870s saw organized white violence in the form of hate organizations like the Ku Klux Klan, the White Brotherhood, and the Knights of the White Camelia (E. Foner, 2005, p. 171; Hodes, 1997). Between 1892 and 1903, white people lynched nearly two thousand Black men and women (J. D. Smith, 1993, p. xiii; see also Berg, 2011; de la Roche, 2008; and Wells, 1892, 1895). Well into the 1900s, white violence in the form of lynchings, wholesale destruction of Black neighborhoods, and sexual assault against Black women and girls maintained a presence on the American landscape and was often legitimated tacitly or explicitly by the popular press and political leaders like Hoke Smith and Benjamin Tillman.

Organized group violence against Black communities occurred regularly through the first half of the twentieth century. In Wilmington, North Carolina, in 1898, white businessmen and members of the "professional class," heavily armed and numbering over a thousand, destroyed the offices of the city's Black newspaper, *The Record* (Shapiro, 1988, p. 70); fired into the homes of Black people (Zucchino, 2020, p. 200); murdered Black men one after the other; and forcibly removed Black men from the city (Zucchino, 2020). In August 1908, white residents of Springfield, Illinois, acting on the commonly circulated rumor of the Black rape of a white woman, lynched two men, set the homes of Black residents on fire, and effectively drove Black residents out of town (Shapiro, 1988, p. 104). White violence occurred from New York City to Houston, Texas, throughout the ironically named "Progressive" era, into the 1920s, Shapiro writes, with the police often abetting the violence and with backing from the National Guard (p. 362).

Lynching—coupled with Jim Crow laws, disenfranchisement, and peonage—provided an extralegal method for extending slavery's white terroristic rule over Black people that had nominally ended with the passage of the Thirteenth Amendment in 1865. Lynching was a spectacle of white violence that worked to instill terror in the hearts and minds of Black people, to limit Black mobility, and to stand in as representative of what could befall any Black person who was perceived to challenge white supremacy. Public displays of white violence also communicated signals to white spectators "about their own supposed racial dominance and superiority" (A. L. Wood, 2009, p. 2).

Importantly, Black communities did not stand by idly but formed organizations like the Niagara Movement (1905), the National Association for the Advancement of Colored People (1909), and the National Emergency Committee Against Mob Violence (1946). They also established Black newspapers and magazines, like those explored in the following chapters, to counter the vast and widely circulating cultural resources that fostered a strategic and carefully constructed white collective memory that dehumanized Black people, erased Black history, and perpetuated myths of racial hierarchy.

Leveling or "One Crime Always Breeds Another"[3]

Articles on lynching and white violence recast the memory of slavery and severed the historical connections between early twentieth-century white violence and the systemic violence of slavery. At times, leveling took the form of a refashioned history—reflective of Lost Cause ideology—in which slavery was depicted as either equally good or equally harmful for both whites and Blacks. Lost Cause discourses refer to the nostalgic sentiments widely expressed in political and popular discourses after the Civil War wherein the South was portrayed as having fought valiantly for a just cause (think *Gone with the Wind*). Lost Cause framings rely on selective amnesia (Hoerl, 2012) to deny the inherent racialized violence in the institution of slavery, violence that did not end with the passage of the Thirteenth Amendment.

The remarks of the president of Bowdoin College, writing in *The Outlook* in May 1904, captured this picture of history that leveled enslaved and enslaver: "The relation between the white and colored races has been fruitful of misunderstanding, alienation, injustice, war between North and South. Both sections have blundered, sinned, suffered, and are sincerely sorry," and "both sides" must make concessions (Hyde, 1904). A writer in *The Independent* noted that "white people as well as black . . . are still suffering" from the effects of slavery ("The Safest of All Crimes," 1903, p. 277). *McClure's*, the magazine often described as the mouthpiece for Progressive Era causes, thought fit to publish a three-part series by Thomas Nelson Page, a writer widely known for his racist depictions of Black people and his espousal of Lost Cause ideology. In the March 1904 installment and again in a 1907 piece, Page put North and South on par, explaining that "when the war closed, the friendship between the races was never stronger" (1904b, p. 553). Leveling was further supported by another *McClure's* writer, William Archer (1909), as well as by then-President Theodore Roosevelt (1905) who celebrated the "glory won . . . by those who followed Grant and by those who followed Lee, for both fought with equal bravery and with equal sincerity of conviction, each striving for the light as it was given him to see the light." Some writers went so far as to suggest slavery was harder on those who owned enslaved persons. Theodore Roosevelt, a frequent contributor to *The Outlook*, wrote that slavery brought more degradation "on the white man who championed it and profited by it than on the black man who suffered under it" (1910, p. 241). Writers in *The Independent* and *The Outlook* noted that white people were "more cursed by slavery than slaves" (Blair, 1902, p. 442) and that after the abolishment of slavery, the "master [was] put at the bottom and the slave at the top" ("The Way Out," 1903, p. 984).

White magazines' coverage of lynching suggested that, although the crime was awful, there was equal blame to go around, pinpointing causes such as poor social conditions, provocation of otherwise law-abiding white people, or Black criminality. These framings suggest a "strategic forgetting" that provides an ahistorical understanding of early 1900s white violence. Strategic forgetting is a form of memory work that silences histories and, in this case, the systemization of white violence encoded in slavery. Lynchings, murders and assaults of Black women and men, and destruction of Black businesses and neighborhoods hang "suspended in time" as if there was no history of sustained, legal, and long-standing white violence against Black people.[4] Magazine writers often framed lynching violence as the result of a bad environment or Black provocation. In Part II of his series "What Is a Lynching?," the muckraker Ray Stannard Baker (1905b) covered race violence in Ohio and Illinois. According to Baker, the "underlying conditions in Springfield [Ohio]" created a "soil richly prepared for an outbreak of mob law—with corrupt politics, vile saloons . . . non-enforcement of vice, a large venal negro vote, lax courts of justice" (p. 425). The Black area of town, he said, was "composed of saloons and disorderly houses, where the lowest of the low, negro men and both negro and white women" gathered (p. 423). According to Baker, Black residents were susceptible to bribery on the part of both Republican and Democratic candidates. Similarly, an article in *The Outlook* asserted that "race riots and lynchings are a product of imperfect, and sometimes unhealthy, social conditions" ("The Medicine for the Mob," 1907, p. 249). The writer referred to the "evil of lynchings and race riots" and in the following sentence explained that Black people were inferior and "difficulties arising from such inferiority cannot be remedied by treating the negroes as if they were all racially mature" (p. 250).

Another writer in *The Independent* noted that the "provoking cause" of race violence in New York and New Orleans was crime on the part of "negro roughs" ("The New York Riot," 1900). Similarly, a writer in *The Outlook* explained the "negroes' best defense against the evils charged against their race is the cure of them. There is no doubt that negroes are continually guilty of brutal assaults upon white women, and that among negroes there is widespread indolence and shiftlessness" ("The Best Defense," 1903, p. 928). According to Ray

Stannard Baker (1905b), lynching was bad for the white man as it "tends to bring [him] down to the lowest level of the criminal negro," so that through lynching the "white man becomes as savage as the negro" (p. 429). This sentiment was shared by Albert Bushnell Hart (1905), a Harvard history professor, who wrote in *The Independent* that race violence "has the disadvantage of demoralizing the white race" (p. 993). Baker (1905) concluded that although not defensible, lynching was understandable as it is "complicated ... by an ignorant, inferior, defenseless, often criminal negro population" (p. 429).

In the autumn of 1906, the Atlanta massacre, one of numerous acts of white terrorism on Black residents, garnered attention from newspapers and magazines alike. On September 22, 1906, more than five thousand white people filled the streets of downtown Atlanta, many heavily armed, and terrorized Black residents into the night, killing at least twenty (Dittmer, 1977, p. 126; see also Burns, 2006; Godshalk, 2005). Dittmer (1977) described a scene wherein white men beat and shot Black barbers who were at work in their shops and then dragged their bodies to the "Henry Grady monument, where souvenir hunters went to work" (p. 125). White men dragged Black women and men from streetcars and beat them, and they demolished Black businesses and homes, sending Black residents to the outskirts of the city to hide. Atlanta police and thousands of white residents participated or cheered on the terrorism. Newspapers like the Atlanta *Evening News*, *Georgian*, and *Journal* had stoked white rage and panic through false headlines reporting Black assaults on defenseless white women (Dittmer, 1977, p. 124).

In the weeks following the violence, magazines like *The Independent* and *The Outlook* served as vehicles for popular analysis of the causes and remedies of racial discord. Largely white, middle-class readers, attracted to the reform orientation of these outlets, were exposed to strikingly different perspectives on the violence, ranging from the right to interracial marriage to repealing the Fourteenth Amendment. Magazines provided the space for in-depth coverage and dialogue among contributors. A month after the violence, *The Independent* ran an article written by an "educated negro, a life-long resident of Georgia," whose name it was not safe to print, according to the editors ("The Atlanta Massacre," 1906). The author described a *planned* white attack on Black Atlanta residents, which stood in contrast to more typical accounts of race violence that suggested they were spontaneous episodes on the part of white "roughs." And this writer emphasized, the violence was provoked not by Black crime but by local white newspapers that printed trumped-up charges of Black assaults and by white business owners angered at the competition from successful Black businesses.

In the same month, October 1906, *The Outlook* ran the article "Racial Self-Restraint" (1906), which suggested, ironically, that the "cure" for preventing "riots" was "some method of requiring the black race to exercise self-control"—notably, "controlling the vicious and lawless elements of [the Black] race" (p. 309). In November 1906, the magazine published the competing perspectives of Carrie Clifford, a writer, activist, and one of the founders of the Ohio Federation of Colored Women's Clubs, and A. J. McKelway, assistant secretary of the National Child Labor Committee. Clifford turned the call for self-restraint on its head with a stinging observation: "when for three days a white mob had control of Atlanta, attacking, maiming, and killing whomsoever it wished, provided only his face was black—I say that when this is the spectacle presented by the proud white race to a gaping world, a lecture to blacks on self-restraint becomes indeed a roaring farce!" (1906, p. 564).

In striking contrast, A. J. McKelway (1906), whom *The Outlook* described as a "southerner of high character," mirrored the Black provocation frame, specifically tapping the by-this-time widespread stereotype of the Black rapist. He claimed, "if there had been no [Black] assaults upon white women in and near Atlanta, there would have been no mobs and no riots" (p. 558). McKelway concluded by suggesting there should be a "local law preventing the sale of rum to negroes," which might enable white people to "protect the negro from what has caused the destruction of the weaker races elsewhere" (p. 562). McKelway's sentiments were echoed by another writer who responded directly to what he called Clifford's "unfortunate mistakes" by expressing alarm at Clifford's call for the right to race assimilation. The writer conflated interracial marriage with the "nameless crime" (rape) and noted that both are "red flags" in the ongoing race conflict (Hall, 1906, p. 685).

The Clifford-McKelway exchange illustrates how the magazine format facilitated dialogue within its own pages, if only at a superficial level. Aronson (2000) suggests that the variety of magazine content, a mixture of essays, fiction, poetry, and polemic, "encouraged discursive revisions" and "new meanings to emerge" over time (p. 198). Readers of *The Independent* and *The Outlook* quite possibly felt they were getting a balanced account of the violence inflicted on Atlanta's Black residents. Yet, the rhetorical strategy of leveling situated the voices of a handful of Black activists in a sea of white writers who suggested there were good and bad people on both sides. Leveling is a forerunner to what, in the twenty-first century, is called "bothsidesism" or "false balance" wherein journalistic coverage suggests valid evidence exists to support both sides of an issue (Lalami, 2019). Levelling lent itself to both the format and audience of *The Independent* and *The Outlook*, fostering a sense of reader enlightenment on issues of racial conflict, while enabling readers to feel beyond reproach.

Writing three months later, Georgia lawyer Hooper Alexander (1907) noted "a general state of criminality among the negroes was in some measure . . . the immediate provoking cause of the Atlanta outbreak" (p. 259). Alexander waxed nostalgic about the good old days of slavery when enslaved Black men and women expressed loyalty and good will to their white masters and mistresses: "the aggregate affection and attachment between the races" are disappearing and "being superceded [sic] by an increasing antagonism which promises to aggravate" racialized crimes and riots (p. 261). Alexander proposed eradicating the Fourteenth and Fifteenth Amendments and leaving the status of Black Americans up to the states, a move that was an "imperious necessity . . . against conditions which will otherwise become morally intolerable" (p. 262).

McKelway was just one of many magazine writers who appealed to latent fear of threats to white male control over white female sexuality by evoking the stereotype of the Black rapist. The rape myth (Black male beast stalks and sexually violates innocent, pure white woman) hinged on an ironic twist of history that turned on its head the widely sanctioned and systematic rape of enslaved Black women by their white masters. References to the Black rapist replaced the memory of the white rapist documented in historical accounts including slave narratives such as Harriet Jacobs's *Incidents in the Life of a Slave Girl*.[5] *The Independent* covered a speech given by Theodore Roosevelt, who acknowledged that lynchings were acts of "savagery" but said they were "caused" by the "hideous crime of rape" ("The Lynching of Negroes," 1906, p. 1370). Ray Stannard Baker (1905a) conjured the image of the shiftless, "floating, worthless negro" who "prowls the roads by day and night" and "makes it unsafe for women to travel alone" (p. 302). With journalistic detachment, other articles described a Black "brute" who was lynched because he "insulted a refined white woman" (Levell, 1901, p. 731); a Black man "burned at the stake for having made an assault upon the wife of a local merchant" ("Race Conflict in Louisiana," 1901, p. 2615); a Black man "accused of a crime against a young woman" ("Lynching," 1909, p. 637); a Black man lynched for an "atrocious assault upon . . . the wife of a farmer" ("Mob Violence, North and South," 1903, p. 1769); and a lynching "caused" by an "attack by a negro upon a white woman" ("The Riot at Springfield," 1908, p. 869; see also "The Lynching of Negroes," 1903b; and "The Negro Question," 1903a).[6] An article by a white woman carried in the October 1907 *Independent* suggests the magazine's openness to inserting views that challenged the white mainstream. The writer provided a contrasting view of lynching that called out white hypocrisy. She wrote, "It might save the life of a considerable number of negroes if he who is without sin among the lynchers could be required to fire the first shot. If womanhood is indeed so sacred a thing, it is hard for me to understand why it is only to be revered and guarded when accompanied by a white skin" ("The Negro and Justice," 1907).

From early twentieth-century magazines to contemporary discussions of racial unrest, leveling has provided a way for popular press writers to lament the atrocities of lynching—or more recently, police shootings of Black men and women—by attributing blame evenly. Additionally, early 1900s magazines expressed regret over lynching because of its perceived threat to established law and order, another maneuver of memory work that disconnected lynching from the long-standing history of white violence against people of color.

The Fiction of White Civilization

The labels used in public debates to discuss lynchings—"mob law," "mob spirit," and "lynch law"—call up the stinging irony with which many Black people viewed the law and police protection. Black people knew that mobs and lynchings had little to do with "law." The defense lawyer, Clayton, in Attica Locke's 2017 novel, *Bluebird, Bluebird,* summons this view when he notes, "law is a lie Black folks need protection *from*—a set of rules that were written against us from the time ink was first set to parchment" (2017, p. 17). Magazines such as *The Independent, The Arena, The Outlook,* and *McClure's* often expressed horror, outrage, and distress over the occurrence of lynchings. But their framings of lynchings—as the work of "mobs," as "outbursts," and as threats to "law and order"—tell us something about how memory work functions in these accounts—namely, to obscure the ways this manifestation of racist violence was situated in a longer history ("from the time ink was first set to parchment") of colonialist violence, both physical and legal, against non-European peoples.

White magazines such as *The Independent, The Outlook, The Arena,* and *McClure's* addressed larger social issues like race relations without offending their white readers and advertisers who funded their business. The magazine format, with its extended essays (e.g., Sheldon's 1906 *Arena* piece), contributions from politicians and academics, and featured "forums," supplied a space to provide a seeming more complex account of lynching. Framing lynching as a matter of law and order was not wholly inaccurate, but neither did it capture the entire story. The frame, however, fit into a larger epistemological stance that relied on willful not knowing, selective remembering, and establishing a fictive past that assuaged white anxieties over increased Black mobility and attainment. These magazines shaped reader identities as morally superior whites through accounts that were not completely unsympathetic but yet managed to elide white accountability by pinning white violence on a few bad apples.

Between 1900 and 1910, white magazines framed lynchings as the result of "mobs," "anarchists," and the "lower elements" of the white population and criticized the atrocity not for its racist violation of human rights but because it represented a breakdown in law and order and thus challenged the fiction of white civilization.[7] Typical of this framing is an article in *The Independent* that quoted the Illinois governor who said lynchers in Danville were "nothing but anarchists" ("The Lynching of Negroes," 1903b, p. 1834). *The Independent* similarly described a Springfield, Missouri, lynching as the result of a "mob of 3,000 persons" who stormed the sheriff's residence, "took the key to the jail, dragged out the arrested black men, and lynched them" ("Negroes Lynched in Missouri," 1906, p. 892). An article in *The Arena* examined the "psychology of the lynching mob," a rhetorical move that rendered lynching the result of an unhinged "mob-mind" as opposed to part of well-established and far-reaching practices both legal and extra-legal that maintained white supremacy in the wake of emancipation (Babbitt, 1904, p. 589). The article went on to say that the "mob impulse" provoked otherwise ordinary people to do unthinkable things at the behest of a "master-mobbist" who acted as leader.

In 1908, Springfield, Illinois, was the location of widespread white violence, loss of lives, and destruction of Black property in the wake of a thwarted lynching. *The Outlook* covered the event by describing the "passion of the rioters," their "unrestrained frenzy," and the ways Black residents "fought viciously and aggressively" ("The Riot at Springfield," 1908, p. 869). The article concluded that "this outbreak is a dreadful proof of the contagious violence of vicious and lawless passion. To meet crime with crime is to multiply crime" (p. 870). This account of the Springfield violence relied on both leveling ("meet crime with crime") and references to "law and order" to frame the violence, which resulted in at least sixteen deaths and personal and property damages suffered by Black residents that amounted to $4 million in present-day dollars (de la Roche, 2008; Shapiro, 1988, p. 103). *The Independent* published a contrasting account by the socialist and reformer William English Walling.[8] Walling (1908) pointed to the wholesale involvement of the Springfield community including women, children, and "prosperous businessmen" who "calmly looked on" as the violence unfolded over a period of two days. Rather than pin part of the blame on supposedly criminal Black men, Walling underscored the "whole awful and menacing truth—that a large part of the white population of Lincoln's home, supported largely by the farmers and miners of the neighboring towns, have initiated a permanent warfare with the negro race."

Describing violence as an "outbreak" obscures the remarkable consistency of white violence against Black people from slavery, throughout Reconstruction, and into the twenty-first century. Whether it was 1906 Atlanta or 1908 Springfield, white violence was rarely a "spontaneous explosion but rather the product" (Shapiro, 1988, p. 97) of a number of intertwining variables including race and class tensions (de la Roche, 2008, p. 10) and "political opportunism and journalistic sensationalism" (Shapiro, 1988, p. 97). Eric Foner (1988) detailed the "pervasiveness" of white violence against freed Blacks during Reconstruction, which "reflected whites' determination to define in their own way the meaning of freedom and their determined resistance to Blacks' efforts to establish their autonomy, whether in matters of family, church, labor, or personal demeanor"

(p. 120). Between the early 1800s and the 1940s, nearly five thousand people were lynched in the United States, with most of the victims being Black (Berg, 2011, p. 92). While popular magazines decried lynchings for the threat they posed to law and order, in reality lynchings played a role in supporting the larger web of racist policies and practices—the so-called "laws" of "law and order"—that denied rights and physical safety to Black people going back to slavery. Mary Church Terrell, president of the National Association of Colored Women, suggested as much in her June 1904 article in the *North American Review*, writing that "lynching is the aftermath of slavery," the "legitimate offspring of slavery" (1904a, p. 861). She continued, "It is as impossible to comprehend the cause of the ferocity and barbarity which attend the average lynching-bee without taking into account the brutalizing effect of slavery upon the people of the section where most of the lynchings occur, as it is to investigate the essence and nature of fire without considering the gases which cause the flame to ignite" (p. 862). Tolnay and Beck (1995) explain lynching was "more than an infrequent interruption of the region's otherwise tranquil racial relations. Rather, it was a routine and systematic effort to subjugate the African-American minority" (p. 17). Likewise, Berg (2011) notes, "racial violence in the age of Jim Crow ran a broad gamut, from individual bullying to wholesale pogroms with dozens of Black victims" (p. 93). Importantly, lynchings were visible and designed to send a message to Black communities of what would befall them should they challenge white supremacy (Berg, 2011; A. L. Wood, 2009).

Additionally, reporting lynchings as the result of "unrestrained frenzy" ("The Riot at Springfield," 1908, p. 869) or the "anarchy of rioters" ("Mob Law," 1910, p. 809) masks the extent to which white violence was well planned and highly orchestrated. Scholars have explained lynchings as "race terror staged as communal ritual" (Berg, 2011, p. 93) and elaborate spectacle in the form of "theatrical entertainment," which worked to attract eager white onlookers (A. L. Wood, 2009, p. 10). White people—men, women, and children—boarded trains and carriages to get a view of the violence. Atlanta's white population deemed the day of Sam Hose's lynching a holiday and commissioned two trains for special trips to the location of the lynching. White onlookers "scraped for hours among [Hose's] ashes in the hope of finding a sufficient number of his bones to take to their friends as souvenirs" (Terrell, 1904a, p. 859). Lynchings such as this one acted as a public reinforcement of white supremacy (A. L. Wood, 2009). Onlookers, according to Wood, "cheered, hooted, clapped, grabbed souvenirs [body parts such as fingers and toes].... Spectators heard the speeches of the mob, the shouts of the crowd, the confessions of the victim, and most of all, his dying shrieks and cries.... And, in all instances, the feel and push of the crowd created the sense of belonging and commonality that sustained the violence" (p. 11).

Magazines often appealed to law and order by referencing lynching as a breakdown in "civilization." *The Outlook* condemned lynchings for their "demoralizing" influence on publics, and besides, the writer noted, lynchings lacked "efficacy ... as a deterrent for the crimes committed by the victims" ("The Epidemic of Savagery," 1901, p. 9). Mob violence was dangerous because it resulted in the "destruction, not physical but moral, of the white race" ("Torture and Lynching," 1902, p. 533) and it "humiliated" cities in both the North and South ("Mob Law," 1910, p. 809). Georgia lawyer Hooper Alexander, writing in *The Outlook*, denounced the "indiscriminate violence" against Black people in Atlanta in 1906, then noted "these conditions are ... very dangerous to organized society, and tend to produce a decline in public and private morality" (1907, p. 261). Another article in *The Outlook* described white violence in Illinois on November 11, 1909, as regrettable because it "brought disgrace" to the city, the state of Illinois, and the "American Republic" ("Lynching," 1909, p. 638). That account deracialized the destruction wrought by white people, noting "every such act of mob violence is an indication that the American people have not yet learned how to govern themselves" (p. 638). Likewise, *The Independent* quoted

Chief Justice Lore of Delaware who exclaimed, "mob law is the end of free government.... Obedience to law is the life-breath of our republic" ("The Negro Question," 1903b, p. 2309).

An extended article in the September 1906 *Arena*, written by Winthrop D. Sheldon of Girard College in Philadelphia, exemplified the way white writers positioned sympathy for Black victims and horror at the atrocity in a larger setting of a "professedly civilized, law-governed and Christian land" (1906, p. 225). Sheldon described the "mob violence" and "reckless fury" of "savage beasts" who commit lynchings (p. 226). Lynching was bad, in part, he wrote, because it bred the conditions and "aggravate[d] the very trouble it was intended to correct" (p. 228) and "disgraced and dishonored" the country "in the estimation of the civilized world" (p. 227). Further, "security for the whites as well as for the blacks depends upon the orderly enforcement of law" (p. 228). Notably, Sheldon does not only implicate "mobs" but acknowledged that, at times, the "best citizens" in a community participated in these rituals of white terrorism, pointing out the guilt of coroners who declined to identify actual causes of death and grand juries that refused to indict lynchers (p. 231).

It is true that lynchings and racialized violence were threats to law and order in the decades following Reconstruction. It is equally important to situate these events in the broader history of white terrorism against Black and indigenous peoples, which includes US genocide against Native Americans, government-sanctioned "resettlement" programs, Jim Crow segregation, chain gangs, and in the twentieth and twenty-first centuries, mass incarceration. These institutionalized forms of violence call into question the notion there ever was a white "civilization" to begin with. Magazine accounts of lynchings performed memory work by dehistoricizing "law and order," suggesting they were neutral constructs, frozen in time, detached from a context, as opposed to imbued with the racist beliefs of a specific era. As the scholar George Lipsitz (1998) explains, "Contemporary whiteness and its rewards have been created and recreated by policies adopted long after the emancipation of enslaved persons in the 1860s and even after the outlawing of *de jure* segregation in the 1960s" (p. 4). Historically, US policies have been directed at controlling and delimiting the rights of a host of marginalized groups. Post-Reconstruction vagrancy laws targeted unemployed Black people; literacy tests and poll taxes disenfranchised Black men; interracial marriage laws attempted to control Black sexuality; Jim Crow laws delimited Black peoples' access to everything from housing, health care, and hotels to public facilities; New Deal legislation denied public benefits to Black workers; and on and on.[9]

Black Abstraction

Black abstraction refers to the ways cultural representations, political practices, legal systems, and economic structures deny Black people subjectivity. Thomas Ross (1997a) explains the "essential purpose of Black abstraction is to deny, or obscure, the humanness of Blacks" (p. 90). Slavery, segregation, discrimination, disenfranchisement, and white racist violence rely on the erasure of Black humanity and render Black people as purely corporeal. Focus on the hypervisible Black body reinforces the "distance from the privileged ranks" of white citizenship with Black corporeality standing in opposition to the disembodied white subject (Wiegman, 1993, p. 455). Black abstraction operates in tandem with white innocence to render slavery and segregation "intellectually coherent and tolerable" (Ross, 1997a, p. 94).

In addition to erasing humanity, abstraction operates to "comfort" or "shelter" white readers by providing a distance between themselves as subjects and "others" as objects.[10] Early 1900s magazine discussions of white racist violence relied on Black abstraction to assuage white guilt and to historically cleave the connections between slavery and lynching. In 1903, *The Independent* ran a number of short articles that listed lynching occurrences with a fact-based ethos, a blitheness that focused on the Black body with a sense of journalistic disinterest and objectivity ("Negroes Lynched and Burned," 1903; "The Lynching of Negroes," 1903a; "The Negro Question," 1903a; "The Negro Problem," 1903). Two articles listed lynchings and "race conflicts"—that is, white violence on Black people—alongside reports of pending legislation and stories of political leaders (e.g., Senator Benjamin Tillman of South Carolina, a white supremacist, and former president Grover Cleveland) who spoke on the issue of race ("The Negro Question," 1903a; "The Negro Problem," 1903). "The Negro Question" (1903a) quoted extensively from Tillman's racist speech including his comment that he would "gladly at any time have led a party of men who were out to lynch a black man" without any other commentary (p. 410; see also "The Lynching of Negroes," 1903b). The listing format of other articles ("Negroes Lynched and Burned," 1903; "The Lynching of Negroes," 1903a; "The Negro Problem," 1903) suggested lynchings were mundane occurrences, which provided a way for white readers to erase personhood from the Black bodies therein described. "The Lynching of Negroes" (1903a) logged three occurrences of white attacks on Black people; "Negroes Lynched and Burned" (1903) cited five such attacks; and "The Negro Problem" (1903) summarized two.

Significant in these portrayals is the rendering of the Black body as a hypervisible object upon which white violence is marked. The Black speaking subject is mute. Typical is *The Independent*'s coverage of the lynching of William Cato and Paul Reed, who were accused of killing a white family in Statesboro, Georgia. The article described the scene with precision, including the amount of fuel poured on the fire: "They were chained to a tall stump, pine wood was heaped about them, and twenty gallons of kerosene were poured over their bodies. There, at 3 p.m., after an hour's delay, during which they were photographed, the two men were burned to death" ("Negroes Burned at the Stake," 1904, p. 413). Similar descriptions found their way to other *Independent* articles between 1903 and 1906 ("Lynch Law and Riot in Ohio," 1904; "Negroes Lynched in Missouri," 1906). The article "Lynch Law and Riot in Ohio" detailed the events surrounding white terrorist violence in a small Ohio town, described as the "lynching of a negro named Richard Dixon . . . followed by the burning of twenty buildings in the negro quarter" (1904, p. 580). A crowd of over a thousand white persons stormed the facility where Dixon was jailed, according to the article; they "battered down the door with a railroad rail, took Dixon out, shot him to death and suspended the body from a telegraph pole, where many bullets were fired into it." Another report noted three Black men were lynched in Springfield, Missouri, "hanged from an electric light tower that is surmounted by a statue of the Goddess of Liberty, and their bodies were burned in the public square, near the foot of this tower" ("Negroes Lynched in Missouri," 1906, p. 892). That article further noted the "charred bodies were lying in public square, where they could be seen by persons on their way to church." Lynchers often left their victims' bodies on display in public spaces, often with warning signs attached, sending a message to other Black residents of their fate should they cross the lines set by white supremacy (see Berg, 2011, p. 93).

The explicit language used to detail the method and location of the killings directed the reader's attention onto the Black body, "charred," "suspended," visible to passers-by, while denying the Black victim any other marker of humanity. Black lynching victims were not described as "residents" although they were, nor was it mentioned they left families and livelihoods behind.[11] Instead, articles mentioned the crime for which lynching victims had been jailed, underscoring the Black-male-as-criminal stereotype used as a pretext for lynchings in the first place. In their historical account of southern lynchings, which they define as "state-sanctioned terrorism" (p. 19), Tolnay and Beck (1995) describe how the rhetorical process of abstraction played a key role in facilitating white violence. Pervasive "debasing" images of Black people, they write, "depersonalized and dehumanized the victim, reducing him or her to a hated object devoid of worth" (p. 23). Referred to repeatedly by politicians, academics, and scientists and detailed in news outlets including the magazines, these narratives depicted Black men as "ignorant and lazy" (R. S. Baker, 1905a, p. 301), even "animal-like" (R. S. Baker, 1905b, p. 427) and thus provided the needed rhetorical link to render lynching "logical" or "coherent" in the minds of racist whites.[12] Although accounts often explained that state governors and local sheriffs attempted to restore law and order and, as described above, castigated the outlaw mentality of white lynchers, such emphases reinforced the agency of white actors while denying humanity to Black people.

Black abstraction hinges on a "hypervisible/invisible paradox" (J. D. Phillips & Griffin, 2015) wherein magazines magnified Black lynching victims as objectified bodies while erasing their subjectivity (p. 37). The hyper-scrutiny of the disembodied Black body is described by the Black philosopher Lewis R. Gordon (2000) who explains that "Black invisibility involves a form of hypervisibility. The Black is . . . not seen by virtue of being seen" (p. 88). Elsewhere, Gordon (1995) explains, "To see [the Black person] as Black is to see enough. Hence to see him as Black is not to see *him* at all. His presence is a form of absence. Like [Ralph] Ellison's Invisible Man, the more present he is, the more he is absent" (p. 99). Rhetorically, Gordon (2000) writes, the processes that render Black people (in)visible function as "epistemic closure" (p. 88), as Black lynching victims are reduced to charred and mutilated bodies on public display.

In contrast, history shows us that Black people often resisted white violence and dehumanization. The African American scholar LaRose Parris (2015) points out: "The fact that enslaved Africans constantly reaffirmed their humanity, actualized their resistance, and maintained their adherence to African ancestral and cultural expressions, in spite of the torrent of punishments and legislative measures employed to crush their will, speaks to a collective ontological self-awareness and self-worth" (p. 56). Black writers and philosophers—such as those whose writings are explored in subsequent chapters—created a body of Africana thought covering ontological, existential, and teleological questions that contrasted to Euro- and androcentric theorizing by Western thinkers (Gordon,

2000; Mills, 1998). And Black citizens formed organizations large and small to combat white violence and segregation. As one example, the Citizens Protective League was formed in New York City in September 1900 in the wake of widespread racialized violence, including on the part of city police, against Black residents (Shapiro, 1988, p. 95). With more than three thousand members, the league filed a lawsuit against the city, provided testimonials to the violence, and published its members' perspectives in a book, *Story of the Riot*. Black-owned periodicals such as *The Voice of the Negro* and *The Colored American Magazine* relied on a host of rhetorical strategies to counter leveling, appeals to white fictionalized civilization, and Black abstraction.

Contemporary political discussions on issues of migration and policing continue to draw on abstraction by presenting people of color as one-dimensional and lacking a history, as bodies detached from mindfulness, feeling, or intellect. References to "illegal aliens" center the nonwhite body as a dangerous force threatening to corrupt a stable and civilized American way of life and figure into the broader ways that the time-worn racist tropes continue to shape the white public imaginary. People of color become at once hypervisible as objects and invisible as human subjects.

The first decade of the twentieth century was marked by the spread of industrial capitalism, city growth, and the passage of racist policies that undermined the Fourteenth and Fifteenth Amendments and that were reinforced by white terrorist activities (e.g., lynchings, incarceration, white riots), further marginalizing Black people and at times destroying their communities and their businesses. During this time, magazine readership flourished with self-identified socially conscious publications leading the way, publications like the muckraking *McClure's* magazine; the explicitly anti-slavery magazine *The Independent*; *The Arena*, whose primary interest was social reform (Mott, 1957); and *The Outlook*, which regularly published articles by Theodore Roosevelt and Booker T. Washington. These periodicals addressed the "race question" or, as it was often called, the "race problem" in the context of lynching, relying on memory work to at once express dismay at these violent acts while deflecting attention from long-standing histories that were inextricably woven into the early 1900s context. Using strategies such as leveling, appeals to civilization, and Black abstraction, these magazines were rhetorical forerunners of twenty-first-century debates over racially infused discussions. Memory work continues to play a significant role in the way willful white ignorance works rhetorically to elide the historical roots of racial violence.

CHAPTER 3

Memory Work and a Cult of White Purity

> I ... have never come in contact with but one negro woman whom I believed to be chaste.
> —"THE NEGRO PROBLEM: HOW IT APPEALS TO A SOUTHERN WHITE WOMAN," 1902, P. 2226

> Epistemic oppression arises from a situation in which the social experiences of the powerless are not properly integrated into collective understandings of the social world.
> —MIRANDA FRICKER, 1999, P. 208

The Black female body has been subjected to scripting by white writers and philosophers in ways that differ from that of the Black male (Collins, 1991; hooks, 2015). Historically, narratives and images of Black women served as the foil to white female purity and a means for displacing histories of white male sexual and physical violence against Black women.[1] Long-standing cultural narratives perpetuated the image of the hypersexual, immoral, unchaste Black woman, cast in stark contrast to the image of white female purity. This image of Black women performed memory work by erasing the history of intergenerational and routinized rape on the part of white enslavers against Black women, which was an "embedded, systemic, and self-replicating feature of American slavery" (Livesey, 2018, p. 275) and by obscuring the roles of white women in slave-holding families (Jones-Rogers, 2019).

The years following Reconstruction represented a time of "terrorism in the American south . . . and control over the sexual agency of black men and women" (Hodes, 1997, p. 148). White attackers often invoked threats to the purity of white womanhood as a pretext for murdering Black men who were viewed as economic threats to white dominance (Hodes, 1997, pp. 153–155). In the context of widespread white violence against Black people and their communities, antimiscegenation laws were reinstated after the Civil War (Van Tassel, 1997), underscoring how the construction of race is not only about bodies, but also "about the reproduction of those bodies through heterosexuality" (Dyer, 1997, p. 25). Interracial relations or what was referred to as "amalgamation" became increasingly taboo as race mixing threatened white purity (Dyer, 1997, p. 25) and blurred the difference upon which the idea of race hierarchy depended (Hodes, 1997). White literature pre- and post-Civil War became a vehicle for transmitting the "white panic" (Knadler, 2002) over blurred racial lines, which often centered on the figure of the "tragic mulatta" (C. L. Peterson, 1995, p. 155).[2]

As daily publications, southern white newspapers effectively stoked white anxiety and, often, immediate violence by reporting falsehoods about Black male rape and criminality, as in the example of Atlanta newspapers that fueled the 1906 Atlanta massacre (Dittmer, 1977). Magazines such as *McClure's*, *The Independent*, *The Arena*, and *The Outlook* appeared on a weekly/monthly basis and defined themselves as reform-minded (as in *McClure's*, *The Arena*, and *The Independent*) or "high-minded . . . but readable" (as in *The Outlook*).[3] Magazines provided space for series, forums, and symposiums that offered contrasting views of Black female sexuality by both white and Black writers. Inclusion of articles by Black men and women alongside those of white writers who expressed disquiet over race "mixing" and "amalgamation" illustrates how popular magazines of the early 1900s served as a public space for debate over the race question. As cultural artifacts, magazines played a role in the "uneven development" of beliefs and narratives concerning race, capturing hegemonic struggle through representation of both racist and resistant voices (White 1992, p. 167). The variety of viewpoints appealed to a broad base of middle-class readers with differing tastes and beliefs, according to White, but captured them in a "regulated latitude" that "moderated," contained, or reframed anti-racist voices (pp. 190, 187). Without gainsaying the importance of publishing articles written by Black women, it is important to recognize how the sheer repetition of alarmist articles that relied on the pseudoscience of race hierarchy worked to both trigger alarm and legitimate the notion of white superiority embraced by white readers and advertisers steeped in the racist social imaginary of the time period.

Hodes (1997) points out that, with the abolishment of slavery, "white Southerners had to rely on the fickle categories of 'black' and 'white' to define white supremacy" (p. 157). To underscore those categories and establish a clear color line, magazine writers (along with others) contrived a "cult of white purity," the rhetorical dimensions of which are explored in this chapter. I use this term here to refer to the ways writers and editors used memory work—in this case, selective forgetting—to conjure white anxiety over the dire consequences of race mixing. For its success, the cult of white purity leveraged memory work through narratives that denied histories of systemic white male rape of Black women and rendered the idea of consensual interracial relationships implausible. The notion of white purity stood at the center of this rhetoric. First, writers racialized purity and pollution, often through references to blood, which came to symbolize cleanliness or contamination. Second, anxiety-inducing articles detailed what may happen when mixing occurred.

Historical Context: White Anxiety and Constructions of Race

Constructing Blackness in popular magazines was equally about constructing whiteness during a period in US history marked by great change. The early 1900s saw the expansion of industrial capitalism, growth of urban spaces, migration of Black southerners to the north, labor unrest, and suffrage activism. All of these forces, in some measure, represented a threat to white male supremacy in and outside the home. The movement of work from home to factory meant white male workers were subjected to the regimen of the time clock and the directives of bosses. White women's continued advances in the paid labor force meant competition for white male workers and increased economic independence for wives and daughters. White factory owners often hired Black male workers to undercut white male wages and to break strikes.[4] Lisa Duggan (2000) explains, "out of the materials of a broad range of social conflicts, economic changes, and cultural wars," a new version of whiteness emerged and was ideologically deployed to justify continued white terrorist violence against Black people (e.g., lynching), Native Americans (e.g., 1890 Wounded Knee), Chinese people, and numerous other populations categorized as nonwhite (p. 15; see also Gunning, 1996). Testimonies given to Congress in the early 1900s over incidents of white violence against Black people revealed time and again that "white anxiety over sexual liaisons between black men and white women was linked to both party politics and successful crops" (Hodes, 1997, p. 153). In other words, Black economic success and political influence stood as a threat to white male supremacy. Casting Black women as sexually immoral reimagined the white home as a bastion of chastity and civility, a rhetorical move that entailed erasing white male sexual violence against Black women.

Academics, journalists, political figures, and religious leaders expressed white anxiety over threats to "race distinction" in books and sermons.[5] Their writings mirrored themes found in popular white magazines that I am calling a "cult of white purity" for the heightened sense of anxiety expressed around racial mixing that came to stand in for perceived threats to white supremacy. In these discourses, pure whiteness symbolized order over chaos, mind over body, and chastity over sexuality. Whiteness became the template for "citizenship" as constructed in Enlightenment writings. Wiegman (1993) explains: "In constituting the citizen through the value system of disembodied abstraction, the white male is 'freed' from the corporeality that might otherwise impede his insertion into the larger body of national identity" (p. 455). In contrast, Blackness stood for disorder, bodily motives, and sexuality, which symbolically distanced the Black body from the "privileged ranks of (potential or actual) citizenry" (Wiegman, 1993, p. 455). Purity became synecdochal, standing in for stability and social order. The Black home and by extension the Black female symbolized immorality, heightened corporeality, and thus a threat to white male control over domestic life and women's bodies, political activity, and the economic sphere.

Academics claimed to have found a scientific basis for their racist theories in Charles Darwin's *The Origin of Species* (Hollandsworth, 2008, p. 13). In the field of psychology, "stereotypical racial difference [was] constituted as a standard area of analysis" (Otten, 1992, p. 238). For example, G. Stanley Hall, a psychologist in childhood development and the first president of the American Psychological Association, tapped the time-worn stereotype of Black people as a "child race" in his 1904 book *Adolescence*. His views were typical of other scholars who drew on the fiction of a hierarchy of races, including statistician Frederick Hoffman (1896) and ethnologist Daniel Garrison Brinton (1890).[6] The American Economic Association (AEA), founded in 1885, published Frederick Hoffman's essay, "Race Traits and Tendencies of the American Negro," in 1896. In it, Hoffman (1896) used numerical data and the arguments of other academics to suggest that a "low state of sexual morality" was the reason for the poor "physical and moral condition of the colored race" and to raise alarm over the dangers of mixing white and Black blood, noting that, although the "mulatto is undoubtedly the superior of the pure black," "race amalgamation" is a "fundamental error" that would lead to "disastrous consequences" including social decay (pp. 207, 185, 191). Importantly, the AEA's publication of Hoffman's essay was an "indication of the degree to which scientific racism had become institutionalized" in the United States by the early 1900s (Hollandsworth, 2008, p. 84). In 1902, the AEA also published an essay by Alfred Holt Stone, a lawyer, politician, southern planter, and associate of various academic institutions (Hollandsworth, 2008). Stone, according to Hollandsworth, "was an ideal spokesperson to defend the institutionalized racism of northern scholars" due to his personal experiences living in the south and his ability to paint white supremacy as benign (p. 100).

Tulane University mathematics professor William Benjamin Smith and lawyer Thomas Nelson Page similarly emphasized blood purity and the dangers of contamination in their respective books. Page (1904a) feared the "peril of contamination from the overcrowding of an inferior race" and the "evil of race-degeneration from enforced and constant association with an inferior race" (p. 213). Smith (1905) noted it was "sheerest folly" to expect that education for black people could "affect the blood . . . or smooth down the inequalities between individuals" of different races (p. 165). Indeed, Smith claimed that just the growth in the Black population—racial intermingling aside—represented a threat to white dominance: "we hold it to be certain that all forms of humanitarianism that tend to give the organically inferior an equal chance with the superior in the propagation of the species, are radically mistaken. . . . Their error may be very amiable, but it is none the less mortal" to the "stronger" race (p. 191). Even President Theodore Roosevelt (1905), who was much more ambivalent about his racism, stated in his address at the Lincoln Dinner: "Full recognition of the fundamental fact that all men should stand on an equal footing as regards civil privileges in no way interferes with recognition of the further fact that all reflecting men of both races are united in feeling that race purity must be maintained."

The popular press, especially "conscientiousless [sic] newspaper editors," buttressed by "dishonest, unscrupulous, ambitious politicians," also fomented racism, which often resulted in white terrorism inflicted on Black communities (Barber, 1906, p. 474). For instance, the newspaper editor and politician John Temple Graves notoriously defended lynching in a 1903 Chautauqua, New York, speech quoted extensively in a *New York Times* article. The problem was not how to prevent lynching, according to Graves; it was how to "destroy the crime which always has and always will provoke lynching" ("He Defends Lynch Law," 1903). Continuing, Graves asserted the lynch mob represented the "most potential bulwark between the women of the South and such a carnival of crime as would infuriate the world and precipitate the annihilation of the negro race."

White Atlanta-area newspapers that printed sensationalized stories about supposed Black assaults on white people played a key role in sparking the Atlanta Massacre of 1906, a white terrorist attack on Black Atlantans that resulted in over a hundred injuries or deaths (Dittmer, 1977). On September 22, 1906, according to Dittmer, the Atlanta *Evening News*, *Georgian*, and *Journal* published a series of extras one after the other about "black fiends" attacking innocent white women; by five that evening, white Atlantans were panicked and, armed and stoked by anger, formed a large crowd that began indiscriminately beating up Black residents and destroying their businesses and neighborhoods (pp. 124–131).[7]

Popular novels like Thomas Dixon's *The Leopard's Spots* (1902) and *The Clansman* (1905) and later films like *The Birth of a Nation* (1915), which was based on Dixon's novels, further contributed to a white racist cultural imaginary (Slide, 2004). *The Leopard's Spots* and *The Clansman*, which together sold hundreds of thousands of copies, reinforced Lost Cause ideology, cast Black people as a danger to southern white power and white innocence, argued against integration, and glorified white violence against Black people (Slide, 2004, p. 30). *The Clansman* was made into a play that was shown in Atlanta in 1906, further contributing to the racism that would result in the Atlanta Massacre (Shapiro, 1988, p. 97).

Political and popular discourses were not spoken or printed in isolation but rather acted intertextually, that is, often in dialogue, drawing from shared cultural resources (e.g., images, narratives, events), or speaking off of one another. Racist academics found a home in popular magazines; local newspapers carried the words of segregationist politicians; and both Black- and white-controlled magazines dialogued about the race question. *The Colored American Magazine* editor and contributor Pauline Hopkins (1903a) lambasted the press that printed "details of hideous crimes attributed to 'brutal Negroes' . . . in flaring headlines with a minuteness of account that is sickening, while the thousands of brave and unselfish deeds wrought by these same 'brutal negroes' for the benefit of the Anglo-Saxon, are relegated to an obscure corner, perhaps at the foot of some advertising page" (p. 286). The popular, white-controlled magazine *McClure's* carried three articles by Thomas Nelson Page that painted a nostalgic picture of the white supremacist South. And *The Independent*, with a tone of detachment and lacking condemnation, published excerpts of racist addresses given by Senator Tillman ("The Lynching of Negroes," 1903b; "The Negro Question," 1903a). White-controlled magazines also published pieces by W. E. B. Du Bois and Booker T. Washington. For their part, Black magazines like *The Colored American Magazine* took on the racism of Thomas Nelson Page as when Carrie Clifford (1907), president of the Ohio Federation of Colored Women's Clubs, called out the "fallacies of Mr. Page's reasoning" and called his southern nostalgia "laughable" (p. 368). And *The Voice of the Negro* editor J. Max Barber (1906) pointed in no uncertain terms to the editor of the Atlanta *News* as the "man who deliberately fomented and precipitated" the Atlanta Massacre (p. 475) and to *The Outlook* writer A. J. McKelway as perpetuating rape myths used to justify white violence (p. 477).

With slavery no longer available to clearly demarcate the lines between white and Black, subject and object, citizen and savage, popular magazines such as *The Independent, The Arena, The Outlook,* and *McClure's* tapped into the widely circulating fears of racial mixture and contamination by reinforcing a fixed and immutable whiteness, one that relied on memory work to rewrite histories of race, gender, and sexual assault in the lives of Black Americans.

Cult of White Purity: Rhetorics of Contamination

In 1902 and 1904, *The Independent* published a series of articles that placed contamination and purity at the heart of the "negro problem." The 1902 articles contrasted viewpoints from a "Southern Colored Woman" and a "Southern White Woman." The editor described the contributions as "extraordinarily frank expressions of the views held on this painful question by the women of both races in the South" ("Editor's Note: The Negro Problem: How It Appeals to a Southern Colored Woman," 1902). The Black writer summoned memories of slavery to counter dubious white claims to Black immorality. She implicated the actions of white slaveholders, "Christian men and women of the South sold wives away from their husbands and compelled them to live with other men. [White] fathers sold their own children. Beautiful girls brought large sums to their owners when sold, especially for mistresses to the fathers and brothers of these same women who now marvel that the negro is not chaste" ("The Negro Problem: How It Appeals to a Southern Colored Woman," 1902, p. 2222).

That writer's strategic recollections of systematic white rape of enslaved Black women were rebutted by the article that followed, written by a white woman who asserted she had never "come in contact with but one negro woman whom [she] believed to be chaste" ("The Negro Problem: How It Appeals to a Southern White Woman," 1902, p. 2226). According to this writer, Black immorality polluted politics as it is impossible to make a "virtuous citizen" of a Black person (p. 2225). White people, she wrote, are "ready to tempt or destroy rather than to endure even a hand to hand political contamination with the negro" (p. 2226). The writer's conflation of sex and politics was typical of white anxiety discourses from Reconstruction to the early 1900s. In 1868, an Arkansas Democrat worried that were Black men given the right to vote, it would mean that "he would be taken into the parlors of all that vote for him—to marry their daughters, and, if necessary, hug their wives!" (quoted in Hodes, 1997, p. 167).

In 1904, *The Independent* published three articles in the March issue that presented the "race problem" from the perspectives of a "southern white woman," a "northern woman," and a "southern colored woman." An editor's note asserted there were "no women in the whole South better qualified to write on this painful topic from their various standpoints" than the three writers ("Editor's Note: The Race Problem—An Autobiography," 1904, p. 586). In her revealing account described as an "autobiography," the southern Black woman turned the idea of Black contamination on its head by giving lie to prevailing notions of white purity. Laying claim to her story of sexual harassment not unlike women and girls of the contemporary #MeToo moment, the writer pointed a finger at supposedly upstanding white men:

> Out of sight of their own women they are willing and anxious to entertain colored women in various ways. Few colored girls reach the age of sixteen without receiving advances from them. . . . I have had a clerk in a store hold my hand as I gave him the money for some purchase and utter some vile request; a shoe man to take liberties, a man in a crowd to place his hands on my person, others to follow me to my very door, a school director to assure me a position if I did his bidding. ("The Race Problem: An Autobiography," 1904, p. 587)

The southern Black woman's contribution was rebutted by an account penned by a southern white woman whose father, she explained, was a member of the Ku Klux Klan. The author detailed her experiences growing up around Black people, noting she "had affection" for Black people "but there was not the least conception of equality in it. I was not taught these race distinctions. I was born with them" ("Experiences of the Race Problem," 1904, p. 592). She continued, Black people have "no sense of race integrity" (p. 592), and Black women were the leading cause of community contamination: "They are so nearly all lacking in virtue that the color of a negro woman's skin is generally taken . . . as a guarantee of her immorality"

(p. 593). Black women were "the greatest menace to the moral life of any community where they live" (p. 593). The third article, written by a "northern woman," offered support for the southern Black woman's perspective by calling up a "resistive memory" (Dyson, 2003, p. 119), a retrospection that opened the door to a new understanding of Black women's experiences. She pointed out that the "scandal of miscegenation" has been going on for generations and that "one-half of the parties to the crime have been gentlemen" of high social standing ("Observations of the Southern Race Feeling," 1904).

Together, these three articles generated so many letters to the magazine that the editors decided to run a fourth article in July that "supplements the others," noting that the four "taken together picture the negro problem from the feminine standpoint in the most genuine and realistic manner shown in any articles we have seen in print" ("Editor's Note: A Northern Negro's Autobiography," 1904). The public reaction to the issues discussed underscores the unrest surrounding Black female sexuality, particularly as it symbolized a threat to the stability of domestic and social life. Fannie Barrier Williams, a widely known Black writer, activist, and club woman, wrote the July article, in which she addressed the issues of Black women's sexuality by invoking the memory of white rape of enslaved Black women. Addressing the southern white woman of the March issue, Williams (1904) noted that we should "look to American slavery" as the source of the problems concerning sexuality:

> It ought not to be necessary to remind a Southern woman that less than 50 years ago the ill-starred mothers of this ransomed race were not allowed to be modest, not allowed to follow the instincts of moral rectitude, and there was no living man to whom they could cry for protection against the men who not only owned them, body and soul, but also the souls of their husbands. . . . Slavery made her the only woman in America for whom virtue was not an ornament and a necessity.

Further underscoring the dubious nature of white claims to knowledge about racial purity, Williams related a story of how she passed as white by speaking French in order to get a seat in the white section of the Jim Crow train cars.

These counternarratives notwithstanding, most articles used the concept of a cult of white purity in writing about the race problem. In 1903, *The Independent* published an article by Samuel Douglas McEnery, United States senator from Louisiana, along with an editorial reflecting on the senator's sentiments. Like many other writers of the early 1900s, McEnery's focus of concern was "social equality," which would lead to supposedly dangerous physical proximity between Black and white people. On this view, purity necessitated distancing to avoid contamination. Blackness came to represent the threat of pollution or corruption. McEnery's exhortations elide the history of slavery wherein Black people had daily intimate contact with white families in their roles as servants, maids, wet nurses, and caregivers. This move to selectively forget the daily close proximity between white and Black people underwrites the cult of white purity.

In his article, McEnery (1903) emphasized that physical distancing would preserve the "integrity and purity of the white race" (p. 426). Allowing Black people to hold government positions posed a danger in that these persons "will come in contact with white men and women," which would be "degrading" (p. 426). Interracial marriages, he wrote, were particularly troublesome and may require retaliation on the part of southerners in order to "save the white race from deterioration and white women from degradation" (p. 426). According to McEnery, anything other than purity was a near impossibility. He noted "that [a Black person] can never be on a plane of social equality with the whites is certain. This is fixed in the unalterable laws of nature. No amount of education, no distinction in any calling or profession can alter the characteristics of the race which make an insurmountable barrier between" the races (p. 424).

The Independent's editorial in the same issue cautioned against taking McEnery's argument at face value as it relied on a pseudoscience of blood mixing to ensure that purity would not be contaminated. The writer pointed out that "no evidence has yet been adduced which proves that the negro is physically, intellectually, essentially, necessarily an inferior race" ("Editorials: Race Purity and Social Equality," 1903, p. 453). This acknowledgement notwithstanding, the writer posited a curious logic that reassured white readers of the predominance of white purity. Interracial mixing—the "admixture of blood"—has not, in fact, he wrote, resulted in "deterioration of white blood.... There has been infusion of white blood in the black race, but no infusion of black blood in the white race." Further, he continued, the "number of pure whites has not at all been decreased, while the number of pure blacks has been greatly decreased, and the negro race is being gradually Caucasionized" (p. 454). His argument suggests blood can be determined "black" or "white," that the offspring of an interracial couple has "mixed" blood, and that "white blood" is stronger or wins out over Black blood. Such reasoning sought to allay white "fear of a black planet," presaging Public Enemy's 1990 album of that name. The hip hop group called attention to the persistent white racist paranoia over the presence of African Americans and centered lyrics on "racist concerns over the effect growing miscegenation would have on the white gene pool" (Reeves, 2008, p. 85).

A forum published in *The Arena* similarly debated issues surrounding "race integrity." The "Have We an American Race Question?" section featured the perspectives of George Allen Mebane, a formerly enslaved man and general superintendent of the Normal and Industrial Institute in North Carolina; Walter Hawley, a white newspaper reporter; W. S. Scarborough, a Black scholar at Wilberforce University; and Walter Guild, a white writer and slavery apologist. Hawley's contribution, "Passing of the Race Problem," expressed fear over Black people in numbers. Hawley (1900) noted: "Idle negroes soon become criminals and dangerous to the peace of any community where they congregate in large numbers, but there is never a race problem where they are in a minority." When the "social lines are clearly and firmly drawn . . . there is no political agitation," he wrote. Likewise, Guild (1900) explained that the race problem is a "'paramount issue' where the negro population equals or exceeds the white."

In *The Arena* forum, Mebane (1900) countered fears of Black corruption by providing statistics demonstrating the Black population grew at a slower rate than the white population in the last half of the nineteenth century and that criticism of interracial mixing should be pointed equally at white men who maintain secretive sexual relationships with Black women outside of their marriages to white women. Mebane's recollection of this practice dating back to the rape of enslaved Black women called up white sexual hypocrisy: "If the white man maintains a high social position among white people, why should not the negress and her children (the latter in no way responsible) occupy a position of equal elevation?"

The Outlook likewise published concerns over the maintenance of "race integrity." In his rendering of the domestic and work habits of formerly enslaved persons, southern farmer William Baxter Poe (1903) relied on the prevailing stereotype of Black people as a "child-race" (p. 497) with an "undeveloped moral consciousness" to arouse anxiety over threats to race integrity (p. 496). He explained that with the removal of slavery to act as a barrier between the races, "other methods" were needed to "safeguard" "race purity" (p. 494). An *Outlook* reader expressed similar anxiety in a letter published the next year. The letter writer used contamination language, noting that "race antipathy" is an "instinct," a "moral antitoxin developed by nature in the individual whose environment involves constant and close contact with an inferior race in large numbers" (E. B. Taylor, 1904, p. 670). Separation by race, he continued, operated for the "salvation of the purity of the superior race." *The Outlook* editor and a regular contributor, Ernest Hamlin Abbott, placed racial integrity at the center of the preservation of civilization in his July 1904 installment of the series "The South and the Negro." He stated, "it is only doing that which is intelligent to recognize that the feeling which insists on race integrity is consistent with a determination to preserve the fabric of civilized society" (E. H. Abbott, 1904, p. 594). In two book reviews, *The Outlook* editors emphasized the desirability of retaining "race distinctions" "for all time" ("Race Prejudice," 1907, p. 452) and stated unequivocally that it is not prejudice but rather a "constitutional feeling, an indomitable and innate determination to preserve racial integrity" that explains the South's desires for separate schools, churches, and train cars ("A Study of the Race Question," 1906, p. 88).

Cult of White Purity: The Dangers of Race Mixing

The "one-drop rule" referred to the prevailing idea in the late 1800s–early 1900s that one drop of "Black blood" qualified a person as "Black." Codified into some state laws, the one-drop rule classified people according to supposedly fixed notions of race through reference to blood contamination by as little as "one drop." The one-drop rule facilitated racial segregation by providing a means for determining a supposedly static race classification. Increased mobility and the growth of urban areas made "ascertaining racial identity" even more important to sustaining white power but was always problematic because it relied on the vagaries of a supposedly visually recognizable race (M. M. Smith, 2006, pp. 7, 75). The 1896 Supreme Court ruling in *Plessy v. Ferguson* brought to the fore the instability of race, color, and blood identification but "sidestepped" how race was supposed to be determined, affirming that "separate but equal" facilities were sufficient (M. M. Smith, 2006, p. 75).[8]

Fannie Barrier Williams's (1904) account in *The Independent* of how she outwitted a ticket taker and passed for white on a train underscores how regulating race and rights was a chancy affair for white people. The uncertainties of race led writers to ponder the dangers should mixing occur. Amalgamation, as it was often referred to, was variously a "red flag" (Hall, 1906); an "impossibility"

(McCurley, 1899); "unthinkable" ("Southern Points of View," 1906); and may result in "defects" and an "inferior race" (Harris, 1899a; McCurley, 1899). Fears over the "product" or the "creature" (Harris, 1899a) resulting from sexual relationships between Black and white obscured a centuries-long history of interracial mixing, the result of white male rape of enslaved Black women.

In 1899, *The Arena* published a symposium on "The Race Problem," with contributions from notably competing voices. In his piece, "The Impossibility of Racial Amalgamation," W. S. McCurley (1899), a white writer, warned against the results of mixing white and Black blood: "In general, the mixture has always produced an inferior race, both in physical and mental capacity" (p. 454). Both white and Black parents experience "remorse of the unlawful cohabitation" that affects the "child in the womb," he wrote. The result is an "unnatural production; and instead of a superior race, it brings into the world beings neither white nor black, with physical and mental defects" (p. 454). In contrast, the formerly enslaved man and educator W. H. Councill (1899) called attention to the atrocities of slavery, shined light on white violence against Black people, and noted that amidst these obstacles Black people continued to progress. Turning the tables on the notion that race was a "problem," he wrote, "I cannot understand all this talk about the negro problem" (p. 432). If in the face of all the obstacles erected by white people, the Black person "has done splendidly . . . [then] what is the negro problem" (p. 433)?[9]

Other magazine writers echoed McCurley's unease over the results of mixed-race reproduction. A regular *Independent* contributor, Mrs. L. H. Harris (1899a), suggested a serious consideration of how the "negro brute" is produced: "He is nearly always a mulatto, or having at least enough white blood in him to replace native humility and cowardice with Caucasian audacity. . . . He is sure to be a bastard. . . . Can such a creature be morally responsible?" And four years later, one of the US senators from Louisiana, Samuel Douglas McEnery (1903), agreed that the "disposition, morals and radically different racial characteristics" of Black people "should forever forbid the amalgamation of the races" (p. 426). Writers for the allegedly socially conscious muckraking magazine were similarly alarmed at the prospects of race mixing. Thomas Nelson Page, author of the racist 1904 book *The Negro*, wrote a "special plea" in *McClure's* in 1907. Page's concern was palpable as he pondered the consequences of an educated Black populace: "Negroes in power—political, commercial, social! In the legislature; on the supreme bench; at the bar; in the medical faculty;—in all hotels! All parlors full of negroes! For the new negroes' aspiration is to mix with the whites. It means miscegenation—the mongrelizing and, at last, the destruction of the American people" (1907, p. 569; see also Hall, 1906). *McClure's* writer William Archer (1909) expressed similar distress over the issue of interracial sexual relations, particularly as the immorality of Black women "left the white male exposed, from boyhood upward, to a stimulation of his animal instincts which, in the peculiar circumstances of the case, cannot be otherwise than unwholesome" (p. 330). Indeed, the white race was endangered, he wrote, by the "instinctive, half-conscious desire of the black race to engraft itself on the white stock, and the no less instinctive horror of the white stock at such a surrender of its racial integrity. This horror is all the more acute—all the more morbid, if you will—because the white race is conscious of its own frailty" (p. 330). Page's and Archer's writings craft Black female sexuality as a contagion that may be released upon unsuspecting white men. The result was an "inferior breed of citizens" (Archer, 1909, p. 333). Notably absent from this appraisal was the routine and systemic sexual assault of Black women on the part of their white enslavers.

The Outlook addressed the "race problem" in editorials that confirmed the impossibility of mixing. In March 1903, its editors wrote that the "negro race is here and is to remain here," but "blacks and whites" will "not intermarry" and "never intermingle" as there is "no prospect of any such absorption of the negro race by the white race in our time" ("The Race Problem," 1903, p. 608). "Intermingling," the editorial continued, would result in the "deterioration of one race, if not of both" (see also "Southern Points of View," 1906; "The Negro: A Portrait," 1910). With similar certitude, the editors wrote five years later that the "amalgamation of the negro and white races is a thought not [to] be entertained" ("Nearing a Solution," 1908, p. 860).[10] In contrast, *The Independent* ran an article by the Black scholar and writer W. E. B. Du Bois (1910) supportive of the right to interracial marriage, noting that a "grown man of sound body and mind has a right to marry any sane, healthy woman of marriageable age who wishes to marry him." Du Bois countered the questionable science undergirding assertions that mixing was dangerous and maintained that white oppression of Black people was far more deleterious that anything that may result from racial amalgamation.

Additionally, a defense of Black morality found voice in two articles in *The Independent* in 1901. Bishop Alexander Walters, president of the National Afro-American Council, appealed to what Reyes (2010) calls "Black critical memory" to recall slavery's impact on the Black family, observing that "when it is remembered that for more than two centuries the marriage vows [of Black men and women] were disregarded and the sanctity of the home ignored by the master class, is it to be wondered at that when we were emancipated our moral stock in trade was almost at zero?" (Walters, 1901, p. 652). Mary Church Terrell (1901), co-founder and first president of the National Association of Colored Women, wrote a letter to *The Independent* detailing her work as a teacher of Black women and men and explaining that in all her years of teaching young Black women not one that she knew was "leading a life of shame" (p. 633).

Still, on the whole, according to white magazine writers, amalgamation or interracial mixing resulted in a contaminated (white) society. The stereotype of the immoral Black women served as foil to white female purity and a means for rhetorically supplanting histories of white male sexual and physical violence against Black women. Historically, their bodies have been "public and exposed" on display for purchase and perceived as an "uninhibited laboring body that was masculinized" (C. L. Peterson, 1995, p. 20). Mid- to late nineteenth-century white writers, wrote Peterson, often figured Black women in "degraded terms as abnormal excessive sexual activity," as a "form of social disorder that confirmed notions of the Black female body as unruly, grotesque, carnivalesque" (pp. 20, 21). White magazines that upheld these depictions performed memory work by shifting attention from past experience to present spectacle, from white sexual control to a supposed Black hypersexuality.

White women penned articles in *The Independent* and *The Outlook* condemning Black women for their "depravity" ("Experiences of the Race Problem," 1904, p. 592); lack of chastity ("The Negro Problem: How It Appeals to a Southern White Woman," 1902); "decadence" (Tayleur, 1904, p. 266); and immorality. Mrs. L. H. Harris (1899b), whose writings appeared numerous times in *The Independent*, claimed this lack of morals ran throughout generations in Black families. At the heart of the "negro race," she wrote, is a "debased" woman herself raised in a home where father and mother are not married; this woman is "seduced before she reaches the age of puberty. She becomes any man's mistress, every man's victim." The Black girl is "victim of savage moods and brutal chastisements from infancy. On this account she falls an easy prey to the first wretch who approaches her with deceitful kindness. The conditions of her life are inhumanly hard, and, tho her tastes are still barbarous, she is the most beauty loving of all women" (p. 1688).

Notably, according to these accounts, Black women enter into a cycle of immorality. Harris (1899b) claimed the Black mother passes sexual corruption along to her children who "draw in with their mother's milk lust and prostitution." An anonymous "southern white woman" stated with conviction that she was "ready not only to affirm but to prove" that, of her Black servants, "there was not one of them who did not have illegitimate children or was not herself an illegitimate" ("The Negro Problem: How It Appeals to a Southern White Woman," 1902, p. 2226). *The Outlook* writer Eleanor Tayleur (1904) lamented the lack of decent home life for Black women—the "beds are unmade, the dishes unwashed.... Here children are born to be thrust out into the street as soon as possible to get them out of the way" (p. 267). Other *Outlook* writers rendered similar observations of the supposedly immoral Black home with one frequent contributor, Lovick P. Winter (1906), noting a "lack of primal moral traits" in Black men and women and going so far as to say Black families "need a pure home" more than an education (p. 845; see also Hammond, 1903; Poe, 1903).[11] These accounts illustrate how the white notion of the Black home as chaotic and depraved is both long-standing and culturally ingrained. Over a half century later, "culture of poverty" discourses drew on this image in a narrative that updated the hierarchy of races to mean a hierarchy of cultures: a wholesome white culture, "protective and benign," and an "unwholesome" Black culture, "aberrant and dangerous" (Solinger, 2000, p. 61).[12]

Popular white magazines instigated a hypervisibility of the Black female body—unchaste and degraded or matriarchal and avaricious—that continues to serve as a scapegoat and a form of Black abstraction that silences the history of white male control over those bodies (J. D. Phillips & Griffin, 2015), a silence that Broussard (2013) describes as "palpable" (p. 388). Lurid descriptions of Black women's supposed impurity and lust centered white anxiety onto the magnified and dangerous Black body, in effect displacing the histories of white male violence and sexual assault of Black women. White men subjected Black women and girls not only to rape but "sexual harassment, domestic violence, and forced reproduction" (Livesey, 2018, p. 271; see also Blassingame, 1972; Broussard, 2013; Davis, 1972; West, 2018). Black women and girls were often the "long-term victims of rape by the same man over an extended period" (Livesey, 2018, p. 271), gave birth to children by these men, and often had their children taken away from them, sold off sometimes to the "fancy trade" where lighter-skinned girls went for a higher price as sexual commodities for buyers (p. 269; see also Bridgewater, 2005, p. 116). Black women's subjectivity was silenced by legal structures (Broussard, 2013), by white wives of slave-holding rapists (Bridgewater, 2005,

p. 117), and by popular writings that focused on the virtuous white female as the victim of sexual exploitation (P. D. Hopkins, 2011, p. 5). During slavery, Black women were property and so not protected as citizens, and into the twentieth and twenty-first centuries Black women have been portrayed as "promiscuous and immoral" and thus as unable to be considered victims (Broussard, 2013, p. 387; Bridgewater, 2005; J. D. Phillips & Griffin, 2015). The systematic rape of Black women hinged on the erasure of Black humanity in order to render Black women as purely corporeal and thus as "unrapable" (Broussard, 2013, p. 387). Perhaps not surprising then is Thomas Nelson Page's (1904c) observation that the "crime of rape was substantially unknown during the period of slavery" (p. 102). Of course, he meant the rape of white women, who were supposedly safe in the presence of their subservient enslaved Black men.

The depiction of Black women as controlling matriarchs who emasculate sons and husbands performs similar memory work, erasing the ways white enslavers controlled Black families, "forcibly coupl[ing] men and women" in order to extract more laboring bodies (Davis, 1972, p. 83), denying parents the right to raise their own children, and separating husbands, wives, and children. Angela Davis (1972) explained, "An accurate portrait of the African woman in bondage must debunk the myth of the matriarchate. Such a portrait must simultaneously attempt to illuminate the historical matrix of her oppression and must evoke her varied, often heroic, responses to the slaveholder's domination" (p. 82). In fact, Davis continued, enslaved Black women, through their efforts to care for the kin with whom they lived, played a crucial role in community survival, which should be considered a "form of resistance" (p. 87).

Into the twenty-first century, Black women's experiences of sexual assault continue to be ignored or downplayed by courts and the wider community. Black women are less likely to be believed when they report their assaults, and men found guilty of raping Black women receive shorter sentences than men found guilty of raping white women (S. Tillman et al., 2010, p. 60). But then as now, Black women practiced their own form of memory work—a resistive memory or countermemory (Triece, 2016)—that filled in the gaps and silences surrounding the place of slavery in shaping politics, the economy, and family life. These countermemories challenged a social imaginary that relied on a hegemonic collective forgetting, a form of willful ignorance that shaped the public imaginary in ways that have facilitated and supported segregation, disenfranchisement, and white violence against Black families and their communities well into the twenty-first century.

Memory work, or the culturally negotiated ways that public recollections are pieced together in partial and politically motivated ways, shaped how early 1900s white-controlled magazines discussed issues surrounding race, gender, and motherhood. Articles about the race question consistently situated Black women as negligent, hypersexual mothers who contributed to the debasement of the Black family and acted as a threat to the purity of the white home and community. A cult of white purity—or fixation on Black sexuality as contamination—muted white female sexuality and erased the history of routinized rape on the part of white men against Black women and girls. White writers frequently expressed a white anxiety when addressing the dangers of interracial mixing, eliciting a moral panic over the dire consequences of amalgamation.

Black magazines similarly proliferated during the early 1900s and provided a quite different understanding of the race question. Many are aware of the writings of African American men such as W. E. B. Du Bois and Booker T. Washington, whose opinions at times found a space in white magazines. Lesser-known writers such as Pauline Hopkins, Fannie Barrier Williams, Ruth D. Todd, Louise Burgess-Ware, and numerous others played an important role in providing countermemory work or "resistive memory" (Dyson, 2003, p. 119), to remember and bear witness to the legacy of slavery in the lives of Black men and women.

CHAPTER 4

Countermemory Work: Reconsidering Black History and White Racism

> To the encouragement of those who faint, or would slavishly bend under the weight of a mistaken popular prejudice; and to the inspiration and aid of all our noble men and women, who are fearlessly and successfully vindicating themselves and our people, the *Colored American Magazine* has been and is devoted.
>
> —R. S. ELLIOT, 1901, P. 44

In their debut issue, *The Colored American Magazine* editors expressed their desires for the magazine to enhance the "bonds of ... racial brotherhood" and to motivate readers to speak out against race discrimination ("Editorial and Publishers' Announcements," 1900, p. 60). They prompted reader engagement, adding that the "management respectfully requests that every man and woman who desires that the present perils, and wrongs endured by our race, should be averted and dispelled, will not only aid this work by a personal subscription, but will so far as is possible contribute" articles in the form of "biography, history, adventure, tradition, folk lore poetry and song, the accumulations of centuries of such experiences as have never befallen any other people." Four years later, the editors of the inaugural issue of *The Voice of the Negro* explained, "they believe that through the columns of this magazine the men and women of this race, who are the doers and thinkers, can reach the thinking people of the nation better than through any other periodical" ("Editorials," 1904, p. 34). They pointed out the launch date of the magazine was the "forty-first anniversary of the liberation of the ancestors of the contributors and editors" (p. 34). It is of significance that both publications emphasized the relevance of history—recalling and remembering—to their missions and to the identities of Black readers.[1] An early issue of *The Colored American Magazine* spoke to this point, noting, "Slavery has existed in other countries . . . but nowhere but here has there been a large negro population subject to conditions which furnish an incentive to authorship on so large a scale" ("Here and There," 1900a, p. 125).

Black magazine writers of the early 1900s saw the importance of acting as historians to rewrite and reset the "inverted epistemology" (Mills, 1997, p. 18), the social imaginary rooted in pseudoscientific racism and hinging on Black invisibility. Their contributions to *The Colored American Magazine* and *The Voice of the Negro* point to the importance they placed on asserting Black visibility and recalling the violence of slavery particularly as it was directed at women. Theirs was a sort of "liberation historiography" that went beyond "historical recovery" to "historical intervention" (Ernest, 2002, p. 415), a process Studs Terkel (1992) called disinterring the buried history of racism (p. 18). As Ernest (2002) so aptly put it, "Writing history is an act of moral imagination, and what can be apprehended as historical truth is revealed in the ways in which the narrative *doesn't* add up" (p. 416; see also Sweeney, 2019, p. 150). Ernest's observation points to the importance of reading Black- and white-controlled magazines in dialogue for the ways white culturally crafted memories do not "add up" when read against the resistant memories emphasized by Black men and women.

Black writers called out the epistemological gaps in white-created collective understandings of Blackness or, more specifically, the "race question." Their efforts illuminate the importance of creating a countermemory (Dyson, 2003; Lipsitz, 1998, p. 162; Reyes, 2010) that gives lie to white collective (mis)remembering. Countermemory work contributes to knowledge production and is needed when the culturally shared epistemic resources are insufficient for recognizing, naming, and explaining one's experiences. This insufficiency is part of a "substantive epistemic practice"—not merely a form of neglect or benign nonknowing—that sustains a *white* social imaginary. A "double consciousness" is an epistemological device that inheres in countermemories, a double knowing that indicates oppressed Black writers know both their own experiences of oppression and how white people view or willfully misunderstand their experiences.[2] Countermemory work represents an important rhetorical resource for marginalized groups (Dunn, 2011). Countermemories created by Black magazine writers sought visibility, a recognition and reinterpretation of history that centered both the accomplishments of Black people and the white terrorism that denied them basic rights to work, raise their families, and participate in the democratic functioning of their communities and the nation.

Importantly, Black women stood at the center of efforts to craft countermemories and expand cultural narratives for understanding race and racism in the early 1900s. The fiction and nonfiction writings of Pauline Hopkins, Fannie Barrier Williams, Josephine Silone Yates, Addie Waites Hunton, and Albreta Moore Smith refuted prevailing accounts of Black women steeped in racist stereotypes that derided their sexuality and denied them visibility as mothers, wives, and contributors to their communities. These and other lesser-known writers employed *documentation* and *haunting* to reverse the "indictments" of white histories and to present "data to refute" those histories (Quarles, 1979, p. 89).[3]

The Importance of Black Women's Magazine Writing

Anna Julia Cooper is exemplary for her contributions to understanding how Black women's experiences shaped knowledge; the extent to which Black women's perspectives could illuminate the shadows cast by willful white ignorance; the relevance of history; the importance of visibility; and the intersectionality of race and gender oppression. She began *A Voice from the South* by framing the ongoing debate surrounding the race question as one between plaintiff and defendant, wherein the lawyers have "theorized and synthesized with sublime ignorance or pathetic misapprehension of counsel from the black client," continuing, "one important witness has not yet been heard from. . . . [We've received] no word from the Black Woman" (1892/1988, p. ii). Underscoring the importance of the "situated knower" whose knowledge and approach to the world stems from social positioning and lived experience (Alcoff, 2006, 2007; Collins, 1991; Pohlhaus, 2012), Cooper explained that the "'other side' [of the issue] has not been represented by one who 'lives there.' And not many can more sensibly realize and more accurately tell the weight and the fret of the 'long dull pain' than the open-eyed but hitherto voiceless Black Woman of America" (p. ii).

Cooper (1892/1988) revisited women's accomplishments in "religion, science, art, [and] economics" (p. 57), made a "plea for the *Colored Girls* of the South" who faced the constant threat of white male sexual exploitation (p. 24), and landed on a foundational element of Black women's lives, the intersectionality of race and gender oppression, which resulted in a double-valenced invisibility. She wrote, the "colored woman of to-day occupies . . . a unique position. . . . Her status seems one of the least ascertainable and definitive of all the forces which make for our civilization. She is confronted by both a woman question and a race problem, and is as yet an unknown or an unacknowledged factor in both" (p. 134). Her reference to the "double jeopardy"[4] of race and gender oppression was echoed by Fannie Barrier Williams (1905), who wrote eloquently of Black women's absence from popular discussions of the race "problem": "She [the Black woman] is not known and hence not believed in; she belongs to a race that is best designated by the term 'problem,' and she lives beneath the shadow of that problem which envelopes and obscures her." Situated "beneath the shadow" of the race problem, she continued, Black women navigate a dual oppression and epistemic silencing ("not believed in") overlooked by white women and Black men. Her words foreshadow the writings of Black feminists such as Frances Beal and women who formed the Combahee River Collective, including Gloria T. Hull, Patricia Bell Scott, and Barbara Smith, whose edited anthology is titled *All the Women Are White, All the Blacks Are Men, But Some of Us Are Brave.*

Scholars have excavated the complex history of periodicals (both magazines and newspapers) and their relationship to white women and Black men (Aronson, 2002; Gallon, 2013; Patterson, 2020; S. Williams, 2015). From their earliest days, magazines have been intertwined with issues of race and gender, serving as outlets for reactionary and liberatory discourses that, prompted by their growing reach, shaped the larger cultural imaginary. The "collective desires" of a growing magazine readership became the target of magazine publishers (Thompson, 2018, p. 2). As early as the mid-1700s, magazines scripted racial identities through slave advertisements, underscoring the "mutually dependent relationship between slavery and the periodical" (Zackodnik, 2015, p. 140). More optimistically, visuals in the form of cartoons provided a way to cultivate the "practice of looking through African American eyes" (S. Williams, 2015, p. 124) and to situate Black readers' observations as a "means of self-assertion" (p. 125).

Much less attention has been devoted to the unique contributions of African American women magazine writers, including their serialized fiction, that broadened understandings of the contours of political intervention (Gallon, 2012; A. N. Williams, 2017, p. 27). Instead, historians have tended to "make the black press synonymous with an elite black male perspective" that centers on the accomplishments of individual Black men and narrowly conceiving what counts as political content (Gallon, 2012, p. 208). And yet, the regular columns, fiction, and nonfiction series of women like Pauline Hopkins and Albreta Moore Smith played a key role in keeping Black magazines afloat, given the challenge of relying on advertising revenue from white-owned companies.[5]

Further, Black women represented a significant part of the growing literate Black magazine public. With the post-Civil War establishment of elementary and high schools for Black students, illiteracy dropped precipitously between the 1880s and 1920. Notably, Black females had a higher rate of literacy than Black men, with "83 percent of females in 1910" able to read and write, "compared with 77 percent of males" (Margo, 1990, p. 9). Royster (2000) describes early twentieth-century Black women's "quest for literacy" as part of their "desire for agency and autonomy" (p. 109). A diverse readership meant editors needed to offer an array of content, a little something for everyone, which the magazine format facilitated. Examination of women's contributions to and influence on *The Colored American Magazine* and *The Voice of the Negro* suggests these often-overlooked writers blazed a trail for Black women activists and writers who worked to expose the intersectional nature of their experiences. Regular columns like "Chicago Notes" and "Here and There" and compelling fiction can be viewed as demands for Black female visibility as writers anchored their experiences of racism and sexism to America's slave past. Black women's contributions addressed a body politics that rendered the culturally silenced issue of white male sexual assault and rape of Black women salient. The magazine stories (examined in chapter 5) provided a way to discuss the taboo issue of sexuality and race in a format that sustained a readership eager to devour the next month's installment. Pauline Hopkins's *Hagar's Daughter*, which ran from March 1901 to March 1902, kept readers engaged and also fulfilled Hopkins's didactic goal of crafting stories of "political and social critique" (Carby, 1987, p. 145). Fiction writers like Hopkins drew on a "seriality dividend," which enabled magazines to "outperform other cultural forms in establishing and extending vital infrastructural networks of American literary culture" (Thompson, 2018, p. 16).

The influence of women who wrote for *The Colored American Magazine* and *The Voice of the Negro* can be seen in magazines like *The Liberator* and *Conditions* from the 1960s–1990s. In the 1960s, *The Liberator* magazine engaged the issue of Black women's rights, "served as a forum for black women's political agency, ideas, and perspectives," and put women in leadership positions (Tinson, 2017, p. 75). *Conditions* magazine, published from 1976 to 1990, started as a lesbian feminist publication, but became multiracial in scope when it published a "Black Women's Issue" that created a space for "black women's creative work and contributed to the development of the field of Black Women's Studies" (Enszer, 2015, p. 162). From the perspective of the Black writers and editors of early 1900s Black magazines, the goals of these magazines would have looked similar to theirs: to create a Black women's public arena to document Black women's accomplishments and to address the ways they experienced misogyny and racism differently from white women and Black men.

To understand Black women's writings, which were at the forefront of race and gender activism, it is central to situate them in dialogue with the writings of Black men and white women and men who also addressed issues of racism and sexism. Laying a foundation for the abolitionist Frederick Douglass, Maria Stewart relied on Biblical references to a jeremiad—the notion of slavery as a moral wrong and the need for national redemption—in her speeches of the early 1830s. Anna Julia Cooper, a contemporary of Elizabeth Cady Stanton and Susan B. Anthony, wrote extensively about the status of women in America, expanding the analyses of white women to encompass the double jeopardy (race and gender oppression) faced by Black women. And Pauline Hopkins contributed numerous articles detailing the accomplishments of Black women in her "Famous Women of the Negro Race" series, situating Black women in the sweep of history as formidable figures and challenging the male-centeredness of W. E. B. Du Bois's "talented tenth" (Gillman & Weinbaum, 2007; James, 1997). So, while Du Bois and Booker T. Washington are familiar names associated with race rights activism in the decades surrounding the turn of the twentieth century, the "period was in fact one of intense activity and productivity for Afro-American women" (Carby, 1987, p. 96; see also Higginbotham, 1993).[6]

Cooper, Du Bois (the Black academic and eventual co-founder of the NAACP), and Ida B. Wells (the journalist, anti-lynching crusader, and co-founder of the NAACP) were contemporaries who were often members of the same organizations although Du Bois rejected both women's offers to work together (James, 1997, p. 42). Du Bois (1903) suggested a "talented tenth" that would play a key role in the progress of African Americans.[7] The talented tenth, wrote Du Bois, consisted of "exceptional men," the "educated and intelligent of the Negro people," who would lead and "elevate" their fellow Black Americans. Although Du Bois's gender politics were "advanced for his era" (James, 1997, p. 19), the notion of a talented tenth was imbued with gender and class inequalities. His writings "assumed and privileged a discourse of Black masculinity" even as he "advocated equality for women" (Carby, 2007, pp. 235, 237; see also Cooper, 2017). He often turned a blind eye to the activism of Black women such as Wells and Cooper (James, 2007). Du Bois eventually rejected the concept of a Black elite or "talented tenth," soured by his own experiences of racism in the academy and by his recognition of the influence of Black working-class activists (James, 1997, pp. 21–23).

A core theme in Black women's writings has been self-definition (Collins, 1991), which includes the right to define one's experiences from knowledge generated by firsthand experience.[8] This chapter explores two rhetorical strategies Black women magazine writers utilized to challenge the willful white ignorance that denied Black women subjectivity. First, they relied on *documentation*, which served both a forward-looking and a re-writing function. Documenting Black women's public activities reconstituted readers and refuted histories of Black women appearing in white magazines. Second, Black women writers asserted subjectivity through a rhetoric of morality, or what Higginbotham (1993) has called a politics of respectability, that gained traction as a resistance discourse through *historical haunting*, a rhetorical process that calls to light a past, culturally repressed memory of violence (Foss & Domenici, 2001; Gunn, 2004; Lozano, 2019). Appeals to respectability functioned not only to reinforce traditional gender norms dictating modesty and purity, but to reinvoke the memory of white male rape of Black enslaved women and girls in an effort to rewrite the script of Black women's sexuality.

Documentation as Reconstitution

In the decades bookending the turn of the twentieth century, Black women wrote prolifically through fiction and journalism. Henry Louis Gates Jr. (1988a) noted the time period 1890–1910 could aptly be called "The Black Woman's Era" (p. xvi). The year 1892 alone saw the publication of three seminal books: Cooper's *A Voice from the South*, *Iola Leroy* by Frances Ellen Watkins Harper, and Ida B. Wells's condemnation of lynching, *Southern Horrors*. *The Colored American Magazine* serialized three of Pauline Hopkins's novels between 1901 and 1903, and both *The Colored American Magazine* and *The Voice of the Negro* carried hundreds of fiction and nonfiction writings from Black women. The importance of these works becomes clearer when we see them through the lens of reconstitution.

Reconstitution refers to the rhetorical process whereby messages can "liberate listeners to think and act more creatively, intelligently, and humanely" (Hammerback, 1994, p. 184). As a rhetoric of possibility, reconstitution taps an idealized vision that encourages readers to "discover and activate latent qualities in themselves" (Jensen & Hammerback, 1998, p. 128). In the context of white violence, discrimination, disenfranchisement, and Jim Crow laws, Black women writers recognized a need to encourage readers to rethink who they were and what was possible for them. As *The Colored American Magazine*'s R. S. Elliot explained in the epigraph to this chapter, the magazine provided "encouragement of those who . . . would . . . bend under the weight of a mistaken popular prejudice" (1901, p. 44). The magazine centered club work and club women in order to create a bold persona that suggested to readers a *becoming*. Without this rhetorical effort, some audience members may be left without the linguistic resources to envision a different and more empowered view of themselves and their communities. In a way these efforts represent a precursor to the contemporary "see it to be it" cultural tide taken up by women and people of color in recent years in efforts to expand the narrow white-male-cisgender representations in popular culture.[9] Through reconstitution, Black women wrote themselves into existence and encouraged their readers to view themselves in new more empowering ways.[10]

Black women's club work has an impressive history (Giddings, 1985; Higginbotham, 1993) that, when shared in the pages of *The Colored American Magazine* and *The Voice of the Negro*, suggested the possibilities for women readers and visualized them at the center of race progress. Specifically, writers used reconstitution to expand what counted as the "new negro" and the "new woman" (Smith-Rosenberg, 1985). The "New Negro" is a term often attributed to the literary figures of the Harlem Renaissance like Alain Locke who sought to create a new image for Black masculinity (Gates, 1988b; Pochmara, 2011). The New Negro is a "trope of reconstruction" (Gates, 1988b), one that enabled Black writers, particularly in the decades surrounding the turn of the twentieth century, to rewrite the image and narrative of the Black experience against those created by white writers such as those explored in previous chapters. The New Negro was a gendered concept, an effort on the part of Black men to assert a Black masculinity that at once "pose[d] a challenge to white constructions, yet . . . most frequently retain[ed] their sexist dimensions" (Pochmara, 2011, p. 10; see also Lindsey, 2017). Du Bois's concept of the talented tenth is illustrative of the gendered New Negro, which elided the voices and different experiences of Black women. The New Negro was also a classed concept that suggested the "isolated, cultured, upper-class part" might stand for the "larger Black whole" (Gates, 1988b, p. 148).

Black women wrote from and were shaped by their social location at the intersection of racism and sexism, what Barbara Smith (1983) described as the "simultaneity of oppressions" (p. xxvii). Their writings suggest the remarkable effort they undertook to be recognized within the Black community—as part of Du Bois's "talented tenth"—while also being part of the New Woman image that figured women as citizens and actors in their own right (Smith-Rosenberg, 1985). Anna Julia Cooper's (1892/1988) exploration of Black women's "unique position" facing "both a woman question and a race problem" found a ready home in popular Black magazines that served as a vehicle for wide distribution of voices gradually gaining a hearing. *The Colored American Magazine* and *The Voice of the Negro* were influenced by women writers and a female reading public eager to see their needs and desires reflected in print. Through feature columns and fiction, these publications provided a composite of a "new Black womanhood" that "appropriated the independence of the popular New Woman, but . . . used that independence in the service of the African-American community" (Bergman, 2003, p. 99; see also Lindsey, 2017).[11] Along with cameo images that frequently appeared on the covers of *The Colored American Magazine*, Black women's magazine writing served as a forerunner to the African American New Woman (Bergman, 2003, p. 91) or the racially ambiguous "New Negro Woman" (Sherrard-Johnson, 2007) that predominated in the Harlem Renaissance of the 1920s and served as a "resistive standpoint that could embrace the complexity of Black women's experiences" (Lindsey, 2017, p. 15). Importantly, as countermemory work, these articles, columns, and cameos contrasted starkly with the still-entrenched "mammy" and "jezebel" slave-era stereotypes. Taken together these writings created a new history of Black women's accomplishments.

An article in the July 1904 Women's Issue of *The Voice of the Negro* situated women's club activity as "one of the most significant movements of the age" ("The National Association of Colored Women," 1904, p. 310) and called on readers to "eschew" the resolutions and memorials that bog down men's clubs and, instead, to act: "Women of the Negro Race!! Write a Book of Acts for the race" (p. 311). These sentiments were seconded by club organizers and leaders like Anna H. Jones, Cornelia Bowen, and Josephine Silone Yates, who used magazine writing to extol Black women's club work and to underscore the role it played in the larger movement for racial justice. Their articles illustrated for readers a clear path to involvement and fulfillment in something larger than themselves.

Writing in *The Voice of the Negro*, Anna H. Jones (1905b), a suffragist and co-founder of the Kansas City Colored Women's League, asserted the "colored people realize that in the development of their women lie the best interests of the race" (p. 692). Cornelia Bowen (1907), a teacher and leader in the Afro-American Women's League and the Alabama State Colored Women's Federated Clubs, similarly lauded the roles Black women were playing in efforts for race equality: "The question is often asked, What is the Negro woman of America doing to help her own race? The National Federation of Colored Women's Clubs tells the story of organized effort among our women to reach the unreached" (p. 61). And Josephine Silone Yates (1907), then president of the National Association of Colored Women, situated women's club work as essential to solving the race problem: "Here women may show themselves a strong factor in the solution of this part of the problem . . . and the work accomplished by Women's Clubs will do much in the way of counteracting this lack of knowledge [on the part of white people] of the Negro's real status" (p. 45).

Other articles appearing in *The Colored American Magazine* and *The Voice of the Negro* between 1900 and 1909 amplified the activities of numerous clubs—from Kindergarten and Mothers Clubs (Yates, 1905), the YWCA in Baltimore ("Mrs. M. E. Murphy," 1908), and the National Association of Colored Women (NACW), later known as the National Association of Colored Women's Clubs ("The National Association of Colored Women's Clubs," 1908; "The National Association of Colored Women," 1906; Hunton, 1908; Yates, 1904) to clubs in the South and Northeast (Bush, 1900; Hunton, 1905; Terrell, 1904b; "The National Association of Colored Women," 1904)—and specified the names and accomplishments of club women. Encouraging in tone, using terms like "possibilities," "opportunity," and "awakening," these articles underscored the promise in organization and envisioned for readers what they too could accomplish. Writers seemed to suggest that if readers could read about it, they might be able to imagine it and strive for it. The NACW, according to Josephine Silone Yates (1904), was expanding in membership; another article proclaimed the organization's 1906 Detroit convention "closed in a blaze of glory" ("The National Association of Colored Women," 1906, p. 193).[12]

Writers frequently used articles to list the names of organizers and their clubs, giving an identity to African American women whose efforts may well have gone unnoticed (Bush, 1900; McAdoo, 1906; "Mrs. M. E. Murphy," 1908; Frances, 1906; Bruce, 1904; A. H. Jones, 1905a; A. M. Smith, 1903; P. Hopkins, 1902g). Addie W. Hunton (1908), an NACW organizer, identified eleven women whose "character and promise" had successfully led efforts on kindergartens, juvenile courts, domestic science, business, and suffrage (p. 418; see also "The National Association of Colored Women's Clubs," 1908). Olivia Ward Bush (1900), the recording secretary of the Northeastern Federation of Colored Women's Clubs and regular contributor to *The Colored American Magazine*, detailed reports from various clubs and spoke to the "possibilities of greater work in the future" (p. 234).

Writers did not ignore the obstacles posed by racism and sexism; their visions were grounded in the realities faced by their readers.

For instance, Maybelle McAdoo and Fannie Barrier Williams threw into doubt notions of universal sisterhood advanced by white women seeking Black women's support for suffrage. McAdoo (1906), a stenographer, club volunteer, and outspoken supporter of anti-lynching and suffrage campaigns, acknowledged "so much is expected" of Black women in business that they must outdo their white sisters: "But each year is adding to the number who are occupying responsible positions, and the public is beginning to realize that the colored girl promises to be a very important factor in its business affairs" (p. 303).[13] Fannie Barrier Williams (1908) warned against the tendency to become "imitators of white women's clubs," irrelevant to the specific needs of Black women and their communities. She noted that committees on literature, music, and entertainment were "not vital nor at all related to the social and economic life of the people by whom they are surrounded or whose needs they were organized to serve" (p. 282). The writers' efforts to give visibility to Black women's intersectional experiences would be taken up in subsequent decades by Black women's organizations such as the Combahee River Collective, formed in 1974, and the twenty-first century effort, #SayHerName, which raises awareness of police abuse against women of color.

The Colored American Magazine ran three columns that detailed the activism of Black women through club work—"The Women's Department," "Here and There," and "Chicago Notes." Seemingly straightforward accounts of club and business activities functioned not only descriptively but prescriptively as they suggested ways to be or to become. "The Women's Department," which appeared only one time, in June 1900, was edited by Pauline Hopkins, a member of the staff from the magazine's inception in 1900 until 1904 (L. Brown, 2008).[14] Hopkins was a formidable fiction and nonfiction writer, public intellectual, and activist on anti-lynching and other racial justice issues. As an editor and contributor, Hopkins was bold and unwavering during a period of white backlash against African Americans who had made gains during Reconstruction's "stunning experiment" that ultimately failed to advance racial equality (E. Foner, 2005, p. 159). Hopkins's radical ideology underwrote her magazine contributions and eventually led to her dismissal from *The Colored American Magazine* (Knight, 2007). In the midst of white discourses sounding the alarm against miscegenation—many of which found a ready home in popular magazines like *The Independent, The Arena, The Outlook,* and *McClure's*—Hopkins "advocated miscegenation as the ideal solution to racial strife" (Cordell, 2006, p. 61).

Hopkins launched "The Women's Department" with a column in June 1900, optimistically pointing out "one of the most remarkable movements of the twentieth century has been the ramification of women in all directions where she has seen the slightest chance for business or intellectual progression" (1900, p. 121). The column listed activities of the NACW as well as regional clubs in New England. In it, Hopkins identified the names and leadership positions held by numerous women in a variety of clubs—for example, Women's Era Club, Phillis Wheatley Club, Lend-a-Hand-Circle, Ruth Circle, and Dandelion Club "composed of very young girls"—thus illustrating the breadth of Black women's activities (p. 118). Her editor's note with that column spoke directly to readers, encouraging them to "send in the name" of their own club and "its officers for enrollment in the Record" (p. 118).

"The Women's Department" disappeared from the pages of *The Colored American Magazine* after June 1900. But "Here and There" seemed to take up the cause with notes on the "various social movements among the colored race," including numerous accounts of women's accomplishments in club work, philanthropy, business, and the arts. Detailing women's accomplishments month after month expanded readers' horizons and provided a reminder of the possibilities for activism. "Here and There" accounts often linked women's accomplishments to the larger cause of racial justice, something that surely struck a chord with readers. The August 1900 installment featured Eva E. Gay, a student at the exclusive Lillian Middleton-Cox School of Elocution and Dramatic Art in Chelsea, Massachusetts. Gay "won for herself (thereby the race) the praise and good will of her teachers and classmates, opening the eyes of many to the possibilities inherent in the race" ("Here and There," 1900b, p. 188). And Alice W. Wiley, president of the Dorcas Society and third vice-president of the Northeastern Federation of Colored Women's Clubs, was said to be a "race woman in the truest sense of the word . . . an untiring worker in every good cause, and a ceaseless advocate of the possibilities within the grasp of her people in every walk of life" ("Here and There," 1901b, p. 58). Other installments of the column detailed women such as Mme. Tyler who sang at the Grand Opera House; Birdie Crusman, a successful writer who was "reaping a snug sum from their sale" ("Here and There," 1900d, p. 141); Mamie Beck of Jackson, who gave the "best address" at the convention of the Michigan State Federation of Colored Women ("Here and There," 1900c, p. 258); and Lena V. Isham, pictured on the cover and discussed as an accomplished teacher, painter, and musician who held a leadership position in numerous clubs ("Here and There," 1901a, pp. 274–275).

Black women's activities and accomplishments were also detailed in "Chicago Notes," which ran from February to August 1901, and in longer articles that featured the work of specific clubs and conventions. Albreta Moore Smith edited "Chicago Notes," a forward-looking, optimistic column that provided briefs on women's club and business activity.[15] Smith (1901a) viewed Black success in business as a solution to the "opprobrious Negro problem" (p. 285) and asserted the "wonderful progress being made by the women should be a source of great pride to the men" (1901b, p. 469). In the February and April 1901 installments, Smith detailed the formation of the Colored Women's Business Club of Chicago and the Colored Women's Business Club of New York and provided brief sketches of women involved in organizational leadership. Profiles assured readers that business acumen did not replace but rather complemented the attributes of a wife and mother. Smith wrote that Dora A. Millar was "thoroughly conversant with the many needs" of the club and a "woman of extraordinary executive ability" but was also charming, warm, and exhibited "good taste" in home maintenance (1901a, p. 289). Like others described in "Here and There," Millar was a woman for her race: "she has abiding faith in the future greatness of the race, and believes that colored women should combine their efforts in order to overcome the many obstacles met in all walks of life" (p. 289). Smith's descriptions of ideal club women hint at the balance African American women had to strike when challenging traditional gender norms of docility and daintiness. Historically, from slavery through 1960s welfare legislation, Black women have been defined and treated as "employable" and have been denied the option to remain in the home as caretaker for their own children. Once relieved of forced labor, Black women often valued "emotional fulfillment and a newfound sense of pride from their roles as wives and mothers" (J. Jones, 1985, p. 58).

Still, Albreta Moore Smith spoke directly to her readers in additional articles appearing in March and May 1902, urging them to "arise and assert their rights as women who believe in the advancement of womanhood" (1902b, p. 27) and to follow the advice of Booker T. Washington in seeking industrial education along the lines of a specific trade (1902a). In "Women's Development in Business," Smith (1902a) counseled, "To those who have inclinations for the work we would say, you must examine yourself carefully,—physically and intellectually—by the sharpest criticism imaginable before entering the arena.... To be successful your life must be one of self-devotion and self-sacrifice.... Never be discouraged, for the thousands of women in positions of trust today is evidence of the fact that there is a growing demand for the work of competent women in all branches of business" (p. 325).

Documentation as Countertestimony

Black women who wrote for *The Voice of the Negro* and *The Colored American Magazine* also highlighted the accomplishments of specific women through profiles, which served as condensed biographies that documented the achievements of Black women in order to contest the white lie of Black inferiority; they were a written act of "countertestimony" (Mills, 2007, p. 33). Documentation through specific profiles and photographs functioned epistemologically to expand the social imaginary—the tropes, narratives, and imagery directed at making sense of the world—and to reshape and reset collective memories of Black women.

Mary Church Terrell (1904b), writing in *The Voice of the Negro*, echoed Anna Julia Cooper's lament that Black women's perspectives were ignored in discussions of race: "It is almost impossible to ascertain exactly what the Negro is doing in any field, for the records are so poorly kept. This is particularly true in the case of the women of the race" (p. 293). Writers such as Pauline Hopkins, editor of and regular contributor to *The Colored American Magazine*, used biographical profiles of Black men and women as a form of historical intervention, a recuperation of Black history and accomplishment from its violent beginnings in North America to the early 1900s accomplishments of African Americans excluded by the white social imaginary (L. Brown, 2008, pp. 284–317). Other Black women such as the journalist Gertrude E. H. Bustill Mossell, Susie King Taylor, and Anna Julia Cooper created a "portfolio" of Black women's historical contributions that served similar historical work (Dagbovie, 2004, p. 247). Here I explore profiles, both textual and visual, contributed by Hopkins as well as Carrie Clifford and Hallie E. Queen to uncover how these articles and images may be understood as performing memory work that challenged willful white ignorance when read against prevailing images of Black women such as those propagated in popular white-controlled magazines.

Biographical profiles appearing in *The Colored American Magazine* gave Black women readers their own history, something denied them in other literary outlets. These accounts countered white-controlled magazine that portrayed Black women as "lacking in virtue" ("Experiences of the Race Problem," 1904, p. 593) and that warned against "close contact with an inferior race" (E. B. Taylor, 1904, p. 670), images that hinged on willful white ignorance of Black women's experiences as enslaved people. In contrast, Pauline Hopkins's series "Famous Women of the Negro Race" (November 1901–October 1902) situated women's accomplishments as singers, writers, educators, and activists on a historical trajectory that began with the horrors women faced under slavery. Hopkins (1901) began her article on Sojourner Truth with a reminder that slavery "actually existed in all its horrors" throughout the northern states (p. 124). In this and the account of Harriet Tubman, Hopkins drew from historical documents to lend credibility to the narratives, which included enduring sexual and physical assault at the hands of the white men who enslaved people and, in the case of Tubman, serving as a spy for the Union army.

Similarly, Hopkins (1902d) launched her May 1902 piece on educators without mincing words:

> With the subtleness of Satan they [white southerners] proclaimed the inferiority of the Negro intellect and to prove their reasoning correct began to bring about the state they desired by special enactment of laws which should sufficiently degrade the helpless being in their control. The mind befogged and mentality contracted was more effectual than manacles and scourges in giving safety to the "peculiar institution," and would furnish ample excuse for all atrocities. (p. 41)

And her June 1902 installment began: "As we have said, one necessary condition of American slavery was ignorance. By the inexorable laws of Mississippi and South Carolina the Negro was doomed to hopeless moral and mental abasement" (1902e, p. 125). In each piece, Hopkins illustrated the successes of Black women, such as Louisa De Mortie, a "brilliant and gifted woman"; Fanny Jackson, whose "rare gifts and great moral aspirations" have been of "untold value and benefit to her race" (1902d); and Maria Louise Baldwin, who was chosen to deliver the address on Harriet Beecher Stowe to the

Brooklyn Institute of Arts and Sciences in February 1897 (1902e). Hopkins did not skirt the added discrimination Black women faced from white women. In the July 1902 piece, Hopkins (1902f) detailed the racist exclusionary practices of the white-dominated General Federation of Women's Clubs, which allowed state federations to decide for themselves whether or not to allow Black women's clubs to affiliate. She continued, however, in an optimistic light describing how "notable women of color [such] as Frances Ellen Harper, Fanny Jackson-Coppin, Annie J. Cooper, Fannie Barrier Williams, and Hallie Q. Brown, delivered address[es] [at the World's Congress of Representative Women] which drew the eyes of the entire world upon them and their race." Her pieces served to "talk back" or tacitly undermine the sole emphasis placed on Booker T. Washington as educator within the Black community, typical of white magazines. Hopkins's profiles suggested the importance she placed on Black history (see Matter-Seibel, 2003). She "insisted that national progress could be achieved only through reviving abolition as a political force" (Zackodnik, 2015, p. 152), and her efforts ensured readers knew that history of struggle and their place within it.

Profiles also served as some of the first efforts to craft an African American New Woman, an image of Black women that gendered the New Negro and raced the New Woman. Indeed, *The Colored American Magazine* as a whole may be viewed as an effort to craft the African American New Woman (Bergman, 2003, p. 91), given the emphasis placed on Black women's public activities and middle-class status. The African American New Woman illustrated the capabilities of her gender. But unlike the image of her white counterpart, the African American New Woman was community-oriented, directed to uplifting the entire race. In this way, images of the African American New Woman performed memory work, acting as a reminder of the roles enslaved women played in holding together families under slavery (Davis, 1972). Angela Davis (1972) underscored the intersectional experiences of enslaved Black women, their dual oppressions, and double-pronged efforts at race and gender liberation: "Even as she [the slave woman] was suffering under her unique oppression as female, she was thrust by the force of circumstances into the center of the slave community. She was, therefore, essential to the *survival* of the community. Not all people have survived enslavement; hence her survival-oriented activities were themselves a form of resistance" (p. 87).

Pauline Hopkins hearkened back to this history in her "Famous Women of the Negro Race" series.[16] In her March 1902 piece on Black women writers, Hopkins (1902b) spoke directly to her female readers, encouraging them to assume the mantle of the African American New Woman. Despite social injunctions against women's public activities, she explained, the "colored woman holds a unique position in the economy of the world's advancement in 1902" (p. 277). With the insight forged from the double oppression of being Black and a woman, Hopkins explained that in addition to performing traditional roles in the home, the "colored woman must have an intimate knowledge of every question that agitates the councils of the world.... Upon the Negro woman lies a great responsibility,—the broadening and deepening of her race, the teaching of youth to grasp present opportunities.... From the time that the first importation of Africans began to add comfort and wealth to the existence of the New World ... the Negro woman has been constantly proving the intellectual character of her race" (p. 277).

In her three-part series on educators, Hopkins suggested a career in teaching as key in efforts for race progress but also as fitting for women.[17] She described the "heroic efforts" of Black women teachers whose "influence upon her race in building character, inculcating great principles" could scarcely be described (1902d, p. 157). She continued, "The struggle that these women made for an independent, self-respecting manhood for their race was against desperate odds" (p. 157). In the July 1902 installment in the series, Hopkins (1902f) described the accomplishments of Joan Imogen Howard, the "first colored pupil of the grammar schools of Boston," who went on to graduate from New York University and become a teacher:

"Under the broadening influence of such educational methods, Miss Howard has developed into a perfect womanhood" (p. 172).

Above all, the African American New Woman was not afraid to speak publicly for her race and her gender (Hopkins, 1902a, 1902c, 1902e; Queen, 1906). Hallie Queen's (1906) *The Voice of the Negro* profile of Mary Church Terrell described the club activist's speaking engagement at Cornell University as doing "more for us as a race than would be done by the publication of thousands of books and magazines, which never reach the eyes nor hands of the white man or woman" (p. 640). Hopkins wrote of Frances Ellen Watkins Harper's public speaking successes (1902c); explained how the "most refined persons would listen for hours to [Harriet Tubman's] strange and eventful stories" (1902a, p. 134); and described how Maria Louise Baldwin's speech at the Brooklyn Institute of Arts and Sciences astounded white listeners who may have been "unacquainted with her ability" (1902e, p. 128). Baldwin "arose to the occasion grandly and fulfilled out fondest hopes, covering herself and us with new honors" (p. 128). The depiction of Black women as public speakers rewrote the white-controlled image of Black women as passive objects in the form of either the mammy or the jezebel.

Profiles of African American New Women were enhanced by photographs of Black women, which graced the cover of *The Colored American Magazine* consistently for the first four years of the magazine's publication.[18] These cover photographs represent "visual markers of the intersection between race and gender on popular black magazine covers" (Gallon, 2015, p. 14) and performed important "race work" central to Black magazines like *The Colored American Magazine*, *The Voice of the Negro*, and the NAACP's *The Crisis* (Zackodnik, 2015, p. 148). Far from being simply a register of reality, *The Colored American Magazine* cover photos were visionary, suggesting future possibilities, even as they performed memory work by calling up painful pasts and challenging "New Negro politics" that suggested Black people had left slavery in the past (Zackodnik, 2015, p. 152).

We may view photographs of African Americans appearing in *The Colored American Magazine* as a form of documentation that bridged the histories of Black women and the narratives suggestive of a becoming. That is, visuals may play a role in both reconstitution—a future vision—and in rewriting a past. Visuals provide a way for viewers to "'see themselves' in the collective representations that are the materials of public culture" (Hariman & Lucaites, 2003, p. 36) and to simultaneously see themselves as connected to a vital past. Photographs portrayed potential—as in the African American New Woman—and, importantly, established a history that rooted Black women to a past of race struggle, survival, and accomplishment. Reviving past memory "can then have an effect on public opinion and public policy, as well as public perception" (Atkins-Sayre, 2012, p. 79).

In suggesting a way to be, these photos were notable for the direct gaze of those pictured. Direct eye contact was a notable form of resistance in the context of white supremacist ideology that considered direct eye contact on the part of Black people a challenge to white power. In the case of magazine covers, direct eye contact with the camera conveyed power and confidence. Returning the camera's gaze suggested these women would not allow the camera to "still" them or render them passive objects. Theirs was a knowing look. With faces square to the camera, their expressions seem to command attention. The August 1902 cover photo of Birdie High of St. Paul, Minnesota, illustrates the knowing gaze. Her dress features a high collar and decorative bodice with a bow. Her hair is pulled back and up, and she is looking calmly into the eye of the camera. Her profile explained she was a successful stenographer and bookkeeper for "one of the largest wholesale and retail business houses" and that she advanced quickly through the J. D. Hess Business College. Numerous covers from 1900 to 1903 provided similarly commanding images. These women's attire—most often a lacy or ruffled dress, high collar, and bow in hair—marked them as middle class and associated with the status and education of the New Woman. But the frequently accompanying profile suggested these women performed work for the uplift of their race.[19]

Cover of *The Colored American Magazine* (August 1902). Reproduced from *The Digital Colored American Magazine*, coloredamerican.org. Original held at the James Weldon Johnson Memorial Collection in the Yale Collection of American Literature, Beinecke Rare Book and Manuscript Library.

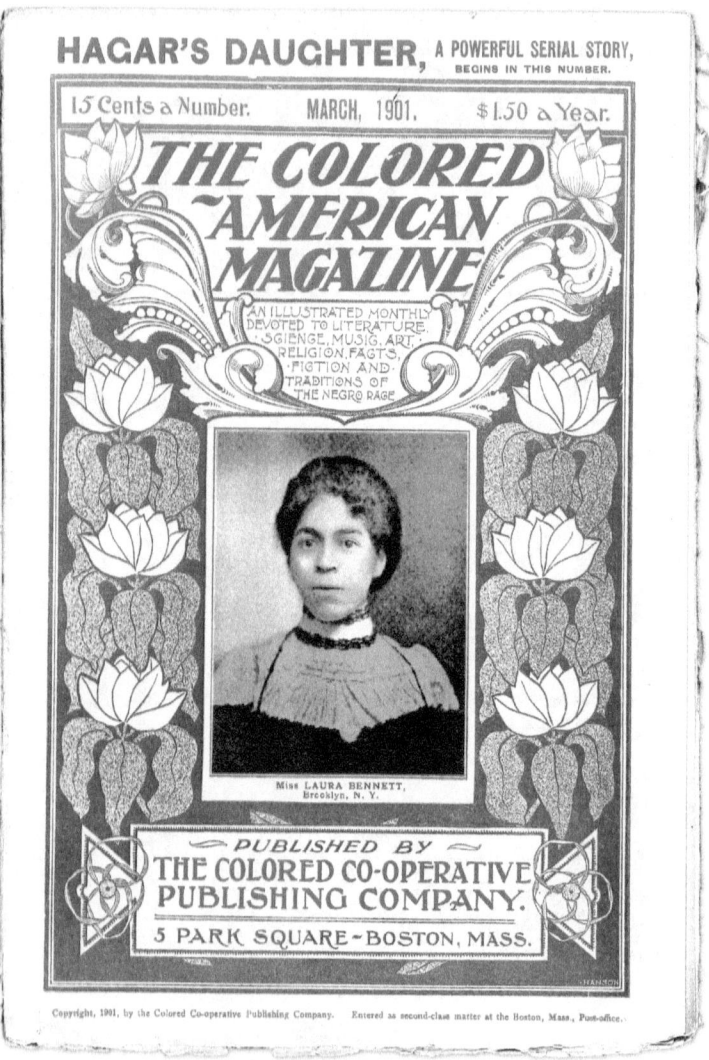

Cover of *The Colored American Magazine* (March 1901). Reproduced from *The Digital Colored American Magazine*, coloredamerican.org. Original held at the James Weldon Johnson Memorial Collection in the Yale Collection of American Literature, Beinecke Rare Book and Manuscript Library.

Cover of *The Colored American Magazine* (July 1901). Reproduced from *The Digital Colored American Magazine*, coloredamerican.org. Original held at the James Weldon Johnson Memorial Collection in the Yale Collection of American Literature, Beinecke Rare Book and Manuscript Library.

Cover of *The Colored American Magazine* (August 1901). Reproduced from *The Digital Colored American Magazine*, coloredamerican.org. Original held at the James Weldon Johnson Memorial Collection in the Yale Collection of American Literature, Beinecke Rare Book and Manuscript Library.

Cover of *The Colored American Magazine* (August 1903). Reproduced from *The Digital Colored American Magazine*, coloredamerican.org. Original held at the James Weldon Johnson Memorial Collection in the Yale Collection of American Literature, Beinecke Rare Book and Manuscript Library.

Cover photos also linked women readers to their powerful and painful pasts. Beginning with the May 1901 cover, the featured photo was flanked on either side by a small profile drawing of Phillis Wheatley, the eighteenth-century poet credited with launching the African American literary tradition (Gates, 1988a, p. vii), and Frederick Douglass, the outspoken abolitionist. This cover design positioned the African American woman as advocate for her race and rooted her in a past of Black accomplishment. These photos challenged painful histories of slavery that at once de-sexed and hypersexualized enslaved Black women. First, the genteel aura of the featured women represented a visual resistance to the memory of Black women as laboring bodies, alongside men, beaten and driven to exhaustion if not death (Davis, 1972, p. 87). And the racial ambiguity of the photos—most of the women featured were light-complexioned—underscored the instability of racial purity occasioned by the systematic white male rape of enslaved Black women. The lighter skin in the photos marked a haunting—a visual conjuring—of the history of sexual assault in the lives of Black women.[20] Like the image of the mulatta prevalent in Black literature of the early 1900s, the image of the light-skinned African American woman "triggers a collective cultural memory of sexual exploitation" (Sherrard-Johnson, 2007, p. 6). Especially when understood in dialogue with white magazine portrayals of African American women, photographs relayed a narrative of Black women and their experiences that belied the degrading accounts provided by writers such as the "southern white woman" who wrote in *The Independent* that Black women "were so nearly all lacking in virtue that the color of a negro woman's skin is generally taken . . . as a guarantee of her immorality" ("Experiences of the Race Problem," 1904, p. 593). This white writer had the historical narrative turned on its head. The color of her skin was an indicator of the history of rape in her family, the immorality of white men who systematically raped Black women during slavery and white men who, after Emancipation, viewed Black women, often without legal protection, as easy prey (Bridgewater, 2005; Broussard, 2013).

Recollecting Rape through Haunting

In her personal narrative, *Incidents in the Life of a Slave Girl*, Harriet Jacobs (1861/2001) explained that, upon discovering her newborn was a girl, "my heart was heavier than it had ever been before. Slavery is terrible for men; but it is far more terrible for women. Superadded to the burden common to all, *they* have wrongs, and sufferings, and mortifications peculiarly their own" (p. 66). The wrongs and mortifications to which Jacobs alluded were the regular occurrences of sexual harassment, assault, rape, and impregnation that enslaved women endured at the hands of white men. Rape haunts Jacobs's narrative as she recounts the daily experiences of girlhood:

> Even the little child, who is accustomed to wait on her mistress and her children, will learn, before she is twelve years old, why it is that her mistress hates such and such a one among the slaves.... [The slave girl] will become prematurely knowing in evil things. Soon she will learn to tremble when she hears her master's footfall.... If God has bestowed beauty upon her, it will prove her greatest curse. That which commands admiration in the white woman only hastens the degradation of the female slave. (p. 27)

Jacobs explained her own fear of Dr. Flint, her white master, who stalked, harassed, and raped her and forced her silence by threatening her life. The white constraint on Black women's voices—the enforced silence—is a theme throughout Jacobs's narrative. For Jacobs and the countless other enslaved females in her position, creating a space for articulating and giving shape to their horrific experiences was a formidable task.[21]

African American women's experiences of rape were deemed unspeakable on two levels. In popular parlance, rape was often referred to as the "nameless crime," as it was viewed as an act that brought shame to the victim as much as punishment to the perpetrator. Additionally, when white men raped Black women, it was not considered a crime at all and thus became nameless insofar as Black women's bodies were not seen as violable within the white social imaginary. White rapists forced silence on Black families. Jacobs (1861/2001) noted that her enslaved coworkers pitied her "but none dared to ask the cause. They had no need to inquire. They knew too well the guilty practices under that roof; and they were aware that to speak of them was an offence that never went unpunished" (p. 27). And the wives of white rapists, well aware of the sexual violence their husbands inflicted, were complicit through their own silence.

Autobiography and essay provided African American women a space to conjure the collective memories of rape through rhetorical "haunting." Haunting refers to the ways language and/or objects may be used to "concretize" and "come to terms with an incomprehensible experience" (Foss & Domenici, 2001, p. 250). Haunting suggests efforts to "mourn," attempts to "presence the dead in traces as a means of knowing" (Gunn, 2004, p. 93; see also Lozano, 2019, p. 89). Writers emphasized Black women's morality as a vehicle for channeling the history of collective sexual abuse. The memory of white rape haunted Black women's writings of morality, providing a way to tacitly *name* the nameless crime and to, in fact, render it a crime, while adhering to norms of decorum and respectability. Rhetorical haunting is a strategy suited to the gender and race politics in which Black women writers engaged in the early 1900s, a cultural context constrained by the seemingly contradictory practices of sexual prudence and systematic sexual assault on Black women and girls. Black magazines like *The Voice of the Negro* and *The Colored American Magazine* provided an apt vehicle to broach the issue of sexual assault as they provided the space for essays and serialized fiction and found a broad-based Black readership eager to engage with the medium (Carby, 1987, p. 127). Writers cloaked rape in a framework of "respectability" that provided a culturally appropriate language to conjure the unspeakable.

The politics of respectability refers to the emphasis Black women, particularly those associated with the Black Baptist church, placed on "temperance, industriousness, thrift, refined manners, and Victorian sexual morals" as a means to uplifting the race (Higginbotham, 1993, p. 14; see also Giddings, 1985). As a concerted reaction to the material and ideological degradation of Black women's bodies, the politics of respectability represented an effort to render Black women's bodies invisible or innocuous, to "serve as a guard against white male sexual objectification," to make their public activity "as safe as possible" given their bodies would "be publicly on display" (B. C. Cooper, 2017, p. 15).[22] The rhetorical challenge for Black women writers was to call forth the past in order to name the crime, but to do so in a language that would not violate social expectations (Gunning, 1996, p. 79; Higgins & Silver, 1991).

In fiction and nonfiction essays, Black women writers couched rape in the language of degradation and violation to render sexual assault present despite the literal absence of direct terminology. Degradation suggests a process, a doing unto, whereby something pure is dragged down, broken down, or eroded (Merriam-Webster Dictionary). For Black women writers, the language of degradation provided a means for "engag[ing] the ghost" (Foss & Dominici, 2001, p. 241) of rape. For example, Pauline Hopkins (1902h) extolled the roles of a "new race of colored women" who were educating their peers and protecting them from the dangers of being around white men: "The benign influence poured upon susceptible youth by the close association between teachers and pupils in four years of academical life can hardly be estimated, especially for a race where every effort has been made to degrade its womanhood." Writing in *The Voice of the Negro*, Sylvanie Francoz Williams (1904) likewise underscored the benefits of education for Black women in providing them the "ability to see and the power [to] feel the degradation of her own race and the injustice of a public opinion fostered by a prejudice which sacrifices her good name to appease its vengeance" (p. 300). *The Voice of the Negro* contributor Mary Church Terrell (1904b) laid blame on the "foul aspersions upon the character of colored women" that were "circulated by the press . . . and especially by the direct descendants of those who in years past were responsible for the moral degradation of their female slaves" (p. 292).

Other articles used ambiguous language to invoke Black women's past experiences of bodily violation and to link it to the actions of white owners of enslaved people. Stories of rape point to how "narrative memory" haunted these writings and provided a "means of translating the traumatic into something speakable, knowable, and manageable" (Foss & Dominici, 2001, p. 242). Equivocal language enabled Black women to name their experiences without transgressing gender expectations for delicacy in such discussions. In her August 1902 sketch of club women, Hopkins (1902g) wrote of the "terrible blow" southern white women had directed at Black women through their exclusionary practices. She continued, "tears and sorrow and heart-burning are the Southern white woman's portion and like Sarah of old, she wreaks her vengeance on helpless Hagar. Club life has but rendered her disposition more intolerable toward *the victims of her husband's and son's evil passions*" (p. 277, emphasis mine). Pauline Hopkins—writing under her pseudonym J. Shirley Shadrach (1903a)—rooted the issues of prostitution and interracial marriage in slave era practices that "weakened moral forces" (p. 201). In the same piece, regarding prostitution, she wrote that the "moral lapses" stemmed from slavery:

> Out of that dreadful condition there was no escape for the female slave but into the cold embraces of death; and the victims were born into that condition; they did not enter into it voluntarily.... It took years to force this condition of immorality upon a helpless sex, but to their everlasting honor, be it said, they have passed from vice to virtue with a rapidity that is amazing. (p. 201)

And regarding interracial mixing, Hopkins writing under the name Shadrach (1903b) reminded the reader that the "'shaded Afghan' which represents the present conglomeration, once pure African, was contributed by the blood of the Southern whites" (p. 208). In her profile of African American writer Frances Ellen Watkins Harper, Hopkins (1902c) detailed Harper's efforts to "speak to women" specifically "along the objects of wrong and abuse under slavery . . . [and] of their morals and general improvement" (p. 150).

The Voice of the Negro's July 1904 Woman's Issue similarly cloaked the issue of rape in terms of violation and im/morality. Nannie Helen Burroughs (1904) wrote of the "encroachments" Black women "had to tolerate before the war and during the war" (p. 279), and Addie Hunton (1904) recalled how the "Negro woman was the subject of compulsory immorality" (p. 281). In the same piece, Hunton called out the irony of the stereotype of the immoral Black woman:

> Wounded by the violence and shame forced upon her in times when she had no voice to speak her woe; bleeding because of the constant irritation of these wounds by those who, while spending their best energies to vilify her to the world, are at the same time ever secretly seeking to make these vilifications true; she asks, Whence comes all this talk about the immorality of the Negro woman? (p. 280)

African American women also used fiction as a channel for discussing systematic white rape of Black women during slavery, a topic taken up in greater detail in chapter 5. Two short stories in *The Colored American Magazine* drew on the trope of passing to raise the issue of slave rape. These stories follow a similar pattern whereby young women, raised by white or white-appearing parents and under the assumption they are white, come to learn they are in reality daughters of a Black woman and a white slave owner. In "Bernice, the Octoroon" (Burgess-Ware, 1903a), Bernice, "refined and fair as an Anglo-Saxon" with a "wealth of golden curls" (p. 608), is exposed as part Black upon learning her mother's mother was her mammy (p. 613). In Fannie Barrier Williams's (1902) story "After Many Days: A Christmas Story," Gladys Winne, a visitor in the Edwards home, learns that her mother and grandmother were enslaved people in the Edwards family. Mrs. Edwards counsels Gladys on the harsh realities of slavery: "She told this chaste and delicate girl how poor slave girls, many of them most beautiful in form and feature, were not allowed to be modest, not allowed to follow the instincts of moral rectitude, that they might be held at the mercy of their masters" (p. 149). Mrs. Edwards's reference to the young women "most beautiful in form and feature" signals what was called the fancy trade, wherein young, enslaved females, often lighter-skinned, were bought as sexual commodities (Livesey, 2018, p. 269; see also Bridgewater, 2005, p. 116).

The two-part story "Scrambled Eggs" by Gertrude Dorsey Brown (1905a, b), which appeared in January and February 1905, told of Black and white babies switched at birth. The story centers on Mr. and Mrs. Grayson, who hire Aunt Caddy as a servant. Mrs. Grayson defends Aunt Caddy against Mr. Grayson's racist treatment stating: "I am not in harmony with your proposed method of dealing with these true but simple minded creatures. Aunt Caddy is a type of one class of Negroes who certainly has proved its legitimate title to our respect and confidence. She has been well raised and for honesty and faithful service was rewarded with treachery. My greatest regret is that *my own father wronged her as he did*" (1905a, p. 33, emphasis mine). On her deathbed, Aunt Caddy provides the big reveal to Mr. and Mrs. Grayson. Mrs. Grayson is her daughter, born on the same day as Aunt Caddy's mistress's baby, Lisbeth. Aunt Caddy had responded to the slave owner Kernal Claybourn's threat to sell her baby: "you wouldn't dar'st to sell my child, for you know that both these children are your own flesh and blood and you know you wouldn't sell the one any sooner than you would the other" (1905a, p. 35). Fearful that her daughter will be sold, Aunt Caddy switches the two newborns, who look strikingly similar. Kernal Claybourn unwittingly sells Lisbeth instead of the baby he fathered with Aunt Caddy.

In an effort to reframe and rename their trauma, Black women writers haunted the memory of rape in order to center these experiences, which were silenced within the white social imaginary. Their essays and fiction served as countertestimony to white-controlled magazines that engaged in a historical rewriting by framing Black women's sexuality as a threat to white purity. In contrast to images of Black women as "debased" (Harris, 1899b) and a "menace . . . to the moral life" ("Experiences of the Race Problem," 1904), their writings recast the roles of victim and perpetrator and restored their experiences of white male rape to public memory.

The writings of Black women that appeared in *The Colored American Magazine* and *The Voice of the Negro* represented counterclaims to the narratives provided in white-owned magazines such as *The Independent*, *McClure's*, *The Arena*, and *The Outlook*. Although these authors wrote from a specific standpoint—they were educated, often from the North, and middle class—their essays and fiction spoke to the experiences of Black women who, regardless of education or class status, were relegated to the margins of history and were often overlooked in debates over the race question.

Their writings went beyond a reinforcement of bourgeois values of uplift and assimilation (see Gaines, 1996) to perform both visionary and countermemory functions. The image of the African American New Woman redefined Du Bois's talented tenth by broadening who may be included in this group. Documentation of club work reconstituted readers into formidable activists capable of speaking out against both race and gender oppression. Profiles and cover photos of Black women redefined what counted as Black history by providing a documentary of Black women's past accomplishments. And through haunting, writers redefined morality and respectability by invoking the history of white rape of Black women.

Black women's magazine writings did not only or merely reverse dominant images and narratives, but they also disrupted and dislocated them from their "privileged position of authority" (C. L. Peterson, 1995, p. 14) within the broader social imaginary. They troubled prevailing racist cultural narratives by rethinking and reframing collective pasts. Part of their project was to unsettle the notions of a secured race and the cult of white purity through narrative inversion.

CHAPTER 5

Countermemory Work and Narrative Inversion

> Never until we welcome the Negro, the foreigner, all races as equals, and welded together in a common nationality, will we deserve prosperity and peace.
> —Pauline Hopkins, 1902g, p. 277

> While individuals differ, biological differences are small. There is no reason to believe that one race is by nature so much more intelligent, endowed with great will power, or emotionally more stable than another.
> —Franz Boas, 1940, pp. 13, 14

The cultural anthropologist Franz Boas, referred to as a "renegade" scholar who challenged the notion of racial hierarchies, has been credited with shaping modern understandings of race, sex, and gender (King, 2019). His research regarding various ethnic groups conducted in the first decades of the 1900s debunked long-standing cultural beliefs that race was a fixed biological category and that some races were "backward" while others "advanced." Boas argued that environment played a more important role than race in shaping people's experiences, beliefs, and practices. King (2019) asserts that Boas and his fellow anthropologists—Margaret Mead, Ruth Benedict, and Zora Neale Hurston—were "on the front lines of the greatest moral battle of our time . . . the struggle to prove that—despite differences of skin color . . . humanity is one undivided thing" (p. 4).

Thirty-plus years prior to the publication of Boas's *Race, Language, and Culture*, African American women wrote short stories, serialized novels, and essays that directly challenged the idea of race fixity. Their writings, largely overlooked by scholars across disciplines, inverted and unsettled ideas of racial hierarchy circulating in the white social imaginary. As rhetorical strategies, inverting racial hierarchy and unsettling racial purity figured prominently in Black women's efforts to create countermemories that called attention to the history of white sexual violence against Black women.

Inversion as Rhetorical Strategy

Perspective by incongruity refers to a rhetorical strategy of disruption or dissociation, a process that creates new meanings "by taking a word usually applied to one setting and transferring its use to another setting" (Burke, 1954, p. 90). Burke goes on to explain that any given word is associated with a context, but when we "wrench apart" familiar associations, we create new understandings, as when we might "observe mosquitoes for signs of wisdom" or "discuss sneezing in the terms heretofore reserved for the analysis of a brilliant invention" (pp. 120, 121). By adjoining incongruous terms, using ambiguous language, or juxtaposing unfamiliar terms and images, speakers/writers may startle the listener/reader into a new understanding of the world. Perspective by incongruity serves a specific rhetorical function: by creating an "identity crisis" (Whedbee, 2001, p. 49) and a new framework for understanding experiences, it acts as critique and clears a path for social change (Blakesley, 2002; Triece, 2007; Whedbee, 2001).

African American women writers used inversion—a form of perspective by incongruity—in two ways. First, inversion ruptured what Mills (1998) called the color-coded morality found in popular narratives (e.g., cult of white purity) and images (e.g., the "debased" Black woman) that associated Blackness with danger and immorality and whiteness with superiority. Second, inversion upended the notion of race fixity circulating within the white social imaginary. Through essays, short stories, and serialized novels, Black women suggested the opposite—that race was fluid, in flux, and often indiscernible and thus a threat to the one-drop rule.[1]

The Colored American Magazine's fiction written by Black women such as Ruth D. Todd, Louise Burgess-Ware, Gertrude Dorsey Brown, and Pauline Hopkins represents some of the earliest efforts to use the trope of passing in ways that contrasted with the "tragic mulatta" image that garnered sympathy from white readers (Charles, 2020, p. 24; Sherrard-Johnson, 2007, p. 4). These stories use the experiences of mixed-race women to reveal the "malleability of racial identities" and to demonstrate how "disguise" could be used as "resistance" (Charles, 2020, p. 7). But the passing stories of *The Colored American Magazine* writers such as Todd, Burgess-Ware, and Brown went further in two ways. These authors used female characters to push cultural standards of decorum that circumscribed popular sentimental domestic novels of the 1800s. With bold storylines that told of suicide and babies switched at birth and that conjured slavery's history of the rape of Black women, these writers entered the "aggressive territories of irony, sarcasm, and parody" (Fabi, 2001, p. 4). And their narratives inverted pseudoscientific racial hierarchy by concluding with light-complexioned characters embracing their Black identities. These stories at once showed race to be unfixed while celebrating Black identities and spaces. These authors forged a new take on passing as a tool or means to an end that resolves with a celebration of Blackness. Stories drew on the instability of race as a clear marker to relate a story of the agency and acumen of Black female characters.

They deployed racial ambiguity as a plotline to show how light-complexioned characters could outwit or trick unknowing white characters who get their comeuppance in the end. For these writers, the "tragic mulatta" was far from pitiable; rather, she engaged in activities that undermined white oppression and resulted in her own independence and happiness as a Black woman.

For white readers, inversion acted as a sort of "symbolic atom-cracking" (Burke, 1937/1984, p. 308; see also Whedbee, 2001, p. 48) that forced a new interpretation of Black experiences in early 1900s America that contrasted with the narratives found in the mainstream white press. Inversion forced an epistemic opening, a way to resist the closure engendered by white images that figured Black Americans as visible objects and invisible subjects (Gordon, 2000, p. 88). For Black readers—the majority of the readers who were exposed to *The Colored American Magazine* and *The Voice of the Negro*—inversion served as "race vindication," an exercise in truth-telling and the exposure of lies (Franklin, 1985; Franklin & Collier-Thomas, 1996). African American intellectuals put their knowledge "in service to 'the race' to deconstruct the discursive structures erected in science, medicine, the law, and historical discourse to uphold the mental and cultural inferiority of African people" (Franklin & Collier-Thomas, 1996, p. 1). In their writings and speeches, African American preachers and professionals of the mid- to late 1800s supported slave insurrections, highlighted Black accomplishments, celebrated Black history, and challenged racial hierarchy, all to support the effort of vindicating the race.

African American women took up the torch in their writings for *The Colored American Magazine* and *The Voice of the Negro* by using inversion to suggest for readers a new way of understanding race and remembering racism. Inversion provided a tool for creating countermemories by subverting slavery-era ideas of racial hierarchy, instead foregrounding the ways, past and present, Black women have revealed race to be mutable. These writings served as literary forerunners to anthropological studies that proved race a construction.

Inverting Racial Hierarchies

Writers addressed accusations of Black violence and immorality such as those carried in white-controlled magazines by pointing to racist laws and histories to suggest where the violence was actually situated. In so doing, they inverted the widely accepted idea of racial hierarchy by recoding im/morality. Tapping the history of slavery and the nation's founding provided a way to attach immorality and violence to whiteness and thus to force a reinterpretation of who inflicted violence against whom. Pauline Hopkins (writing under both her own name and her pseudonym J. Shirley Shadrach) referred to slavery as the "sum of all villainies and the slave holder the greatest of villains" (Hopkins, 1902d, p. 156) and noted that the "negro is susceptible to the same temptations that beset the rest of the human family, but many of his moral lapses are the result of inherited traits inbred by slavery" (Shadrach, 1903a, p. 201; see also P. Hopkins, 1903b, and Shadrach, 1903b). Writing as Shadrach (1903b), Hopkins began her March 1903 article on interracial marriage with a reference to the history of interracial mixing: "As a class, Negroes are what any other people would be so long subjected to the terrorism of tyranny which blurred the relation of the sexes and thereby weakened the physical, intellectual and moral forces of an entire race" (p. 208). Josephine Silone Yates (1905), then president of the National Association of Colored Women, noted that slavery rendered the sanctity of motherhood meaningless for Black mothers who often were unable to locate their stolen children after Emancipation (p. 305).

Often these writings articulate a rhetoric of shame characteristic of the Black jeremiad. Henry (2014) explains: "To shame the white racist, then, is to transform what had previously been a mechanism for establishing white honor and superiority into a mark of white shame. It is to invert the order of things, stigmatizing beliefs and behaviors that had once been essential to defending one's status and one's honor" (p. 304). Writers such as Carrie Clifford, Emma F. G.

Merritt, and M. Cravatt Simpson drew on jeremiad language of warning and redemption to stoke the memory of slavery.

In her speech to the Northeastern Federation of Colored Women's Clubs reprinted in the October 1903 *Colored American Magazine*, M. Cravatt Simpson[2] (1903), then president of the Woman's Era Club, set lynching on a continuum with slavery. This position was in contrast to popular magazines such as *The Outlook* and *The Independent*, which suggested lynchings were "outbreaks" or aberrations within an otherwise civilized community (see, for example, "Negroes Lynched in Missouri," 1906; "The Lynching of Negroes," 1903b; "The Riot at Springfield," 1908). Simpson (1903) asserted that the "barbarism of these so-called civilized lynchers is analogous to the atrocities of their forefathers, who . . . had ships plying the African coast, laden with thousands of human souls to sell into bondage" (p. 708). Carrie Clifford, president of the Ohio Federation of Colored Women's Clubs, unseated the "negro problem" by transforming it into an American problem in her *Colored American Magazine* article "The Great American Question." Invoking the memory of slavery, Clifford (1907) argued, "Civilized people agree that it [slavery] was the arch-crime, and that from it flowed all the dehumanizing influences that come from ignorance, rape, bastardy, inhumanity and hate" (p. 365). Clifford turned the narrative of Black inferiority on its head. She asked, "Shall the Negro then be blamed for his degradation? Rather shall not the guilty South suffer for her own sins?" And using vitriolic language reminiscent of the early African American speaker Maria Stewart, who drew on the Black jeremiad in her speeches of the 1830s (M. Richardson, 1987), Emma F. G. Merritt (1905), pronounced: "Wherever the American flag is planted, wherever its symbolic folds are unfurled, the air becomes immediately surcharged with a noxious venom exuded from the poisonous body of a whimpering, whining creature that follows close in its trail" (p. 466). Merritt goes on to link the poison to the practice of slavery and subsequent Jim Crow policies. In contrast to the image of the illiterate freedman in need of white uplift, Mary

Church Terrell (1905) wrote with characteristic wit and irony about a "service which should be rendered the south" by Black people—namely, "freeing the white south from the thralldom of its prejudices, emancipating it from the slavery of its petty, narrow views which choke the good impulses ... of even its worthiest citizens" (p. 182). Terrell urged a discussion on the part of Black leaders for "enlightening, and civilizing the thousands of ignorant, slothful, unaspiring and vicious white people of the South" (p. 183).

Rejecting popular language that framed slavery as a "blunder" (Hyde, 1904) or a curse to white people (Blair, 1902) as did white-controlled magazines, Black women inverted the association by invoking memories from the standpoint of those whose families lived it. Slavery was "terrorism," a "noxious venom," and "barbarism." Their use of inversion illustrates Burke's perspective by incongruity whereby "incongruous word combinations" (Whedbee, 2001, p. 47) are used to force a new worldview and to simultaneously create a new sense of self. They used rhetorical reversal to invalidate conventional white understandings of morality and to vindicate the efforts of African Americans who labored through writings and speeches to get their perspectives on racism accepted into the wider social imaginary.

Other women gave the lie to the cult of white purity that so often served to justify lynchings of Black men. Writing as Shadrach (1902b), Hopkins pointed out that when a community discovered a southern white woman was having a relationship with a Black man, the woman was quick to "sacrifice her dusky lover to save her reputation" (p. 415). Mrs. Booker T. Washington (1904) set Black women's purity, "virtue and constancy" on par with if not superior to that of white women, who "boast of a line of ancestry that may have descended from the *savagery of the Britons*" (p. 290; emphasis mine). Sylvanie Francoz Williams (1904) noted the "immorality" of white people (p. 299), and Nannie Helen Burroughs (1905) pointed out that "white men" have "outraged" "women of both races" for centuries (p. 107). Ida Joyce Jackson (1907) took President Theodore Roosevelt to task for chastising Black people who failed to assist police seeking men accused of raping white women. She responded that Black people "despised" anyone who would "assault a poor defenseless female of any race" (p. 352). But Jackson vindicated the Black community for not assisting in police searches by pointing to the white violence so often inflicted on innocent Black bodies. An angry mob, she wrote, "strings up the first Negro whom it meets, innocent though he may be, to a beam and hangs him higher than Haman and then tortures his dangling body by shooting it full of bullets, or else set fire to the body while yet alive" (p. 352).

Unfixing Race

Black women writers upended the notion of racial biology and hierarchy years before anthropologists like Jean Finot (1907) and Franz Boas (1940) published their studies suggesting race was a superficial category. Essays and short stories established countermemories through narratives of interracial relationships to demonstrate race as indeterminable and thus unreliable as a foundation for policies such as the "one-drop" rule. Serialized love stories invoked and then rewrote popular white memories of the loving and obedient "mammy/servant." Plotlines featured biracial Black women who fooled white lovers, embraced their Black identity, or sought revenge upon ruthless white paramours by switching babies at birth.

Pauline Hopkins used irony to deride the anxiety expressed by white writers like Thomas Nelson Page (1904a) who feared the "evil of race-degeneration from enforced and constant association with an inferior race" (p. 213). Hopkins, writing as J. Shirley Shadrach (1903a), asserted that "legitimate offsprings of miscegenation form a large and increasing portion of the population of Massachusetts. It's a hard pill to swallow, but if you go at it right it is warranted not to cause instant death" (p. 206). With similar wit, Shadrach (1902a) asked in a September 1902 essay, "who can tell when the drop of black blood will inadvertently filter back to the *American channels from whence it started*, and its possessors be placed by popular vote in the presidential chair?" (p. 347, emphasis mine). Fannie Barrier Williams (1905), writing in *The Voice of the Negro*, noted that "great nature has made her what she is, and the laws of men have made for her a class below the level of other women" (p. 400). Likewise, Carrie Clifford (1907) reminded readers of the unreliability of physical appearance when determining race and thus the ever-present possibility that a Black person might be passing as white: "In many instances the slight mixture of color is not apparent, and these people ride on railroads, eat in restaurants, stop in hotels unmolested; and strange to say, these terrible racial characteristics . . . remain undetected by the wide awake, sensitive white Americans who marry them, and live happily with them to the end of the chapter" (p. 368).

Between 1900 and 1906, *The Colored American Magazine* published fiction by writers such as Ruth D. Todd, Louise Burgess-Ware, Gertrude Dorsey Brown, and Pauline Hopkins that together represent a body of literature significant for the ways they subverted the notion of race as a fixed category. "Mulatta iconography" and the "vocabulary of racial ambiguity" have a history dating to at least the mid-1800s with the publication of William Wells Brown's *Clotel, or, the President's Daughter* (Sherrard-Johnson, 2007, p. 3). According to Sherrard-Johnson, Brown's story (and others that relied on the tragic mulatta image) elicited reader identification and sympathy from white women (p. 4).

The Colored American Magazine stories of mixed-race women stand out for the ways they challenged norms of gender and sexual propriety and centered candid characters who subverted racial hierarchy, gave the lie to racial purity, and won their own happy endings through agency and self-determination. Writers used plot lines (e.g., switching babies) to undermine the social control of white men and place agency in the hands of mixed-race female characters. Additionally, these women inventively utilized the literary device of passing, the "conscious decision to use a white appearance to hide a Black heritage for social advancement" (Carby, 1987, p. 158), to explore the consequences of shifting racial identities.

In "Bernice, The Octoroon," Louise Burgess-Ware (1903a, b) used the story of the "cultured octoroon" Bernice to convey how race ancestry can be kept hidden not only from an unsuspecting white population but even from oneself. Bernice, who is "covered with golden curls" and has a "blonde complexion, dainty mouth, and deep blue eyes," teaches at a school for Black children (1903a, p. 608). Bernice, unaware of her "Negro ancestry," becomes engaged to Garrett Purnello, whose mother is a racist. When a jealous cousin, Lenore, reveals to Bernice, Garrett, and his mother that Bernice is mixed race, Mrs. Purnello "moved away from Bernice as if the air were contaminated" (p. 612). Bernice responds, "My skin is fairer than many of our acquaintances. My parents are cultured. Why should I be persecuted because mamma is of mixed origin?" (p. 613). Bernice then reveals racial hierarchy to be a house of cards, calling out the history of white male rape of Black women: "Let me ask you, how did it happen that your ancestors, whom you claim were so chivalrous and aristocratic, stooped to mix with an inferior race, and thus flood the country with the mulattoes, quadroons, and octoroons that are so bitterly despised by many of both races? Well may you blush when you think of such chivalry?" (p. 613). Burgess-Ware used the outspoken Bernice to foreground the hushed subject of white male rape, slavery's systematic sexual violence that relied on the power of not-naming to remain a nonissue, an act rendered incapable of being addressed.

When Bernice expresses her desire to devote her life to uplifting her race, Garrett intervenes and implores her to marry him and pass as white (Burgess-Ware, 1903a, p. 613). Bernice rejects Garrett's offer, explaining she "would feel like a woman wearing a mask" (p. 613). She has a "deep sense of right and wrong . . . [and] knowing the depth of the chasm existing between the two races, was not willing to remain in a false position" (p. 614). Bernice seeks employment teaching Black students at Black schools. Shocked by the poverty and ignorance of her students but dedicated to their intellectual and social improvement, Bernice observes the "mixture" of students under her charge. As the omniscient narrator, Burgess-Ware conjures the issue of white rape and hypocrisy, explaining, "It never entered her [Bernice's] pure mind that many of these [children] knew no father; it did not dawn upon her that a race despising hers was at every opportunity flooding the country with children, born to be despised and persecuted . . . whose fathers lived in luxury" while their (Black) mothers struggled alone (p. 614).

In the second installment of the story, Bernice temporarily leaves the Black school where she is teaching to visit Baltimore and to "enjoy a farewell peep into the world where once she had figured so prominently" (Burgess-Ware, 1903b, p. 653). She quickly realizes how easily she could be mistaken for white: "She smiled as she thought of the stigma resting on her. Such chivalry, such gallantry, but let it be whispered that one drop coursed through her veins, she would be scorned and disgraced" (p. 653). After a time, Bernice's visit "was no longer pleasant" but "only a ghost of a happier past"; thus, she leaves Baltimore, never to "wear the mask again" (p. 654).

The story winds down with the revelation that Garrett's racist mother was herself of mixed race, which, of course, renders Garrett, who had lived into adulthood as a wealthy white man, Black. At the close, Garrett and Bernice marry, with Garrett earning money as a "lawyer of much repute, and greatly beloved for the good he does for the race with which they are identified" (Burgess-Ware, 1903b, p. 657). The character of Bernice appeals to readers' experiences in what Julia S. Charles (2020) calls "That Middle World," a concept that suggests the connectedness between race and space in racial passing. That Middle World, writes Charles, is a "permeable," "metaphysical space" that reveals race as performative, an act of existing in-between (p. 23). Bernice experiences work and social spaces as racialized: philanthropy work was "white," the school where she taught was "Black." With "skin fairer" than most, Bernice could perform whiteness, but Burgess-Ware has Bernice and, by story's end, Garrett reject passing, suggesting it is a betrayal of their race.

Three stories used the plot of switching babies to examine the idea of unknowing passing. "The Octoroon's Revenge," by Ruth D. Todd (1902a), told the story of a forbidden love between Lillian, the "daughter of one of Virginia's royal blue bloods," and the "young mulatto coachman in her father's employ" (p. 291). Early in the story, Todd provides literary cues in the description of Lillian's appearance to cast doubt on the purity of her whiteness. Lillian has "masses of silken hair of a raven blackness, and . . . eyes large and dreamy, of a deep violet blue" (p. 291). Due to the perceived racial difference between Lillian and the coachman, the relationship is, of course, forbidden, so the couple decide to elope. Lillian's father, the well-to-do Jack Westland, commits suicide one month later.

The key to the "deep mystery connected" to Jack's death is held by one of Jack's longtime servants, an "octoroon woman" named Nellie who had an eighteen-month love relationship with Jack shortly after she joined the Westland family years earlier. Despite his promises to remain forever with Nellie, Jack abandons her for a white woman whom he marries. Nellie, left pregnant by Jack, finds herself with a "thirst for vengeance" against Jack (Todd, 1902a, p. 294). As it turns out, Nellie and Jack's white wife give birth to girls within four months of each other. The wife dies in childbirth, and Nellie is forced to be a wet nurse for the baby of Jack's wife. Spurned by Jack and forced back into her role as a commodity for the Westland family, Nellie plans her revenge. While Jack is abroad for two years, his white infant dies. Nellie, observing her daughter and the white wife's daughter bear a close resemblance, decides to pass her own daughter off as the baby of Jack's deceased white wife. Upon his return home and unaware his white baby has passed away, Jack is duped when presented with a "beautiful, blue eyed baby girl, with jet black curls about her little neck" whom he believes is the daughter of his deceased wife (p. 294). At the close of the story, we learn the daughter raised in wealth among "Virginia's most exclusive circle" is, of course, Lillian, the alleged white daughter of Jack Westland, who had committed suicide. Upon learning her own mixed-race history, Lillian, left with a substantial inheritance, decides to marry the coachman, Harry, and along with her mother, Nellie, "the octoroon avenger," they go abroad where race prejudice is less prominent (p. 295).

"After Many Days" by Fannie Barrier Williams (1902) related a similar story of a Black servant who had her own mixed-race daughter raised in the white family. In the story, Aunt Linda reveals to the "lovely Gladys Winne," raised by white foster parents, that she is really the granddaughter of Aunt Linda. Aunt Linda's daughter, Alice, had eloped with the young Master Harry Winne and gave birth to Gladys. Alice died shortly after childbirth and made Harry promise to raise Gladys in the Winne home and to never tell her "that her ma was a slave or dat she has a drop of my blood, make it all yours" (p. 148). Further undermining the trustworthiness of race identification upon (white) sight, Aunt Alice, as she tells the story to Gladys, takes Gladys's hand—"pink and white and delicate as a rose leaf"—into "her own old and yellow one" and asserts, "Look chile, look, could any one ever fin' the same blood in dese two hans by jest looking at en? No, honey, I has done kep dissecret all dese years, and now I pass it on to you an you mus' keep it for yourself for the res' of de time" (p. 149).

Unwilling to forsake her own racial family background, Gladys reveals that she is part Black to her fiancé Paul, who responds with incredulity that it is "nonsense," "impossible, worse than improbable . . . is it possible that there can be concealed in this flawless skin, these dear violet eyes, these finely chiseled features, a trace of lineage or blood, without a single characteristic to vindicate its presence?" (F. B. Williams, 1902, p. 152). Paul channels the white fear of indeterminate racial markers that threatened to crumble the foundation of racial discrimination. The two decide to part ways, but, upon Paul's urging, they meet once more for a final goodbye, whereupon Gladys states, "Look at me, Paul . . . have I changed since yesterday;

am I not the same Gladys you have loved so long?" (p. 153). Gladys's remark underscores the spuriousness of "contamination" from Black blood that would result in what Thomas Nelson Page (1904a) called "race-degeneration" (p. 213). In Williams's story, an enlightened Paul realizes, "there is no such thing as life without Gladys" (p. 153), and the two live happily ever after.

A similar revelation that confounded race identification came from the Black servant Aunt Caddy in the two-part short story "Scrambled Eggs" by Gertrude Dorsey Brown (1905a, b). Aunt Caddy works in the home of the well-to-do Grayson family, headed by the racist Mr. Grayson who is offended that Aunt Caddy wishes to be called by her chosen post-slavery name, Mrs. Caroline Somebody (G. D. Brown, 1905a, p. 32). Lying on her deathbed at the Grayson home, Aunt Caddy reveals that she is actually Mrs. Grayson's mother. Caddy gave birth to Mrs. Grayson on the same day as her mistress gave birth to a daughter. Caddy describes her own baby as a "pretty plump little girl, as much like missus' babe as could be 'ceptin' mine had darker hair and much more of it" (p. 36). Caddy's white owner, Kernal Claybourn, concerned that Caddy would devote more attention to her own child than his wife's, threatened to sell Caddy's baby. Caddy responded: "Kernal Claybourn, you wouldn't dar'st to sell my child, for you know that both these children are your own flesh and blood and you know you wouldn't sell the one any sooner than you would the other" (p. 36). Claybourn, unable to tell the two baby girls apart, inadvertently sold his white daughter "up-river to a speculator in Memphis" (p. 37). Caddy, aware of the "mistake," kept quiet and followed Claybourn's orders to "scramble [his] eggs for my breakfast" (p. 37). Caddy, on her deathbed, notes the irony of the scrambled egg, repeating to herself, "I certainly done scrambled your eggs" (p. 37).

In the stories of baby switching, the narrative control remained in the voice of the Black servant responsible for the swap. Nellie, Aunt Linda, and Aunt Caddy related the story from their own perspectives as mothers concerned for the welfare of their infants. Rather than objects of white scorn, and although victims of white male rape, these women fooled the men who assaulted them, putting into sharp relief the constructedness and indeed precariousness of racial difference and thus racial privilege. In the context of the one-drop rule, Aunt Caddy's revelation meant, of course, that the racist Mr. Grayson was unknowingly married to a Black woman, thus mocking Grayson's asserted epistemic superiority—the idea held by white people that they could somehow *know* or readily perceive Blackness. Ruth Todd, author of "The Octoroon's Revenge," gave the wealthy white antagonist, Jack Westland, the ultimate denouement, death by suicide, to critique the depth of hatred white people held toward Blackness. Writers drew on the theme of passing to examine the experiences of women who were unaware of their own racialized past. Whereas traditional narratives of passing explore what happens when African American characters assume a white identity—e.g., Jessie Redmon Fauset's *Plum Bun* and Nella Larsen's *Passing*—writers like Todd and Williams created characters caught off guard upon learning their mothers were Black. Lillian (in "The Octoroon's Revenge") and Gladys (in "After Many Days") embrace their Black identities without pause and marry their suitors of choice. Hopkins's *Hagar's Daughter*, detailed below, suggested a more complicated process of identity realization and acceptance.

"A Case of Measure for Measure," by Gertrude Dorsey Brown (1906a-f), provided a twist on the traditional passing trope, telling the story of Agnes Hein, a young white woman, invited to a "Negro ball" that requires the white attendees to present themselves in blackface to "represent a colored person" (G. D. Brown, 1906a, p. 253). Agnes tasks Ora, her Black maid, with assisting in the effort to make Agnes look Black. Ora, filled with "indignation" and viewing the "white colored ball" with the "same depths of contempt that she reserved for . . . 'The Clansman'" (p. 257), had obtained Black dye and "massaged [it] into the soft white skin" of Agnes (p. 257). Transformed into apparent Black people, Agnes and her fellow white friends experience more than they bargained for—racism "measure for measure." The July and August 1906 installments of the story tell of two white men, made up in blackface to attend the Black ball, who sneak into an open window of the home of Judge King (the host of the ball) in order to steal diamonds. Once caught and having fruitlessly tried to explain they are not really Black, they "were hurried out a rear entrance half fainting and scarcely able to plead for that mercy which is so seldom granted to colored men who are charged with crime, and never to those who are caught with the goods" (G. D. Brown, 1906d, p. 97). Judge King, satisfied with having caught the robbers, suggests a "tree party," a turn of events in which the author hints at just desserts for the white men who have participated in the history of lynching violence on Black bodies.

The August 1906 installment tells of another instance of white "justice" when, at the close of the ball and ready to take the train back home, Agnes and her fellow party attendees discover the Black dye can't be removed from their skin. Standing at the train station appearing as Black passengers, Agnes and her friends are denied entrance onto the cars and are forced to wait for a later train with a Jim Crow car. They plead in vain with the conductor, "Why, you surely can tell by our voices and—well, our diction, that we are not Negroes" (G. D. Brown, 1906d, p. 100). Unconvinced, the conductor allows the train to pull away, leaving the group "standing on the platform in various stages of insanity and chagrin," giving them a dose of their own racist medicine, "measure for measure" (p. 100).

Pauline Hopkins's thirty-seven-chapter serialized novel *Hagar's Daughter*, appearing in *The Colored American Magazine* from March 1901 to March 1902, stands as a signature example of Black women's literature that inverted the notion of race fixity, suggested the absurdity of the one-drop rule, and placed agency in the hands of Black women.[3] Hopkins's fiction has parallels with the genre of domestic fiction created by women writers of the early twentieth century but with significant differences. Her writing "used the heroine's entertaining adventures to repudiate racism" (Tate, 1992, p. 195).

The story, opening in the fall of 1860 as the southern states sought secession and the Civil War heated up, takes the reader across twenty years, through multiple plot surprises, and provides a happy ending with love crossing race lines. The narrative begins with the marriage of the wealthy Ellis Enson to the beautiful Hagar Sargent, who is described as having "pure creamy skin" and "curved crimson lips ready to smile" (P. Hopkins, 1901/1902, p. 35) and elsewhere as "spiritual, and open as the day" (p. 44). But the perfect marriage, made complete by the birth of a daughter, is thrown asunder when the nefarious slave-trader Walker and St. Clair Enson, Ellis's ne'er-do-well disinherited brother, visit the Enson family under the pretext that St. Clair wishes to meet his new niece. The plan, hatched by Walker and St. Clair prior to the visit, is to reveal Walker's secret, that he "bought a slave child from a man in St. Louis, and not being able to find a ready sale for her on account of her white complexion," he "lent her" to the Sargent family who raised her as their own daughter (p. 52). The girl Walker refers to is none other than Hagar, proved when Walker presents the papers of the sale. Ellis, shocked at the revelation that his wife is part Black, pays Walker $6,000 to retain his wife and child. Ellis's reaction to the sale underscores the extent of white anxiety over Black contamination so common at the time: he says, "I would willingly give the money twice over, even my whole fortune, if it did not prove my wife to be of Negro blood" (p. 56).

But then, in a show of white redemption, Ellis decides he truly loves Hagar and his daughter and so plans to leave for Europe with his family where they can live presumably without racial prejudice. Overhearing the family's plan, Walker assaults Ellis, leaving him for dead, reasserts control over Hagar and the baby, and sells them to a New Orleans merchant (P. Hopkins, 1901/1902, p. 73). Hagar, "with her child closely clasped in her arms" (p. 73), makes a night escape but, soon trapped on all sides by pursuers, she has to make an excruciating decision:

She kissed her babe, clasped it convulsively in her arms, saying: "Alas, poor innocent, there is one gift for thee yet left for your unfortunate mother to bestow,—it is death. Better so than the fate reserved for us both." Then she raised her tearful, imploring eyes to heaven as if seeking for mercy and compassion, and with one bound sprang over the railing of the bridge, and sank beneath the waters of the Potomac river. (pp. 74, 75)

The narrative then jumps to 1882 when the reader is introduced to Senator Bowen, his wife, Estelle, and their daughter, Jewel. Estelle is Bowen's second wife but acts as a "mother to the motherless child [Jewel]" (P. Hopkins, 1901/1902, p. 81). Jewel is described as having "beauty ... of the Saxon type, dazzling fair, with creamy roseate skin. Her hair was fair, with streaks of copper in it; her eyes, gray with thick short lashes" (p. 82). Between Jewel and her stepmother, "there was perfect accord" (p. 83). From the time Estelle first met her, "Jewel had been like her very own" (p. 83). After receiving an education and traveling abroad, Jewel meets the Harvard-educated Cuthbert Sumner, and the two fall in love. In the meantime, another nefarious plot is hatched, this time by General Benson (Cuthbert's superior at the Treasury Department), Benson's friend Major Madison, and Madison's daughter, Aurelia. The three plan to swindle the Sumner family of millions of dollars by convincing Sumner to marry Aurelia, thus giving Madison access to the Sumner fortune, and by arranging a marriage between Benson and Jewel, which would presumably give Benson access to the Bowen estate. Through a series of events, Aurelia tricks Jewel into breaking off her engagement with Cuthbert, and Benson frames Cuthbert for a murder, thus sending Cuthbert to jail. Jewel, unconvinced of Cuthbert's guilt, visits him in jail, and they reunite and marry while he remains imprisoned. In the meantime, Senator Bowen passed away, and his will, when found, somewhat suspiciously assigns Benson legal guardianship of Jewel until she comes of age.

Cuthbert's trial provides the backdrop for the big reveal wherein the detective Mr. Henson uncovers the true identities of various characters who have eluded detection. On the witness stand, Henson explains that, after having been beaten up by his brother and Walker, Ellis Enson regained consciousness to find his wife, Hagar, and his child had been sold into slavery (P. Hopkins, 1901/1902, p. 260). Henson then explains that he discovered St. Clair and Walker were still living in the US, although undercover after having been "found guilty as one of the conspirators against the life of President Lincoln" (p. 261). With the judge and those present in the courtroom on tenterhooks, he continues:

> I found that [St. Clair] was in this country, serving the government he had basely betrayed, and still steeped in crime along with his pal, Walker. Gentlemen, General Benson is St. Clair Enson, and his friend, Major Madison, is the notorious trader, Walker. As for me, I no longer need to conceal my identity. Gentlemen . . . *General Benson is my brother—I am Ellis Enson!* (p. 261, italics in original).

Upon this revelation, Mrs. Bowen "sprang to her feet with a scream," approaches Ellis/Mr. Hanson, and exclaims, "Ellis! Ellis! I am Hagar!" (p. 261). General Benson is subsequently charged with the murder for which he framed Cuthbert, Madison is charged with forging Senator Bowen's will, Cuthbert is released from jail and reunited with Jewel, and, happily, Hagar/Mrs. Bowen and Ellis remarry.

A final twist of events leads to the discovery of Jewel's identity. As Hagar is assisting in settling the Bowen estate, she remembers the senator's dying words regarding a "little hair trunk" (P. Hopkins, 1901/1902, p. 274). Hagar gently sifts through the objects of the trunk and discovers infant clothing, "vaguely familiar" in appearance, and her mother's locket, which she recalled was around her "darling's neck" when she last dressed her, prior to her being sold in the slave market. In the locket is a small piece of paper upon which is written:

> March 1862,—Went up the Potomac on the "Zenas Bowen" for oysters. Brought off 100 guns, 300 pounds of ammunition, Charleston, S. C. Picked up log gloating outside the bay with a girl baby less

than one year old attached to it by clothing. Must have floated many hours, but the sleeping child was unhurt. Clothing rich; no clue to parents or relatives. November 1862.—Have adopted the child and shall call her "Jewel." Have placed this mem. [memo] inside locket found on child for future reference. Zenas Bowen, Mary Jane Bowen

Alas, Hagar (and the reader) discover that Jewel is Hagar's daughter.

In writing this story, Hopkins and other women who published fiction in *The Colored American Magazine* drew on common themes, providing a unique perspective on miscegenation and the plight of the mixed-race woman from their own standpoint. Gaines (1996) suggests that for the "Black South, miscegenation was synonymous with the rape of Black women by white men," and the idea of "mulatto degeneracy" prevailed in the Black community (pp. 58, 59). In contrast, Hopkins, Ruth Todd ("The Octoroon's Revenge"), and Fannie Barrier Williams ("After Many Days") created stories of consensual yet forbidden love between white men and Black women, which resulted in the birth of a mixed-race child. Miscegenation, far from being a scarlet letter, was variously framed as undetectable, a device used to trick white men such as Jack in "The Octoroon's Revenge" and Kernal Claybourn in "Scrambled Eggs," or a struggle overcome by true love.

Todd, Williams, Burgess-Ware, and Hopkins provided physical descriptions to hint at the racial ambiguity of key characters as a literary device to show the epistemological gap in white detection that sought to fix race. Their detailed depictions demonstrated the fluidity of race and evaporated the notion of race as fixed and identifiable, which in turn rendered racial hierarchy a sham. Hopkins (1901/1902) rendered Hagar the picture of stereotypical white womanliness—she had "creamy" skin (p. 35) and was a "fair vision in purest white" (p. 53). Her appearance fooled her first husband, Ellis, and even Hagar believed herself to be white. Early in the story, upon learning from Walker about Hagar's true identity as an enslaved woman, Ellis responded with defiance to Walker who claimed to own her: "There is not one drop of Negro blood in her veins; I doubt, sir, if you have ever seen her" (p. 53). His reply suggested the mistaken white belief that Blackness could be seen, detected (as an iniquity), made visible, and thus objectified. Likewise, Jewel's identity as part Black confounded Cuthbert, who said of her when they were initially engaged, "She is an angel, my white angel of purity" (p. 103).

Both Ellis and Cuthbert were ambivalent white men described as holding racist sentiments but coming around to the idea that ultimately race was irrelevant when it came to relationships and marriage. Hopkins (1901/1902) credited Cuthbert's racist beliefs to societal influence. She explained, "Cuthbert Sumner was born with a noble nature; his faults were those caused by environment and tradition. Chivalrous, generous-hearted . . . yet born and bred in an atmosphere which approved of freedom and qualified equality for the Negro, he had never considered for one moment the remote contingency of actual social contact with this unfortunate people" (p. 265). Fearing Cuthbert's rejection, Jewel, Hagar, and Ellis go abroad to Europe. Cuthbert overcomes his prejudices, realizes his love for Jewel is undying, and goes to Europe in search of the three. He returns unsuccessful and goes to the venerable Enson Hall to see if they have returned. Before entering the hall to be reunited with his beloved Jewel, he sees a small graveyard on the Enson premises, goes to explore, and sees a "fair, slender shaft of polished cream-white marble" with the inscription "Jewel, aged 21. 'Not my will, but Thine be done!'" (p. 283). Jewel had died in Europe of Roman fever. And there the story ends: Cuthbert was denied the love of his life, but learned a lesson. Hopkins concluded the story, coming full circle back to the memory of slavery:

> The holy institution of marriage ignored the life of the slave, breed indifference in the masters to the enormity of illicit connections, with the result that the sacred family relation is weakened and finally ignored in many cases. In the light of his recent experiences Cuthbert Sumner views life and eternity with different eyes and thoughts from what he did before he knew that he had wedded Hagar's daughter. (p. 284)

Bookending *Hagar's Daughter* with the historical facts of slavery, Hopkins suggested what Sweeney (2019) calls the "continuity between the traumas of slavery and contemporary struggles for racial justice" (p. 155). The story's tragic ending undermined the traditional domestic novel's conventions, "thereby emphasizing the failure of the U.S. civil sphere of Hopkins's epoch to sustain the ideal ending" (Tate, 1992, p. 196).

―――――◆―――――

The work of African American women magazine writers represents a significant contribution to a field of literature and essays that explored the issues of race as a social construction. Pauline Hopkins and her fellow magazine writers embraced "fiction as a cultural form ... of great historical and political significance" (Carby, 1987, p. 128). Widely known African American women activists and writers such as Mary Church Terrell, Fannie Barrier Williams, Carrie Clifford, Mrs. Booker T. Washington, and Pauline Hopkins sustained a fervent pace of publication in both *The Colored American Magazine* and *The Voice of the Negro* between 1900 and 1907. Equally notable were the voices of women such as Ruth D. Todd, Louise Burgess-Ware, Gertrude Dorsey Brown, M. Cravatt Simpson, Emma F. G. Merritt, Sylvanie Francoz Wlliams, and Ida Joyce Jackson who challenged the masculinist bias of the "talented tenth," called out the taboo subject of rape, and reconstituted their African American sisters as readers capable of leadership and social reform in their communities. These writers engaged countermemory work as a form of cultural resistance, as a way to undermine white nostalgia and recast historical narratives to foreground their experiences as Black women. Their efforts stand as a precursor to contemporary efforts to "say her name" or to raise awareness of African American women's unique experiences of oppression due to race and gender status.

The parallels between the strategies found in white-controlled magazines, particularly white racist nostalgia, and present-day racist rhetorics are striking and point to the relevance of advancing a vocal countermemory narrative of racism-and-resistance-as-American-history similar to that provided in Black magazine such as *The Colored American Magazine* and *The Voice of the Negro*.

CONCLUSION

Persistent White Ignorance and the Optimism of Resistant Cultural Memory

American history is a history of racism and white terrorism against people of color and their communities. Additionally, what is often referred to as "Black history" (e.g., February as Black History Month) *is* American history as African Americans have stood at the center of economic growth, democratic advancement, and cultural development since their enslavement and arrival on the shores of the Americas in August 1619. These two observations often go unnoticed and/or unnamed within the larger "social imaginary," constructed and reinforced through stories, lore, imagery, scripts, and public monuments, which variously shape and reinforce social values and beliefs. Collectively constructed, publicly shared memories figure prominently in a culture's prevailing imaginary. How we choose to recall past events (e.g., slavery or the nation's founding) suggests who and what is important and what is not worth remembering or should not be "stirred up" as the white former prosecutor from Mississippi noted about commemorations of Emmett Till, quoted in the introduction.

Debates over the race question in popular magazines around the turn of the twentieth century represent some of the earliest cultural conversations over how Americans should remember slavery,

American history, and white violence. Memory work becomes palpable during times of widespread economic insecurity, whether it be the early 1900s period of industrialization and increased gains on the part of Black people or the early twenty-first century, marked by social unrest, increased visibility of marginalized groups (e.g., LGBTQ, Black, Indigenous, Asian American, people of color), a widening wealth gap, and the disappearance of well-paying manufacturing jobs. These debates continue to merit our attention. Cultural memories (in)validate experiences, empower/disempower certain groups, frame social problems, and, importantly, establish parameters for conversations on policy change. In the twenty-first century, an iteration of the race question is debated through political rhetorics and media as diverse as school curricula and public memorials. Like the essays in turn-of-the-twentieth-century magazines such as *The Independent*, *McClure's*, *The Arena*, and *The Outlook*, present-day debates leverage cultural memory as they grapple with national identity and notions of citizenship in the twenty-first century. This chapter looks to the ways a contemporary "race question" has been re-animated in both oppressive and progressive ways through twenty-first-century policies, debates, and racial justice efforts.

Communication and Epistemology in the Twenty-First Century: New Framings of the Race Question

Memory work operates both hegemonically and as resistance. Culturally shared memories are not a given, nor static, but must be consistently (re)created and "preserved" (Spelman, 2007, p. 120). The previous chapters sought to take up and expand upon Lisa Flores's (2016) call for racial rhetorical criticisms through an exploration of the ever-presence of race in discussions of national identity and cultural memory. A comparison of widely circulating writings on the "race problem" undercover what rhetorical strategies were employed to differently remember the past, how American history becomes sanitized and severed from white terrorism, and how we may differently conceptualize that past so that we may be able to fruitfully and truthfully participate in current debates over race and racism.

Throughout much of the twentieth century, popular magazines, newspapers, and later radio and television became the vehicles through which stories about and debates over race were conveyed. The extent to which Black- and white-controlled magazines around the turn of the twentieth century referenced each other's articles and authors suggests these writers were, to a degree, dialoging over how to remember slavery, how to understand whiteness and Blackness, and how to view the roles of African Americans in the US post-Emancipation and post-Reconstruction. A comparative study suggests the importance of viewing Black magazine writing as part and parcel of the "broader currents of print culture" (Sweeney, 2019, p. 138).

Popular magazines such as *The Outlook, The Arena, The Independent,* and *McClure's,* dominated by the perspectives of white writers and owners, engaged a selective memory to perpetuate a Lost Cause nostalgia, to (re)conceptualize the notion of a white civilization, to render the Black body abstract and devoid of a history, and to perpetuate a cult of white purity. African American women writing in Black-controlled magazines such as *The Colored American Magazine* and *The Voice of the Negro* penned stories and essays providing a resistive or countermemory framework for recalling slavery and in particular women's experiences within that institution. Creating a Black women's history—a written "portfolio" of their accomplishments (Dagbovie, 2004)—served as refutation to the racist cult of white purity and reconstituted Black women as self-determined subjects in contrast to white portrayals of them as jezebels and mammies. Black women recalled the history of white men's rape of Black women through rhetorical haunting and used strategies of inversion to undermine race hierarchies and to underscore the fluidity of race.

In many respects, early 1900s America looks not unlike the sociopolitical context facing America in the first decades of the twenty-first century. And both eras have given rise to surges in racist and nationalist rhetorics. As Manisha Sinha (2019) observed, "Historical parallelism rarely works in a simplistic manner. But it does work when historians discern broad similarities and patterns that link our present moment to the past" (p. 2). The twenty-first-century racialization of public spaces and the emergence of redemption rhetorics call to light the persistent and long shadow cast by willful white ignorance and hegemonic cultural memory.

Race and Space in the Twenty-First Century

Both digital and physical spaces continue to be racialized, demarcating bodies as white or Black, safe or dangerous, and establishing boundaries that delimit mobility not unlike Jim Crow policies of the early twentieth century. The frame of neutrality that cloaked so-called "scientific" racism in the late 1800s–early 1900s similarly shrouds twenty-first-century digital technologies that come across as colorblind and thus indisputable (Benjamin, 2019; Farr, 2004; Haller, 1971; Mills, 1998; Muhammad, 2010; Omi & Winant, 1994; Parris, 2015). A "new Jim Crow" (M. Alexander, 2010), the mass incarceration of millions of African Americans, has replaced the racial caste system that arose in post-Reconstruction America. And despite progressive reforms in how arrests, jailing, and sentencing are handled, a new "generation of racial and social control" referred to variously as "e-carceration" (M. Alexander, 2018), the "New Jim Code" (Benjamin, 2019), or "weapons of math destruction" (O'Neill, 2017) is relying on technology and algorithms to determine people's fates in courts (M. Alexander, 2018, p. 3) and to "reinforce racism and other forms of inequity" through "biased bots, altruistic algorithms, and their many coded cousins" (Benjamin, 2019, pp. 2, 7). States like Arizona, Kentucky, New Jersey, and Utah rely on Public Safety Assessments ("About the Public Safety Assessment: PSA Sites," n.d.), which are algorithms to assist judges in predicting "failure to appear in court pretrial, new criminal arrest while on pretrial release" ("About the Public Safety Assessment: What Is the PSA," n.d.). These and other technologies appear objective and unbiased on the surface—they rely on mathematical models presumed to be neutral—but are "based on factors . . . highly correlated with race and class" (M. Alexander, 2018, p. 3). Racist "cultural coding" becomes embedded "into the technical coding of software programs" and works to perpetuate racial inequality (Benjamin, 2019, p. 9).

Racist epistemologies remain articulated to physical spaces like parks and neighborhoods that continue to be coded "Black" or "white." Racial profiling, shopping while Black, driving while Black, and what Chan Tov McNamarah (2019) calls "White caller crime" are all ways of naming the experiences of people of color who have been arrested, pulled over by the police, followed by store clerks, kicked out of establishments, and, in the tragic cases of Trayvon Martin, Tamir Rice, John Crawford III, and Ahmaud Arbery, killed by police or white vigilantes simply because they were Black and thus perceived as "out of place" or engaging in misconduct.[1] "Driving while Black" and similar phrases call attention to the ways race tracks with mobility and social control and underscore how public spaces are marked "white" or "Black" even if a sign that says "whites only" is not posted. White caller crime refers to the ways white people weaponize white privilege through calls to police, "racialized police communication," to report "when Black persons are engaged in behavior that would not have been read as suspicious, or otherwise worthy of police involvement had they been White" (McNamarah, 2019, p. 335). Over ninety such calls were documented in 2018 alone, and studies show the phenomenon has been persistent for decades (McNamarah, 2019, pp. 337–341, 346). Importantly, racialized police communication results in physical and emotional harm and "inflicts a multifarious group of intangible injuries" (p. 345).

Perhaps the most widely known example is that of Amy Cooper, a white woman, who called 911 after an African American man, Christian Cooper, asked her to leash her dog in Central Park. Amy

Cooper's recorded call reveals how she leveraged race to tap into centuries-old stereotypes of the dangerous Black brute: "There is a man, an African American man . . . he is recording me and threatening me and my dog. . . . There is an African American man, I am in Central park, he is recording me and threatening myself and my dog" (Vera, 2020). Cooper's race marking and reference to Christian Cooper as a threat even though the recorded video clearly shows the two are at least ten feet apart echoes early 1900s anxieties over the mere presence of Black bodies in what are perceived as white spaces. Amy Cooper sounds not unlike the *McClure's* writer Ray Stannard Baker (1905a) who warned of the shiftless or "floating, worthless" Black men who make it "unsafe for women to travel alone"—or, in this case, walk one's dog in Central Park. The idea of an African American bird watcher in Central Park was not conceivable to Cooper, who fell back on stereotypes of Black men as criminal and dangerous.

Similar racist stereotypes are deployed against Black women who appear out of place as the example of white callers in Oregon and Wisconsin who reported Black women—both canvassing for election to political positions—for walking through the neighborhood "for no apparent reason" or allegedly in search of drugs (McNamarah, 2019, p. 340). Their descriptions are reminiscent of the portrayal provided by *The Independent* writer who noted Black women posed the "greatest menace to the moral life of any community where they live" ("Experiences of the Race Problem," 1904). From 1904 to the 2018 phone calls to police, Black women are viewed through the "white racial frame"[2] that situates them as polluting otherwise white spaces.

Redemption Rhetorics

Politicians and conservative activists have put cultural memory into practice through redemption rhetorics that invoke calls for "restoring America," "renewal," and return to "law and order" that conjure a feel-good, fictionalized past characterized by neighborhood peace and national prosperity. Examination of these rhetorics shows how "civilization" is coded white in and through a strategic invocation of which parts of a culture we are to recall. These discourses perform a racist cultural labor by denying the recollection of painful memories, those that belie American's "greatness" and that continue to impact the lives of Black Americans in the twenty-first century.

Redemption rhetoric often begins by creating and amplifying a crisis and then providing an antidote. In the early 1900s, the manufactured crisis centered on the presence of hundreds of thousands of Black men, free and enfranchised according to the Thirteenth and Fifteenth Amendments, that presented a threat to white supremacy in politics and white control over the economy. Redemption rhetoric was steeped in scientific racism and found its way into political, academic, and popular discourses, even progressive-minded magazines like *McClure's*, *The Independent*, *The Arena*, and *The Outlook*.

In the early 1900s, Congressional leaders like the virulently racist US senator from South Carolina Benjamin R. Tillman (1903) stoked anger and fear over a post-Reconstruction south by fixating on the numbers of Black people compared to white people. Tillman argued:

> While we have opened the door of hope for a while to the whites . . . every man who can look beyond his nose can see that with the negroes constantly going to school, the increasing number of people who can read and write among the colored race, with such preponderance of numbers as they have, will in time encroach upon and reach and overbalance our white men. And then what will happen? Will the door of hope be closed again on us by submitting to negro domination? (p. 19)

His rhetoric reverberated in that of Donald Trump (2018), who fanned the flames of racism when he referenced "large groups" or "large numbers" of "aliens" eight times in his Presidential

Proclamation Addressing Mass Migration in November 2018 (see also Trump, 2019). According to Trump, migrants traveling north from Central America were "unlawful," some were violent, and like a virus, they may spread: "the arrival of large numbers of aliens will contribute to the overloading of our immigration and asylum system and to the release of thousands of aliens into the interior of the United States" (quoted in Santiago & Shoichet, 2018).

Trump's 2016 presidential campaign slogan, "Make America Great Again," typifies redemption rhetoric as it suggests a renewal or a rebirth reminiscent of the 1870s "Redeemers" who sought to restore the South to its days of white supremacy. The phrase, emblazoned on red caps, T-shirts, and bumper stickers, kindles both nostalgia and anger by at once asserting that "greatness" previously existed but is no more and suggesting it was unfairly stolen or is under siege. The phrase belies a violent past, from the forcible removal of Indigenous peoples including the Trail of Tears, to the horrific and sadistic public lynchings of Black men, women, and children, to the wholesale destruction of Black homes and communities through both white violence and federal transportation and housing policies that denied the Black accumulation of wealth.

Redemption rhetorics continue to echo in debates over how to teach American history in K-12 schools—and in some states, on college campuses—an issue that rose to national attention after *The New York Times* August 2019 publication of the "1619 Project," itself a paradigmatic example of resistant memory work in popular media. Organized and edited by the journalist Nikole Hannah-Jones, the project consisted of a series of essays and photos in the newspaper's magazine that encouraged a rethinking of the place of slavery in US history. The collection sought to "reframe the country's history by placing the consequences of slavery and the contributions of black Americans at the very center of our national narrative" (Hannah-Jones, 2019). Contributors drew a line from present-day institutions and practices including the nature of capitalism, suburban sprawl, and inequities in health care back to the institution of slavery. The project extended beyond the initial publication to include curricula that could be used in schools. Soon after publication, the 1619 Project, coupled with references to critical race theory (CRT) made by a fellow from the conservative Manhattan Institute on Fox News's *Tucker Carlson Tonight*, became a lightning rod in debates over how to remember racism in US history (Waxman, 2021).

The 1619 Project's publication—and its association with CRT, which, in its widely misunderstood interpretation, has become a convenient shorthand for perceived threats to white-controlled histories—set off alarm bells in political circles and local school boards and spawned a backlash in the form of calls for restoration and renewal. The criticism from conservative activists received media coverage by outlets from Fox News to National Public Radio, further amplifying the issue of cultural memory and spurring debate in other public spaces like websites and social media platforms where well-funded groups have suggested changes to state laws that would outlaw the teaching of so-called "divisive" topics.[3] In January 2021, then-president Donald Trump established a 1776 Commission, whose goal was the "restoration of American education, which can only be grounded on a history of those principles[,] that is 'accurate, honest, unifying, inspiring, and ennobling'" (The President's Advisory 1776 Commission, 2021, p. 1). According to the commission's report, the "path to a renewed American unity" could be found in a "rediscovery of our shared identity rooted in our founding principles" (p. 1).

Although the 1776 Commission was disbanded by President Biden, its efforts shifted to a political action committee, the 1776 Project PAC, which is active as of this writing and has endorsed candidates in thirty school districts across thirteen states (1776 Project PAC, n.d.-b). The PAC seeks to reform the "public education system by promoting patriotism and pride in American history" and influencing local school boards in their decisions regarding how to teach US history (1776 Project PAC, n.d.-c). Its homepage typifies redemption rhetoric in the way it stokes fear over a looming threat to long-standing institutions and suggests a way to resolve the supposed crisis: "A new and troubling trend has emerged in our nation's public school system" (1776 Project PAC, n.d.-c). Critical race theory, according to the "About" page, advocates dismantling "the cornerstones of American society" and rebuilding America according to a "Marxist vision" (1776 Project PAC, n.d.-a). The 1776 Project PAC is "pushing back against this growing crisis . . . by campaigning on behalf of school board candidates that vow to overturn any teaching of the 1619 Project or critical race theory. . . . We will also support any type of education reform that promotes a patriotic vision of America and its history" (1776 Project PAC, n.d.-c). The 1776 Project PAC and similar efforts across the nation (e.g., the 1776 Action) put memory work to use by insisting on a one-dimensional version of historical recollection that falls within the bounds of "patriotism," a frequently used term that, while undefined, alludes to celebratory and self-congratulatory appraisals of history that whitewash—metaphorically and literally—the terrorism, pain, trauma, and exclusion that were part and parcel of the nation's founding and growth. For example, Florida's Board of Education developed standards for grades 6–8 social studies that included discussion of how "slaves developed skills, which, in some instances, could be applied for their personal benefit," a partial and misleading notion and one that dilutes the horrors of slavery similar to the rhetorics discussed in chapter 2 (Florida's Academic State Standards—Social Studies, 2023, p. 71).

Twenty-first-century protests arising around the dismantling of Confederate-era monuments also center on the cultural construction of memory. Scholars have studied the ways these structures glorify the slaveholding South in the spirit of the Lost Cause ideology. The previous chapters' analyses of popular magazine debates suggest we can more fully understand the relationship between monuments and memory by accounting for the ways conversations take place across communication spheres and platforms. Notably, these monuments "spoke" and continue to speak within the larger cultural discourse over race and American identity, one that was also playing out in popular print materials, political speeches, and congressional debates over antilynching legislation. In tandem with popular and political discourses, these stone and steel symbols of slavery had a hand in broader deliberative debates, reinforcing white supremacy to justify the broader post-Reconstruction backlash against the expansion of civil rights.

Individuals enter into debates over sites of public remembrance with differing experiences, values, and beliefs and thus will attach differing meanings to memorials. The previous chapters point to the insights to be gained from bridging epistemology studies with rhetorical criticism of popular documents to explore how experience and standpoint shape public discourses. Chapter 1 pointed out how powerful groups (e.g., white wealthy, cisgender men) hold a greater influence over these collective resources for knowing; that is, epistemic resources are rarely democratically generated and do not always reflect the experiences of marginalized groups. And also, more optimistically, marginalized groups push back to "recalibrate . . . epistemic resources and/or create new ones" until the tension or contradictions between cultural expressions and lived experience—the "reality gap"—is reconciled (Pohlhaus, 2012, p. 719).[4] Recalibration "can result in new possibilities for knowing" and provide "new tools for organizing and making sense of experience" (Pohlhaus, 2012, p. 719), a particularly important task in the midst of popular and political discourses that shape and legitimate public policy that furthers "state, economic, cultural, and discursive violence" against people of color (Flores, 2016, p. 8). In short, issues of racial justice have become tethered to battles over memory and demonstrate that a good deal is at stake in how we decide to, as a community, remember racism and its legacy.

Resistant Cultural Memory

When a white person says, "All Lives Matter," in response to the assertion "Black Lives Matter," they are conveying a willful white ignorance rooted in a strategic not-knowing, forgetting, or displacing the ways past systems of racist violence and discrimination continue to shape contemporary experiences. Similar white responses such as "My family never owned slaves" or "I'm not a racist" presume a specific start to the discussion, one that begins now, as in today, with "me" or "my history." These responses launch a narrative of race relations from the point of here and now, as if our experiences hang suspended in time, detached from past contexts. In these examples, narrative launch points operate rhetorically to facilitate strategic forgetting. They put memory to work by scripting where and when the story begins. In contrast, if we go back much further in time to commence the narrative, we would then be in a position to tell a different story.

Beginning the narrative in a different historical moment does not guarantee a different outcome for understanding present-day racism. The task for scholars and concerned citizens alike is to put historical knowledge to use—to *make memory work*—in resistant and more democratic ways to highlight how police brutality, health, housing, and education disparities and wealth gaps are rooted in the legacy of slavery. We need to engage discourses of historical connectedness, to show a "history of relationships" over time wherein "earlier episodes are linked to later ones as manifestations of the same system of racialized domination" (McCarthy, 2004, p. 760).[5] As Thomas McCarthy (2002) so incisively argues, "The greater the public familiarity with and knowledge of that history [of racism], the greater are the chances of effectively interpreting current problems as belonging to its accumulated effects and thus of publicly framing them as moral issues or issues of justice" (p. 640). To use language from epistemology studies, the lack of such familiarity with history represents a willful white ignorance, which functions to strategically forget these historical connections.

The cultivation of a "black critical memory" (Reyes, 2010) is key to pushing back against the hegemony of white silence. Michael Eric Dyson (2003) asserts that "one of the most powerful ways of challenging and ultimately destroying the . . . myth of white superiority is to unearth sites of resistive memory, history, and practice" (p. 119). Scholars, journalists, and activists have been putting Black resistant memory to work since the writings of Pauline Hopkins and her fellow magazine contributors of the early 1900s. What is needed is a mobilization of resistive or countermemory narratives publicly shared and accompanied by movement in the streets, much like what the United States saw in late May through July 2020 in the wake of the police homicide of George Floyd.

The words of Karlos K. Hill (2020) illuminate how historical knowledge can function epistemically, expanding how we interpret and come to understand events in the present. He explained:

> When I see footage of George Floyd being killed by the Minneapolis officer, I see the history of slavery. . . . The history of slavery was about dominating Black bodies and specifically dominating Black bodies for profit's sake. We think that because slavery ended the desire to dominate Black bodies went away, it evaporated into thin air. No, it persisted and we saw it in the history of lynching and racial violence in this country that white men had to dominate . . . and control Black bodies through violence that continues in the form of lynching. I believe we see traces of that . . . in the George Floyd murder but most people would not make that connection. And so, if we had real thorough-going conversations about the history of slavery not just as an economic institution but as a violent institution that was about dominating Black bodies we could get so far in this country around thinking about police brutality.

Knowing history—a people's history told from the perspectives of those most excluded from mainstream narratives—is important for expanding cultural knowledge, for enlarging and legitimating what counts as knowledge about the nation and the experiences of those who contributed to the development of communities, the survival and well-being of their families, and the progress of democracy.

Importantly, publicly sharing those histories—that is, the act of telling stories and identifying specific individuals—contributes to how we know history, including the physical pain, the trauma, and the resilience that were part and parcel of the growth and development of the US.

The concept of standpoint sheds light on the relationship, the interdependence, between lived experience and social knowledge. How we come to know or understand something, say racism, is both "limited and enabled" by social location (Code, 1993, p. 39). Alcoff (2007) describes this tenet of standpoint well: "All knowers are situated in time and space, with specific experiences, social locations, modes of perceptual practices and habits, styles of reasoning, and sets of interests that are fluid and open to interpretation but that have some objective elements in regard to the conditions of the knower's material reality" (p. 42). Standpoint, then, recognizes the limitations imposed through a social location of privilege, which holds a vested interest in sustaining a willful ignorance and is less likely to generate critical questions about social relations (regarding inequality, disparities, etc.) (Alcoff, 2006, 2007; Collins, 1986; Harding, 1993; Hartsock, 1983). In contrast, living day-to-day with deprivation, suffering, and lack of access to basic resources may generate an "epistemic advantage" (Alcoff, 2006, p. 96) or a vantage point from which to recognize and critically examine the causes of one's suffering. African American women's "outsider within" position at the intersection of race and gender oppression offers a "special standpoint on self, family, and society" that is indispensable for critiquing patriarchy, racism, sexism, etc. (Collins, 1986, p. S14). Standpoint theory is careful to point out that one's social location does not guarantee a specific perspective, nor does it imply the perspectives of persons occupying a similar position (e.g., African American women) will generate identical perspectives. Standpoint suggests a reflective process whereby one draws from personal experience to make sense of one's surroundings and relationships, what Alcoff (2006) calls "situated reasoning" (p. 94), and then determines how to act (Collins, 1991, p. 28; J. Wood, 2005).

Black women's early 1900s magazine articles and essays—particularly as examined in dialogue with the writings of white-controlled magazines—exemplify recalibration, specifically as these women sought to revive the relevance of history through strategies like rhetorical haunting and inversion. Their writings called up a past of sexual violence against Black women as well as a history of Black women's accomplishments in order to give the lie to long-standing myths and stereotypes deployed to justify race and gender oppression. As writers, they insisted on visibility and created a countermemory that upended white collective misremembering (Dyson, 2003; Mills, 1997); theirs was a "liberation historiography" that served as "historical intervention" (Ernest, 2002, p. 415). Additionally, the essays and stories in *The Colored American Magazine* and *The Voice of the Negro* reconstituted the identities of their readers. Through profiles and lists of Black women's accomplishments, essays prompted readers to identify with and see themselves in the stories of activism and agency. Reconstitution points to the role communication plays in shaping identities, expanding possibilities, and suggesting a becoming.

From the nineteenth to the twenty-first centuries, African American women have unsettled willful white ignorance and collective misremembering through fiction, academic theorizing, magazine journalism, poetry, film, and, most recently, digital activism. The magazine writings of the Black women explored in chapters 4 and 5 provided a scaffolding for late twentieth-century and early twenty-first-century writers and poets such as Toni Morrison, Alice Walker, Audre Lorde, and Claudia Rankine; journalists like Nikole Hannah-Jones; scholars such as Angela Davis and Kimberlé Crenshaw; and activists like the women of the Combahee River Collective, and more recently, Patrisse Cullors, Alicia Garza, and Opal Tometi. These efforts draw from the wellspring of early 1900s Black women's magazine writing and are threaded together by reliance on the establishment of resistant or countermemory as a means for generating critical social knowledge and new ways of understanding race, gender, sexuality, and discrimination.

Like Anna Julia Cooper, who pointed out in 1892 that Black women faced both a woman question and a race question, the Combahee River Collective—a group of African American women who began meeting in 1974—wrote in their 1977 statement that they are "not just trying to fight oppression on one front or even two, but instead to address a whole range of oppressions" (Combahee River Collective, 1977). The importance of critical remembering is apparent in their founding statement in which they invoke the names of influential Black women from the past, some of whom were also summoned by Pauline Hopkins over seventy-five years earlier, including Sojourner Truth, Harriet Tubman, Frances Ellen Watkins Harper, Ida B. Wells, and Mary Church Terrell. Repetition serves as an insistence on recognizing the bravery and acumen of these women and their centrality to the narrative of Black struggle over the past century. The collective's statement acknowledges a path from the accomplishments of these historical figures to 1970s Black women's struggles: "Contemporary Black feminism is the outgrowth of countless generations of personal sacrifice, militancy, and work by our mothers and sisters" (Combahee River Collective, 1977). Within the academy, African American legal scholar and activist Kimberlé Crenshaw (1989) has coined the term "intersectionality" as a means for describing Black women's interlocking experiences of gender and racial oppression. Like the Combahee River Collective, Crenshaw grounds contemporary Black feminism's emphasis on intersectionality in the oratory efforts of Sojourner Truth and Anna Julia Cooper to show the roots of Black women's rhetorical efforts to challenge dominant white understandings of both gender and race.

Resistant memory is at the heart of critical race theory (CRT), described in a body of writings by scholars including Crenshaw that provide a theoretical and legal framework for understanding the ways racism and the legacy of slavery continue to shape and impact US institutions and legal structures. CRT posits that racism is not a matter of personal prejudice but is woven into supposedly equitable laws that have discriminatory outcomes. Initially confined largely to academic discussions, CRT has been catapulted into the mainstream and hijacked by conservatives seeking to promote a distorted history of slavery, at a historical moment when white nostalgia is tapping into a broader white anxiety stoked by both material circumstances (e.g., loss of stable and well-paying jobs) and divisive rhetorics that suggest America's history of greatness is threatened by migrants and racial unrest.[6]

Traditional mainstream magazines continue to address issues of race, at times utilizing resistant memory to cover issues like reparations and racist policing (Coates, 2014; Hannah-Jones, 2021; Luckerson, 2020). Indeed, the argument for reparations is premised on the idea that history matters, as James Baldwin so clearly explained in 1965: "History . . . is not merely something to be read. And it does not refer merely, or even principally, to the past. On the contrary, the great force of history comes from the fact that we carry it within us, are unconsciously controlled by it in many ways. . . . It is to history that we owe our frames of reference, our identities, and our aspirations" (quoted in Grossman, 2016). *The Atlantic* magazine's June 2014 cover story, "The Case for Reparations," sparked a broader cultural discussion over the issue of recompense for Black Americans (Demby, 2014). The magazine's nearly twenty-page think piece by Ta-Nehisi Coates brought to light racist housing and lending policies, in part through a profile of one African American man, Clyde Ross. Coates (2014) drew on statistics and sociological studies pointing to the ways Black families in the twenty-first century continue to experience the ripple effects of past policies. Rebutting the idea that the past no longer matters, Coates points out,

> one cannot escape the question [of reparations] by hand-waving at the past, disavowing the acts of one's ancestors, nor by citing a recent date of ancestral immigration. The last slaveholder has been dead for a very long time. The last soldier to endure Valley Forge has been dead much longer. To proudly claim the veteran and disown the slaveholder is patriotism à la carte. . . . If Thomas Jefferson's

genius matters, then so does his taking of Sally Hemings's body. If George Washington crossing the Delaware matters, so must his ruthless pursuit of the runagate Oney Judge. (p. 62)

By both humanizing the issues through stories of specific African Americans and providing little-known historical information about the normalization and codification of racist laws, Coates encouraged a new way of seeing the issue of reparations.

Nikole Hannah-Jones, the journalist and creator of the 1619 Project, took up the issue of reparations in the June 30, 2020, *New York Times Magazine*, calling up past racist laws like Black codes and those supporting slave patrols to demonstrate how they echo in more recent stop and frisk policies and qualified immunity for police officers. Sources as diverse as *USA Today*, the BBC, CNN, and MSNBC have given space and time to Coates's and Hannah-Jones's articles, pointing to the intertextual nature of diverse media vehicles that recirculate, speaking with and in opposition to one another like early twentieth-century magazines debating the race question.

Similar to the magazine pieces on reparations, the 2016 documentary film *13th*, written and directed by Ava DuVernay, explores the impact of slavery on contemporary mass incarceration and the criminal justice system. The film acts as an accessible popular artifact that employs resistant memory work. The favorable reception of the film in more mainstream circles (it was nominated for an Academy Award for Best Documentary Feature) suggests a larger cultural shift in collective memory and a willingness, however tentative, to use history as an instrument for understanding the present and for policy debate formation. The unwillingness of Congress to even open up discussion of reparations, coupled with the widespread backlash to the 1619 Project in the form of state laws to monitor how history can be taught, shows the amount of heavy lifting still needed to bring about a historical reckoning with racism.

In the twenty-first century, debates over the nature of race and the impact of slavery continue to find a home in poetry, film, and fiction that perform cultural memory labor by shaping accepted histories of race and racism. In her *New York Times*-bestselling collection of poems, *Citizen: An American Lyric*, Claudia Rankine (2014) writes eloquently and incisively about experiences of day-to-day racism, using the notion of history to illustrate how the past continues to haunt and inflict pain on the body. Memory is always already there, she writes, as the "vessel" of one's feelings, its unrelenting nature a "fatal flaw" that one carries through life (p. 7). She explains, "You can't put the past behind you. It's buried in you; it's turned your flesh into its own cupboard" (p. 63), and "Memory is a tough place" (p. 64). Cultural efforts to bury memory work in oppressive ways: "You like to think memory goes far back though remembering never was recommended. Forget all that, the world says. The world's had a lot of practice. No one should adhere to the facts that contribute to narrative, the facts that create lives" (p. 61). In other words, history plays out in and through bodies, "the facts that create lives." But marginalized bodies are denied authenticity and voice through the mantra to "forget all that." Rankine's poetry shows white ignorance to be a form of gaslighting that invalidates and annihilates experiences of oppression, rendering them unspeakable and unimaginable.

Increasingly, digital spaces have become the locus of both (online) magazine writing and activism that seek to re-narrate the Black experience in America. These efforts broaden what counts as journalism, eschewing traditional norms of objectivity, centering on marginalized voices, and oftentimes bearing witness to the past. Increasingly, social media outlets, websites, and podcasts play a role similar to popular magazines by providing a combination of news and entertainment accessible to a middle-class audience. Referred to as a "new Black Press" and "new protest #journalism" (A. V. Richardson, 2020), these media outlets operate rhetorically as a "demand" on the part of Black communities heretofore marginalized by the mainstream press. Black-created and -controlled websites, social media hashtags and livestreaming, and podcasts provide public platforms that may bridge the gap between a people's history and what is currently held to be "true" within the prevailing white social imaginary.[7] Internet sites such as TRiiBE, the Grio, the Root, and ZORA, a news website described as "celebrating and centering experiences of color," have created counternarratives on issues like the coronavirus pandemic and presidential politics in an effort to call out the continued impact of racism that is often ignored in mainstream news coverage ("Meet the New Black Press," 2020; "ZORA," n.d.).

For ordinary people who lack access to formal publishing outlets like popular magazines, hashtag activism represents a "unique fusion of social justice, technology, and citizen journalism" that enables Black feminists to "bring attention and justice to women who rarely receive either" (S. Williams, 2015, p. 343). Hashtag activism and digital media more broadly point to an "evolution in journalism" whereby ordinary people not formally trained as journalists act as "citizen journalists," collecting and disseminating newsworthy stories told from a marginalized standpoint (Russell, 2007, p. 286). Like early 1900s Black magazines, digital media provide a vehicle for sharing an epistemological view that cuts through white willful ignorance, what the scholar Allissa V. Richardson (2020) called "bearing witness while black." In digital journalism and activism, women of color, such as Alicia Garza, Patrisse Cullors, Marissa Johnson, Shellonnee Chinn, Brittany Ferrell, Brittany Packnett Cunningham, Eve Ewing, and Ieshia Evans, have been on the front lines since 2014 (A. V. Richardson, 2020). In solidarity with Black men, these activists use smartphone technology to apply counterhegemonic strategies such as those used by Black women magazine writers of *The Colored American Magazine* and *The Voice of the Negro*. In 1907, Josephine Silone Yates spoke to the importance of "counteracting this lack of knowledge" white readers held of Black women (p. 45). Much like Yates and others who called to light Black women's cultural and economic contributions and countered stereotypes of Black female lasciviousness in early 1900s Black magazines, digital activists have created narratives that counter racist news frames, which, perhaps not surprisingly, show some resemblance to the racist frames of the white-controlled magazines analyzed in previous chapters. The social media platform X (formerly known as Twitter) figured significantly in Black Lives Matter protests by being used for tweeting calls to action, documenting police violence, and upending the myth of Black criminality, in an effort to counter the "law and order" frame that, in contemporary news coverage of racial justice protests, continues to depict white police as necessary for controlling supposedly unruly and violent Black protesters (A. V. Richardson, 2020, pp. 54–71).

Using digital platforms alongside movement activism, Crenshaw founded #SayHerName, a project of the African American Policy Forum (AAPF), to raise awareness of the experiences of Black women and girls who have been victimized by law enforcement but whose stories often go unnoticed in broader public debates about racism and police brutality.[8] The #SayHerName initiative is an interdisciplinary endeavor that has utilized a host of communication outlets (e.g., web presence, hashtags, investigative reporting) and face-to-face actions (e.g., vigils, demonstrations) to raise awareness of and put an end to police violence against women of color. Andrea J. Ritchie (2017), who worked with the AAPF and the Center for Intersectionality and Social Policy to establish the goals of #SayHerName, has conducted extensive research to uncover the names and experiences of women and girls of color who have been brutalized at the hands of police and the legal system in ways that are both similar to and different from the violence experienced by Black men like Eric Garner and Freddie Gray. Some of these women are Breonna Taylor, Charleena Lyles, Rekia Boyd, Shantel Davis, and Sandra Bland. African American women are more likely than Black men to experience police violence in the home and in the context of calling for police help (Ritchie, 2020) and are more likely to experience police brutality in the form of sexual assault ("Black Women's Lives Matter," 2020). Between 2005 and 2013, "police officers in the U.S. were charged with forcible rape and sodomy 624 times" ("Black Women's Lives Matter," 2020).

Crenshaw explained the importance of publicly identifying, voicing, and emphasizing Black women's experiences:

> For our entire history of slavery and efforts to challenge it, the ways that it's experienced by men have been the center of it, and that has created a narrative about what anti-Black racism looks like. That is accurate, but it is not entirely inclusive. . . . We don't tell the stories about the disrespect that Black women experienced. So not too surprisingly, when the police treat Black women in ways that are continuous with that legacy, we don't have the stories. (quoted in Young & McMahon, 2020)

Crenshaw's observations tell us a great deal about history, communication, and cultural knowledge. First, history as we often know it contains strategic gaps; for example, we know a partial story of slavery, one that often excludes how women experienced it. Second, that history, including the gaps, shapes how we know the Black experience today. And finally, telling stories publicly—through social media campaigns, speeches, Black-created television, music, film, and art—fills the gaps in ways that enable us to better understand and address pressing social issues facing us today, such as police brutality, the racial wealth gap, racial health disparities, housing segregation, and mass incarceration. Knowing history enables us to better shape public policy in the present (McCarthy, 2002, 2004; Coates, 2014).

#BlackGirlMagic, a hashtag campaign galvanized by CaShawn Thompson in 2013, seeks to highlight the accomplishments of Black women and girls in order to challenge widespread cultural stereotypes that devalue them and render them invisible (Thomas, 2015). The #BlackGirlMagic hashtag functions much like the profiles that filled the pages of *The Colored American Magazine*, which created a "portfolio" of Black women's activities and achievements and served for readers as a vision of what they might become. Like the magazine writings, #BlackGirlMagic functions to both document and motivate. Likewise, April Reign created #OscarsSoWhite in 2015, and Shardé Davis and Joy Woods tweeted #BlackInTheIvory in June 2020, two campaigns striving to challenge the invisibility and discriminatory treatment of Black men and women in the film industry and higher education, respectively (Aviles, 2020; Ugwu, 2020). #OscarsSoWhite has continued to be used as a way to call out whiteness and white privilege as shapers of cultural identity, norms, and values, as in "#OscarsSoWhite they have a perfect credit score," or as Reign initially tweeted, "#OscarsSoWhite they asked to touch my hair."

Other campaigns such as #StandWithJada, #FreeCeCe, #RememberRenisha, and #MuteRKelly have been used to specifically call out violence against African American women and girls (Berridge & Portwood-Stacer, 2015). Renisha McBride, who had been in a car accident in a predominantly white neighborhood, was shot in the face after knocking on the door of a white man to seek help. The hashtag #RememberRenisha "kept her story alive on social media" after it fell off the pages and screens of the mainstream media (Berridge & Portwood-Stacer, 2015, p. 343). Black Twitter functions as a twenty-first-century public forum for Black women's voices in much the same way as did the early 1900s *Colored American Magazine* and *The Voice of the Negro*.

Notably, it was three African American women, Patrisse Cullors, Alicia Garza, and Opal Tometi, who formed #BlackLivesMatter in 2013, in the wake of the murder of the unarmed Black teen Trayvon Martin. Black Lives Matter has grown into a global movement recognized as key in efforts to undo systemic racism and anti-Black racism in all forms. The movement underscores an intersectional approach seeking to "build a space that affirms Black women and is free from sexism, misogyny, and environments in which men are centered" ("What We Believe," n.d.).[9] The organization is "guided by the fact that all Black lives matter, regardless of actual or perceived sexual identity, gender identity, gender expression, economic status, ability, disability, religious beliefs or disbeliefs, immigration status, or location" ("What We Believe," n.d.). The impact of the movement's campaign to raise awareness can be seen in 2020 polls that show an increase in support for the movement and an increase in the percentage of white respondents who say African Americans "do not receive equal treatment in the criminal justice system" (Langer, 2020).

#BlackLivesMatter and #SayHerName render Black women and their experiences visible through forms of strategic communication that invert, disrupt, and, importantly, reestablish and remember Black women's presence as creators, mothers, workers, activists, and community builders throughout US history. They sit along the historical trajectory of African American women's efforts to "talk back" (hooks, 1989), deploy the "uncivil tongue" (Lozano-Reich & Cloud, 2009), or use the "mother tongue" (Stover, 2003, pp. 156–157), all of which refer to the ways Black women have challenged and "nullified" the prevailing white social imaginary and demonstrated "that they are a power with which to be reckoned" (p. 156).

Podcasts, another outlet for digital journalism, parallel alternative/community radio broadcasts, which have played a role in oppositional efforts since the medium's inception (Russell, 2007). As streamable and downloadable audio files, podcasts offer listeners a convenient way to learn about and engage with anti-racist efforts. Podcasts about race and racism in America are wide-ranging and come from both independent and mainstream publishing efforts. A few examples that draw deeply on resistant memory are Scene on Radio's fourteen-part series, "Seeing White," which debuted in 2017; the 1619 Project produced by *The New York Times*; and Kimberlé Crenshaw's podcast, "Intersectionality Matters!" Crenshaw covers diverse issues impacting women of color, often taking a historical view. The May 2021 episode revived the memory of Black women athletes who played a role in athletic activism—women like Rose Robinson and Wilma Rudolph who, unlike Kareem Abdul-Jabbar and Muhammed Ali, remain largely absent from cultural memory of Black activism in sports. And in the October 2021 episode, Crenshaw revisited the Clarence Thomas–Anita Hill hearings from

1991 to explore how issues of race, gender, and power remain relevant in the twenty-first century.

Coupling Public Communication with On-the-Ground Resistance

Finally, and most importantly, we cannot rely on communication and persuasion alone, whether it occurs through writing, film, music, political debate, public hearings for reparations, or something else. These communicative efforts must be coupled with on-the-ground movement like what we have seen over the course of US history, when hundreds of thousands of ordinary people have taken to the streets, occupied lunch counters, factory floors, and welfare offices, and disrupted transportation to demand basic rights (e.g., a minimum wage, an eight-hour workday, public assistance, an end to segregation and police brutality). In short, we need both coercive and persuasive tactics. Debates over issues as profound and far-reaching as ending racism, defunding the police, abolishing the prison system, and challenging capitalism and imperialism involve more than a controversy or a clash of opinion. They represent a deep-seated conflict where communication, negotiation, and what is otherwise considered civil debate are not adequate, particularly given the uneven material and symbolic ground upon which participants stand (Barnlund & Haiman, 1960; Simons, 1972). As an example, in contract negotiations, employers hold the power to simply fire workers, especially if they are not unionized.[10] In these cases, the "channels for peaceful protest and reform [are] so clogged that they appear to be (and, in fact, may be) inaccessible to some segments of the population" (Haiman, 1967, p. 105). Historically, ordinary people have engaged in direct or extra-discursive actions—that is, physical actions involving bodily presence—to effectively get the message across and win demands. The United Auto Workers' 1936–36 sit-down strike in Flint, Michigan, illustrates how physical presence—sitting down on the factory floor and occupying the building—gave workers the upper hand as they both halted production and prevented scabs from entering to replace them. Their efforts were reinforced by community support, especially from wives, daughters, and sisters of the strikers, who picketed daily, sang rousing songs, and gave speeches (Fine, 1969; Lynch, 2001; Triece, 2007).

In the second decade of the twenty-first century, we have witnessed mass protests, demonstrations, and daily traffic disruption, coupled with communicative efforts as in nationwide organizing, social media outreach, hashtag campaigns, speeches, and policy debates geared to ending systemic racism and mass incarceration and to defunding the police. African American women have stood at the center of these efforts. Black Lives Matter stands as perhaps the signature example in the twenty-first century of coupling extra-discursive or direct actions with strategic public communication and communication technologies like hashtags, websites, and social media, along with traditional forms of communication like speeches, yard signs, T-shirts, etc. In solidarity with groups like the Poor People's Campaign and other unions and social justice groups, Black Lives Matter called for a "Strike for Black Lives" on July 20, 2020. Tens of thousands of workers walked off the job to call attention to systemic racism that has become more entrenched and recognizable in the context of the pandemic (Bogage, 2020).

The twin efforts are not separate but part of a whole that suggest the interdependence of knowledge, communication, and action in the form of democratic struggle. To emphasize communication's role in shaping cultural knowledge is not to necessarily suggest that persuasion is always successful, particularly without collective material pushback. Racism is not only or simply a question of morals that can be settled through changes in ideas, values, or discourses. Racism has always been integral to capitalism, something we saw with the role slavery played in the development of the US economy in both northern and southern states. Without challenging the structures and systems that perpetuate and benefit from racial (and gender, ethnic, etc.) divisions, the root causes of social inequalities will continue to be unaddressed.[11] The words of the abolitionist and women's right advocate Frederick Douglass (1857) are instructive: "If there is no struggle, there is no progress."

We should understand, however, the indispensable role of communication in advancing democratic struggle and facilitating a new nonracist, nonsexist social imaginary that challenges white willful ignorance. African American women's writings of the late 1800s-early 1900s—the voices of Gertrude Dorsey Brown, Carrie Clifford, Anna Julia Cooper, Pauline Hopkins, Addie Waites Hunton, Maybelle McAdoo, Emma F. G. Merritt, M. Cravatt Simpson, Albreta Moore Smith, Mary Church Terrell, Ruth D. Todd, Louise Burgess-Ware, Fannie Barrier Williams, Sylvanie Francoz Williams, and Josephine Silone Yates—provided a foundation upon which future writers could build, one that challenged epistemic invisibility and established credibility. Their writings called attention to intersectional forms of oppression—or as Anna Julia Cooper (1892/1988) emphasized, both the "woman question and [the] race question" (p. 134). And they situated Black women at the forefront of racial justice. In the words of Anna H. Jones (1905b), the "colored people realize that in the development of their women lie the best interests of their race" (p. 692).

As Claudia Rankine's poetry reminds us, for centuries, popular culture and political discourses have practiced forgetting, have recommended a form of not remembering that perpetuates a willful white ignorance. African American women from Pauline Hopkins to Rankine, Crenshaw, Cullors, Garza, Tometi, and the countless women of color whose names may never be officially recorded have stood at the center of efforts to remember, to draw the lines from past to present, in an effort to make the world a more humane place free of exploitation and injustice.

ACKNOWLEDGMENTS

During the 2020 pandemic lockdown, the works of James Baldwin, Pauline Hopkins, and Claudia Rankine kept me absorbed and prompted me to think about the power to be found in voicing memories of pain and resistance. I must begin by thanking the many African American writers whose works—some of which are explored in this book—raised my consciousness and inspired me to think more deeply about the ways cultural memories work to both support and resist racism in America.

I have learned over the years that, even when I write alone, scholarship is rarely a solo project. Many people have had a hand in shaping this book and enabling me to see it through to publication. Thank you to the University Press of Mississippi, editor Emily Snyder Bandy, and the anonymous reviewers who provided detailed and thoughtful feedback on earlier drafts. The faculty and staff at The University of Akron have provided support and camaraderie over the past twenty-five years and throughout the writing of this book. I am especially grateful for the funding received from the university's 2019 Summer Faculty Fellowship and for the encouragement of colleagues including Colleen Barnes, Daniela Jauk-Ajamie, Kathleen D. Clark, and Heather Walter.

A big thank you also goes to Brian Sweeney and Eurie Dahn, directors of the Digital Colored American Magazine online archive, and to the James Weldon Johnson Memorial Collection in the

Yale Collection of American Literature, Beinecke Rare Book and Manuscript Library. Their careful preservation and digitalization of *The Colored American Magazine* have been instrumental to my research and have made widely available this invaluable resource for individuals interested in experiencing the voices of African American writers of the early twentieth century.

Finally, I consider myself incredibly fortunate to have the support of my two children, Lily and Dashiell, my spouse, Mark, and our three cats, Patty, Paul, and Howard, in addition to a circle of dear friends and neighbors who inspire lively debate, elicit lots of laughs, and provide good reason for continuing to extend academic insights to social justice efforts in the broader community.

NOTES

Introduction: Communication, Race, and Popular Magazines

1. Emmett Till was beaten and shot. His murderers wrapped barbed wire and a seventy-five-pound metal fan around his neck, then threw him in the Tallahatchie River.

2. See Pohlhaus (2012) on the idea of using new frameworks from untapped bodies of knowledge to "recalibrate" (p. 719) public understandings of race.

3. Some influential racist white writers of the early 1900s include lawyer Thomas Nelson Page; academics like William Benjamin Smith and Alfred Holt Stone; and political figures like James Vardaman, Hoke Smith, and Benjamin Tillman.

4. For more on Reconstruction, see Foner (1988, 2019) and Gates (2019). For information on Ku Klux Klan violence, see Hodes (1997). For more on white violence against Black communities in general, see Shapiro (1988).

5. Here and throughout the book, if no page number is provided, that indicates there was no page number found on the archived version of the document examined.

Chapter 1: Popular Magazines, Race, and the Construction of Cultural Knowledge

1. See Triece (2013) on the "reality gap" that shaped the protest discourses of African American women in the welfare rights movement of the 1960s–70s.

2. Mills (1997) uses the term "racial contract" to describe how ignorance operates to preserve white dominance. The "racial contract prescribes for its signatories . . . an epistemology of ignorance, a particular pattern of localized and

global cognitive dysfunctions ... producing the ironic outcome that whites will in general be unable to understand the world they themselves have made" (p. 18).

3. See Meyers (2020) on delineating the difference between objectivity and "truthful journalism."

4. See Atton (2002, 2009); Barnard (2018); Deuze (2009); Lewis et al. (2014); Min (2020); Nah and Yamamoto (2019); and Triece (forthcoming).

5. See Gates (1988a, p. xvi) and Carby (1988) for more detail on Black women's literary activity between 1890 and 1910.

6. Andreá N. Williams (2017) calls for more studies of African American women's periodical writing situated "in a more textured knowledge of periodical cultures" (p. 28).

7. Josephine Silone Yates's name sometimes also appeared on her magazine articles as Josephine Silone-Yates, but I am using it without a hyphen here since that is the way it appears in most sources about her.

8. Carby (1987) considers *The Colored American Magazine* a "product of the magazine 'revolution'" that had been taking shape since the 1800s. Due to the parallels in editorial intent, readership, and circulation numbers, I similarly include *The Voice of the Negro* in that category.

9. See "Away from Accommodation" (Johnson & Johnson, 1977) and "Booker T. Washington and the Negro Press" (Meier, 1953) for views on Washington's influence on Black periodicals. Johnson and Johnson (1977) shed light on the rivalry between Booker T. Washington and W. E. B. Du Bois that played out in African American magazines such as *The Colored American Magazine* and *The Voice of the Negro*. Du Bois, who advocated higher education and uplift for Black Americans, was frustrated by what he perceived as Washington's conciliatory approach to racial progress through industrial education and by Washington's financial control over various Black periodicals. Du Bois viewed *The Voice of the Negro*—which frequently published his articles—as a forerunner of the NAACP's magazine *The Crisis*, which would be founded in 1910.

10. See *Daughter of the Revolution* (Dworkin, 2007) for a compilation of Hopkins's biographies published in *The Colored American Magazine*.

11. The quote comes from the Sacramento County District Attorney Anne Marie Schubert who announced in March 2019 that officers who shot and killed Stephon Clark, who was in his grandmother's backyard, would not be charged (Del Real, 2019).

12. This language of anxiety was used by Thomas Nelson Page in 1904.

Chapter 2: Memory Work and White Violence

1. See Shapiro, *White Violence and Black Response* (1988) for a historical account of the ways that Black communities defended themselves and fought back against white terrorism.
2. Journalist and anti-lynching crusader Ida B. Wells published *The Red Record* in 1895. It was a compilation of statistics on lynching and provided an assessment of causes.
3. "The New York Riot," 1900, 27.
4. A similar observation regarding strategic forgetting was made about press coverage of the foreclosure crisis in Cleveland and Detroit in 2008 (Triece, 2017).
5. For historical accounts of the systematic rape of enslaved Black women by white enslavers, see Broussard (2013); Bridgewater (2005); and Livesey (2018). The issue of rape and slavery is discussed more fully in chapter 5.
6. Legal discourses similarly appealed to the image of the Black male rapist as in an article in *The American Lawyer* titled "The Negro War on White Women and How to Prevent Lynching" (Ornsby, 1903).
7. *The Independent* covered lynching in sixty-two articles, *The Outlook* in forty-two articles, *The Arena* in seven articles, and *McClure's* in eight articles.
8. Walling's article was not the only voice to counter the prevailing framings. In 1899 ("The Delegal Riots in Georgia"), 1900 ("White Justice and Black"), and 1901 ("The Rev. Quincy Ewing on Lynching"), *The Independent* published three articles that called out the racist hypocrisy of the justice system. "White Justice and Black" (1900) pointed out that when murderers are Black and victims white, there is a "swift lynching"; but when murderers are white and victims are Black, "it is probable that nothing would have ever been said or done about it" (p. 961).
9. For further reading on the ways racism is built into US laws and policies, see M. Alexander (2010); Bullard (1994); Massey & Denton (1993); Quadagno (1994); and Rothstein (2017).
10. Ross (1997b) explains, "white innocence and Black abstraction comfort us [white people] in our choices" (p. 265).
11. In contrast, consider Mary Church Terrell's (1904a) excoriation of lynching published in the *North American Review*. She described the plight of two Black men wrongly accused and lynched. Terrell gave a full picture of these men, explaining one was a merchant in Atlanta and the other a corn field worker in New Orleans.
12. In a speech given to Booker T. Washington's Tuskegee Institute, Grover Cleveland was quoted as worrying that "among the nearly nine millions of negroes who have been intermixed with our citizenship there is still a grievous amount of ignorance, a sad amount of viciousness, and a tremendous amount of laziness and thriftlessness" ("The Negro Problem," 1903, p. 938). Theodore

Roosevelt (1905) advised that the "backward race be trained so that it may enter into the possession of true freedom . . . while the forward race is enabled to preserve unharmed the high civilization wrought out by its forefathers."

Chapter 3: Memory Work and a Cult of White Purity

1. For histories of rape in the context of slavery, see Blassingame (1972); P. D. Hopkins (2011); and Livesey (2018).

2. Black women authors such as Harriet Jacobs, Harriet E. Wilson, and Frances Ellen Watkins Harper critiqued the tragic mulatta figure in their writings (C. L. Peterson, 1995).

3. See Mott (1958) on *The Independent* (p. 377); Mott (1957) on *The Arena* (p. 402); and Mott (1938) on *The Outlook* (p. 429).

4. For a more detailed history of labor conditions and activism and how they intersected with gender and race, see Philip Foner (1976, 1979, 1980). See Matthaei (1982) for ways capitalism shaped the workplace and family.

5. See, for example, the writings of academics such as William Benjamin Smith and Frederick Hoffman; Catholic priest Thomas Price; politicians such as Alfred Holt Stone, Benjamin Tillman, and James Vardaman; and lawyers like Thomas Dixon and Thomas Nelson Page. For a collection of racist writings, see J. D. Smith (1993), *Anti-Black Thought 1863–1925*.

6. J. D. Smith's (1993) eleven-volume series, *Anti-Black Thought*, contains the racist writings of academics, politicians, and hate groups between 1863 and 1925.

7. Notably, upon the 2018 opening in Montgomery, Alabama, of the National Memorial for Peace and Justice, a memorial commemorating lynching victims, the city's primary newspaper, *The Montgomery Advertiser*, apologized for its dehumanizing coverage of lynching between 1870 and 1950 (see Moench, 2018).

8. Homer Plessy was a light-skinned Black man who contested Louisiana's separate but equal laws by boarding the white railway car and provoking his own arrest. His attorneys, who helped coordinate the action, argued in court that states have no power to force train conductors to "determine" race. The court dismissed the case. Upon subsequent appeals, which eventually landed at the US Supreme Court in 1896, the justices upheld separate but equal policies. The judge for the state court's decision referenced the risks of contamination, noting the dangers of putting the races in "contact" with one another and asserting the "unreasonable insistence upon thrusting the company of one race upon another" (quoted in M. M. Smith, 2006, pp. 73, 74).

9. Other contributors included writer and educator Booker T. Washington, who pleaded for the races to come together for the mutual benefit of Black uplift, particularly through education for Black people; James Theodore Holly, a Black Protestant Episcopal bishop, who pinned the race problem on imperialism; and

J. Montgomery McGovern, a white writer who recommended disfranchisement as a "remedy" for the race problem.

10. *The Outlook* writer and editor Ernest Hamlin Abbott (1904) wrote in part VII of his series "The South and the Negro" that both races were "averse" to "social intimacy" (p. 533).

11. Winter, a prohibition supporter, was a southern "apologist" who believed the 1906 Atlanta massacre was caused largely by alcohol in the hands of Black residents (Luker, 1991, p. 241

12. Press coverage of the police shooting of the African American boy Tamir Rice in November 2014 in Cleveland drew on the century-old stereotype of the unstable Black home. A Cleveland.com article homed in on Rice's domestic surroundings as if to suggest this had something to do with his shooting death: "Tamir lived in a three-unit, brick apartment building off Madison Avenue, across from the park. Graffiti covers almost every surface in sight—a convenience store, a US Postal Service box, a 'No Parking' sign, a used clothes and a shoe collective bin. A few blocks west, near Berea Road, a sign on a mechanic shop nestled between crumbling warehouses warns customers that the business is not responsible for vehicle fires, break-ins or smashed windows.... A few blocks east of Tamir's apartment, at West 98th Street, a once notorious gang wage a 'reign of terror'" (Shaffer, 2014).

This detailed description puts the signs of poverty—a used clothes and shoe collection bin, an abandoned warehouse—to work by associating these physical markers with criminal activity, such as break-ins and gangs. Another article pointed out that Rice's mother had pleaded guilty to drug trafficking and assault in 2001 and his father had a history of domestic violence (Blackwell, 2014). In addition to this article representing shameless victim-blaming, it performs a function similar to early 1900s articles that homed in on the "lack of primal moral traits" (Winter, 1906) and the "immoral" Black mother. Namely, such rhetorical moves situate Rice's home as synecdoche, as a symbol to stand in for the failed Black family with the "bad mother" at the center. The Blackwell article is no longer available on Cleveland.com. The news platform's racist coverage of the Rice tragedy was roundly taken to task by the *Columbia Journalism Review* (Clark, 2014).

Chapter 4: Countermemory Work: Reconsidering Black History and White Racism

1. The Boston Literary and Historical Association placed a similar importance on knowing and calling up history. This organization, founded in 1901, was a "product of the city's African American intellectual and professional elite" (L. Brown, 2008, p. 408). Brown also points out the founders "recognized the importance of asserting and claiming the past, which would enhance their claims on the present day" (p. 409). One of the group's key purposes was to "collect

and preserve hitherto ungarnered data of historical value" to Black Americans (quoted in L. Brown, 2008, p. 409).

2. Pohlhaus (2012) explains that the collective "refusal to recognize alternate epistemic resources, when enacted by those with material power, is hard to overcome.... Such a refusal is *not* an inherent inability, but rather a willful act" (p. 729).

3. Quarles (1979) looks at the writings of antebellum Black men and women who directed their efforts to recovering Black history and contributions to American life. He quotes Maria Stewart who, in 1833, lamented, "When I cast my eyes on the long list of illustrious names that are enrolled in the bright annals of fame among whites, I turn my eyes within, and ask my thoughts, 'Where are the names of our illustrious ones?'" (p. 93).

4. In 1968, Frances Beal formed the Black Women's Liberation Committee as a voice for Black women to critique the "double jeopardy" of racism and sexism. See Anderson-Bricker, 1999, p. 58.

5. Kim Gallon (2020) discusses the challenges faced by Black newspapers to attract advertising revenue in the 1920s–30s (pp. 33–35). She notes that white-held companies often believed their "dollars were better spent in white publications" (p. 34).

6. Evelyn Brooks Higginbotham's influential book, *Righteous Discontent* (1993), elaborates on the "female talented tenth" in order to restore Black women's place within the history of civil rights activism of the early twentieth century.

7. The concept of a "talented tenth" was originally conceived by Henry Morehouse, the executive secretary of the American Baptist Home Missionary Society (James, 1997, p. 17).

8. Standpoint theory need not lead to the conclusion that all Black women's experiences are uniform. Critical consciousness of one's position in society vis-à-vis axes of power is not ready-made but a reflective process that occurs, in part, through communication—for example, conversations with friends and kin, exposure to resistant messages as those found in the Black press, etc.

9. Kwame Anthony Appiah (2019) explains the importance of films like *Black Panther* as stemming from an ability both to establish identification with Black viewers and to offer visions to which to aspire. Black-created films, he argues, serve not just a "see it to be it" but a "see it to dream it" function.

10. See Watson (1999) on how women utilized autobiography to write themselves into existence (p. 1).

11. Lindsey (2017) calls it a "new negro womanhood" and notes Black women's efforts to be recognized were not monolithic but represented a variety of standpoints.

12. Josephine Silone Yates's article also appeared in the May issue of *The Colored American Magazine*.

13. For more on McAdoo and other African American women's activism in the New York YWCA, see Weisenfeld, 1997.

14. It is unclear why "The Women's Department" was dropped after only one installment. The editor's note that headed the column proclaimed, "We bring to this column an enthusiastic desire to do good and pleasing work for our lady patrons" (P. Hopkins, 1900, p. 118).

15. *The Colored American Magazine* publishes her name as Albreta Moore Smith in 1901 articles. Starting in 1902, the magazine uses Albreta Moore-Smith. In her book, *Beauty Shop Politics*, Gill (2010) mentions her as Alberta Moore Smith. In this book, I have chosen to use Albreta as her first name as it appeared that way most frequently in the magazine; and for consistency with the 1901 use, I chose to use the 1901 unhyphenated version of her last names.

16. See L. Brown (2008), Cordell (2006), Gruesser (1996), Knight (2007), Otten (1992), and Shockley (1972) for scholarship on Hopkins's writings and career at *The Colored American Magazine*.

17. For analysis of some Hopkins articles, I used the versions and corresponding page numbers contained in the anthology *Daughter of the Revolution: The Major Nonfiction Works of Pauline E. Hopkins*.

18. Exceptions were October 1900 and October 1901. Beginning in March 1904, *The Colored American Magazine* covers featured successful African American men, indicating the magazine's shift away from its proto Black feminist emphasis (Bergman, 2003). It is worth noting that 1904 was the year Booker T. Washington took control of the magazine and Hopkins left to write for *The Voice of the Negro*.

19. See also the covers of September 1900, February 1901, June 1902, and January 1903. These issues are digitized and available at coloredamerican.org.

20. Livesey (2018) explains that, for historians examining the experiences of Black women, indications of lighter skin may "provide a methodological tool that can be applied to the recovery of sexually violent experiences within other source material" (p. 269).

21. Sojourner Truth's narrative, penned by the abolitionist Olive Gilbert, was notably silent—"from motives of delicacy"—on issues of sexuality, in contrast to Jacobs's story (M. Washington, 2007, p. 57). According to Washington, Truth's biographer believed that including Truth's experiences of sex and sexual abuse would "compromise efforts to bypass the stereotypical images of Black women" (p. 69). In contrast, the choice of Jacobs's biographer, Lydia Maria Childs, to include details of sexual harassment and rape put Jacobs's reputation on the line (p. 69).

22. Scholars have documented and discussed the ways Black families managed the complexities arising from race and economic oppression. Adhering to traditional gender and familial norms was a form of resistance for Black women who seldom had the luxury of staying home to raise their children (J. Jones, 1985;

Higginbotham, 1992). Higginbotham also discusses how the politics of respectability exposed the class tensions within the Black community with its stress on gaining the respect of the white community through adherence to rigid moral and gender norms that may have been attainable only through middle class status. See also Gaines (1996).

Chapter 5: Countermemory Work and Narrative Inversion

1. Dutta (2018) discusses how social change communication that comes from the margins uses inversion to challenge the notion of "culture as static" (p. 87) and "development as economic growth and linear progress" (p. 97).

2. Occasionally, her middle name (which was her birth name) was spelled Cravat or Cravath.

3. See Sweeney (2019) for a detailed analysis of *Hagar's Daughter* as it pertained to Hopkins's efforts to reclaim Black history against the white imaginary's pull to revisionist histories of reunification. Also see Carby (1987) for an analysis of *Hagar's Daughter* that focuses on themes of passing and gender. See Tate (1992) for an analysis of Hopkins's fiction as domestic fiction.

Conclusion: Persistent White Ignorance and the Optimism of Resistant Cultural Memory

1. Trayvon Martin was walking back to his father's fiancée's home in Sanford, Florida, after having gone to the store for a snack. Tamir Rice was playing in Cudell Park in Cleveland, Ohio. John Crawford III was shopping at a Walmart in Beavercreek, Ohio. Ahmaud Arbery was jogging through a suburban neighborhood in Glynn County, Georgia.

2. Joe R. Feagin (2020) describes the "white racial frame" as a "white worldview that encompasses a *broad and persisting set of racial stereotypes, prejudices, ideologies, images, interpretations and narratives, emotions, and reactions to language accents, as well as racialized inclinations to discriminate*" (p. 3, italics in original).

3. Since 2022, seven states have passed laws legislating what K-12 (and in some cases, college-level) teachers can say about gender, sex, race, sexuality, and American history ("Which States Passed Laws Restricting School Curriculum?"). The bills have been inspired by misinterpretations of critical race theory and a white anxiety over history lessons that would address systemic racism, including its role in the nation's founding and its influences on contemporary social institutions (Camera, 2021; S. Schwartz, 2021).

4. I (Triece, 2007, 2013) have used the term "reality gap" to describe the "space between prevailing, widely accepted ideologies that describe or interpret our experiences and the lives of ordinary people as they are experienced day in and day out" (2013, p. 34).

5. McCarthy (2004) borrows terminology from Janna Thomason in *Taking Responsibility for the Past*.

6. Although the theory has been around since the early 1990s, critical race theory has become the latest media buzzword signifying all things "race." Outlets ranging from *Time* magazine, *The Washington Post*, *The New York Times*, and *Scientific American* to CNN and NPR have addressed it and the surrounding controversy.

7. McCarthy (2004) suggests "public hearings" and "commissions of inquiry" on reparations as public platforms whereby the "massive gap between professional historiography and public memory might be narrowed" (p. 765).

8. Crenshaw (1989) developed the concept of "intersectionality" to explain Black women's intersecting experiences of race and gender oppression.

9. The Black Lives Matter organization removed the "What We Believe" page from its website in September 2020 after backlash from conservatives over what was criticized as supposedly "anti-family" and socialist-leaning language (J. Abbott, 2020).

10. Even unionized workers often hold little power over their livelihoods and material fate. Many union contracts have *force majeure* measures in them that stipulate that, in the face of a catastrophic event, the employer has the right to throw out the contract. This is what happened to unionized faculty at the University of Akron in July 2020 when the administration fired ninety-seven faculty members, many of whom were tenured and had worked at the university for decades. Consider also the example of when then-President Ronald Reagan summarily fired air traffic control workers in August 1981 when they refused to return to work after walking out on strike.

11. In "Racism Is Not a Moral Question," *New York Times* columnist Jamelle Bouie (2021) turns to the 1948 book *Caste, Class, and Race* by Oliver Cromwell Cox to make the case that eradicating racism requires dismantling the economic system that relies on social hierarchies to remain in place. Bouie's critique of capitalism and racism appearing in a widely circulating mainstream newspaper is further evidence of the ways public discourses appearing in news outlets have expanded to include counterhegemonic memory of the role of racism in the trajectory of US economic development.

REFERENCES

Abbott, E. H. (1904, July). The south and the Negro: Social equality versus social service. *The Outlook*, 589–594.

Abbott, J. (2020, September 21). Black Lives Matter removes controversial "What We Believe" page from website. https://disrn.com/news/black-lives-matter-removes-controversial-belief-statements-from-website

About the public safety assessment: PSA sites. (n.d.). Advancing Pretrial Policy & Research. Retrieved February 26, 2024, from https://advancingpretrial.org/psa/psa-sites/

About the public safety assessment: What is the PSA. (n.d.). Advancing Pretrial Policy & Research. Retrieved February 26, 2024, from https://advancingpretrial.org/psa/about/

Adams, J. H. (1904, August). Rough sketches: The new Negro man. *The Voice of the Negro*, 447–452.

Alcoff, L. (2006). *Visible identities: Race, gender and the self*. Oxford University Press.

Alcoff, L. (2007). Epistemologies of ignorance: Three types. In S. Sullivan and N. Tuana (Eds.), *Race and epistemologies of ignorance* (pp. 39–58). State University of New York.

Alcoff, L., & Potter, E. (Eds.). (1993). *Feminist epistemologies*. Routledge.

Alexander, H. (1907, February). Race riots and lynch law: The cause and the cure. *The Outlook*, 259–263.

Alexander, M. (2010). *The new Jim Crow: Mass incarceration in the age of colorblindness*. The New Press.

Alexander, M. (2018, November 11). The newest Jim Crow. *The New York Times*, Sunday Review, 3.

Allen, S. A. (1902, December). The test of manhood: A Christmas story. *The Colored American Magazine*, 113–119.

Anderson, H. (2013). Facilitating active citizenship: Participating in prisoners' radio. *Critical Studies in Media Communication, 30*, 292–306.

Anderson-Bricker, K. (1999). "Triple jeopardy": Black women and the growth of feminist consciousness in SNCC, 1964–1975. In K. Springer (Ed.), *Still lifting, still climbing: Contemporary African American women's contemporary activism* (pp. 49–69). New York University Press.

Appiah, K. A. (2019, September 22). What does it mean to "look like me"? *The New York Times*, Sunday Review, 7.

Archer, W. (1909, July). Black and white in the south. *McClure's*, 324–338.

Aronson, A. B. (2000). America's first feminist magazine: Transforming the popular to the political. In L. Brake, B. Bell, & D. Finkelstein (Eds.), *Nineteenth-century media and the construction of identities* (pp. 197–219). Palgrave.

Aronson, A. B. (2002). *Taking liberties: Early American women's magazines and their readers*. Praeger.

Atkins-Sayre, W. (2012). Snapshots of the south: Eudora Welty's photography and contested images of race. *Southern Communication Journal, 77*, 77–93.

The Atlanta massacre. (1906, October 4). *The Independent*.

Atton, C. (2002). *Alternative Media*. Sage.

Atton, C. (2009). Alternative and citizen journalism. In K. Wahl-Jorgensen & T. Hanitzsch, (Eds.), *The handbook of journalism studies* (pp. 265–278). Routledge.

Aviles, G. (2020, June 8). Black women create #BlackInTheIvory and #PublishingPaidMe to reveal inequity in academia and publishing. NBC News. https://www.nbcnews.com/pop-culture/pop-culture-news/black-women-create-blackintheivory-publishingpaidme-reveal-inequity-academia-publishing-n1227626

Babbitt, D. R. (1904, December). The psychology of the lynching mob. *The Arena*, 586–589.

Bailey, A. (2007). Strategic ignorance. In S. Sullivan and N. Tuana (Eds.), *Race and epistemologies of ignorance* (pp. 77–94). State University of New York.

Baker, A., Goodman, J. D., & Mueller, B. (2015, June 13). Beyond the chokehold: The path to Eric Garner's death. *The New York Times*. https://www.nytimes.com/2015/06/14/nyregion/eric-garner-police-chokehold-staten-island.html

Baker, R. S. (1905a, January). What is a lynching? A study of mob justice, south and north. Part I. *McClure's*, 299–314.

Baker, R. S. (1905b, February). What is a lynching? A study of mob justice, south and north. Part II. *McClure's*, 422–430.

Barber, J. M. (1906, November). The Atlanta tragedy. *The Voice of the Negro*, 473–479.

Barnard, S. R. (2018). *Citizens at the gates: Twitter, networked publics, and the transformation of American journalism*. Palgrave Macmillan.

Barnlund, D. C., & Haiman, F. S. (1960). *The dynamics of discussion*. Houghton Mifflin.

Bar On, B.-A. (1993). Marginality and epistemic privilege. In L. Alcoff & E. Potter (Eds.), *Feminist epistemologies* (pp. 83–100). Routledge.

Benard, A. A. F. (2016). Colonizing Black female bodies within patriarchal capitalism: Feminist and human rights perspectives. *Sexualization, Media, & Society*, October-December, 1–11.

Benjamin, R. (2019). *Race after technology: Abolitionist tools for the new Jim Code*. Polity Press.

Berg, M. (2011). *Popular justice: A history of lynching in America*. Rowman & Littlefield.

Bergman, J. (2003). "A new race of Colored women": Pauline Hopkins at the Colored American Magazine. In A. Heilmann (Ed.), *Feminist forerunners: New womanism and feminism in the early twentieth century* (pp. 87–100). Pandora.

Berridge, S., & Portwood-Stacer, L. (2015). Introduction: Feminism, hashtags and violence against women and girls. *Feminist Media Studies*, *15*, 341–358.

The best defense. (1903, August). *The Outlook*, 927–929.

Bhabha, H. K. (1985). Signs taken for wonders: Questions of ambivalence and authority under a tree outside Delhi, May 1817. *Critical Inquiry*, *12*, 144–165.

Black women's lives matter: Breaking the cover on systemic race and gender violence by police. (2020). *The Facts*. https://www.thefactsnewspaper.com/post/black-women-s-lives-matter-breaking-the-cover-on-systemic-race-and-gender-violence-by-police

Blair, H. W. (1902, February). The Negro problem. *The Independent*, 442.

Blake, J. (2019, February 17). Stop "whitesplaining" racism to me. CNN. https://www.cnn.com/2019/02/17/us/whitesplaining-racism-blake-analysis/index.html

Blakesley, D. (2002). *The elements of dramatism*. Pearson.

Blassingame, J. (1972). *The slave community: Plantation life in the antebellum south*. Oxford University Press.

Boas, F. (1940). *Race, language, and culture*. The MacMillan Company.

Bogage, J. (2020, July 20). Thousands of U.S. workers walk out in "strike for black lives." *The Washington Post*. https://www.washingtonpost.com/business/2020/07/20/strike-for-black-lives/

Bouie, J. (2021, November 14). Racism is not a moral question. *The New York Times*, Sunday Review, 7.

Bowen, C. (1907, March). Woman's part in the uplift of our race. *The Colored American Magazine*, 61–62.

Brake, L., Bell, B., & Finkelstein, D. (2000). *Nineteenth-century media and the construction of identities*. Palgrave.

Bridgewater, P. D. (2005). Ain't I a slave: Slavery reproductive abuse, and reparations. *UCLA Women's Law Journal*, *14*, 89–161.

Brinton, D. G. (1890). *Races and peoples: Lectures on the science of ethnography*. N. D. C. Hodges, Publisher.

Broussard, P. A. (2013). Black women's post-slavery silence syndrome: A twenty-first century remnant of slavery, Jim Crow, and systemic racism—who will tell her stories? *Journal of Gender, Race & Justice*, *16*, 373–421.

Brown, G. D. (1905a, January). Scrambled eggs. *The Colored American Magazine*, 31–38.
Brown, G. D. (1905b, February). Scrambled eggs, continued. *The Colored American Magazine*, 79–86.
Brown, G. D. (1906a, April). A case of measure for measure. *The Colored American Magazine*, 253–258.
Brown, G. D. (1906b, May). A case of measure for measure, chapters III, IV. *The Colored American Magazine*, 301–304.
Brown, G. D. (1906c, July). A case of measure for measure, chapter V. *The Colored American Magazine*, 25–28.
Brown, G. D. (1906d, August). A case of measure for measure, chapters VI, VII. *The Colored American Magazine*, 97–100.
Brown, G. D. (1906e, September). A case of measure for measure, chapter VIII. *The Colored American Magazine*, 167–172.
Brown, G. D. (1906f, October). A case of measure for measure, chapter IX. *The Colored American Magazine*, 281–284.
Brown, L. (2008). *Pauline Elizabeth Hopkins: Black daughter of the revolution*. University of North Carolina Press.
Bruce, J. B. (1904, November). The afterglow of the women's convention. *The Voice of the Negro*, 541–543.
Bullard, R. (Ed.). (1994). *Unequal protection: Environmental justice and communities of color*. Sierra Club Books.
Bullock, P. L. (1981). *The Afro-American periodical press, 1838–1909*. Louisiana State University Press.
Burgess-Ware, M. L. (1903a, August). Bernice, the octoroon. *The Colored American Magazine*, 607–616.
Burgess-Ware, M. L. (1903b, August). Bernice, the octoroon. Part 2. *The Colored American Magazine*, 651–657.
Burke, K. (1954). *Permanence and change: An anatomy of purpose*. Hermes Publications.
Burke, K. (1937/1984). *Attitudes toward history* (3rd ed.). University of California Press.
Burns, R. (2006). *Rage in the gate city: The story of the 1906 Atlanta race riot*. University of Georgia Press.
Burroughs, N. H. (1904, July). Not color but character. *The Voice of the Negro*, 277–279.
Burroughs, N. H. (1905, February). Miss Burroughs replies to Mr. Carrington. *The Voice of the Negro*, 106–107.
Bush, O. W. (1900, September). Northeastern Federation of Women's Clubs. *The Colored American Magazine*, 234–235.

Camera, L. (2021, June 23). Bills banning critical race theory advance in states despite its absence in many classrooms. *US News and World Report*. https://www.usnews.com/news/education-news/articles/2021-06-23/bills-banning-critical-race-theory-advance-in-states-despite-its-absence-in-many-classrooms

Campbell, C. (2019, July 28). Trump calls Cummings "racist" in new round of Twitter fury about Baltimore. *Baltimore Sun*. https://www.baltimoresun.com/politics/bs-md-pol-trump-tweets-baltimore-20190728-klambm2qubbxrfg ghacuhev55y-story.html

Carby, H. (1987). *Reconstructing womanhood: The emergence of the Afro-American woman novelist*. Oxford University Press.

Carby, H. (1988). Introduction. *The magazine novels of Pauline Hopkins*. Oxford University Press.

Carby, H. (2007). The souls of black men. In S. Gillman (Ed.), *Next to the color line: Gender, sexuality, and W. E. B. Du Bois* (pp. 234–268). University of Minnesota Press.

Carey, J. (1992). *Communication as culture: Essays on media & society*. Routledge.

Castoriadis, C. (1997). *World in fragments: Writings on politics, society, psychoanalysis, and the imagination*. Stanford University Press.

Center for American Progress. (2020). How white supremacy returned to mainstream politics. https://www.americanprogress.org/article/white-supremacy-returned-mainstream-politics/

Charles, J. (2020). *That middle world: Race, performance, and the politics of passing*. University of North Carolina Press.

Clark, A. (2014, December 2). What a Cleveland news outlet should learn from its flawed Tamir Rice coverage. *Columbia Journalism Review*. https://www.cjr.org/local_news/tamir_rice_northeast_ohio_media_group.php

Clifford, C. W. (1906, November). A northern black point of view. *The Outlook*, 562–564.

Clifford, C. W. (1907, May). The great American question. *The Colored American Magazine*, 364–373.

Coates, T.-N. (2014, June). The case for reparations. *The Atlantic*. https://www.theatlantic.com/magazine/archive/2014/06/the-case-for-reparations/361631/

Code, L. (1993). Taking subjectivity into account. In L. Alcoff & E. Potter (Eds.), *Feminist epistemologies* (pp. 15–48). Routledge.

Collins, P. H. (1986). Learning from the outsider within: The sociological significance of Black feminist thought. *Social Problems, 33*, S14–S32.

Collins, P. H. (1991). *Black feminist thought: Knowledge, consciousness, and the politics of empowerment*. Routledge.

Combahee River Collective. (1977). Statement. https://www.blackpast.org/african-american-history/combahee-river-collective-statement-1977/

Cooper, A. J. (1892/1988). *A voice from the south.* Oxford University Press.
Cooper, B. C. (2017). *Beyond respectability: The intellectual thought of race women.* University of Illinois Press.
Cordell, S. A. (2006). "The case was very black against" her: Pauline Hopkins and the politics of racial ambiguity at the *Colored American Magazine. American Periodicals, 16,* 52–73.
Councill, W. H. (1899, April). Is there a Negro problem? *The Arena,* 426–437.
Crenshaw, K. (1989). Demarginalizing the intersection of race and sex: A Black feminist critique of antidiscrimination doctrine, feminist theory and antiracist politics. *University of Chicago Legal Forum,* 139–167.
Dagbovie, P. G. (2004). Black women historians from the late 19th century to the dawning of the civil rights movement. *The Journal of African American History, 89,* 241–261.
Dahn, E. (2021). *Jim Crow networks: African American periodical cultures.* University of Massachusetts Press.
Davis, A. (1972). Reflections on the Black woman's role in the community of slaves. *The Massachusetts Review, 13,* 81–100.
de la Roche, R. S. (2008). *In Lincoln's shadow: The 1908 race riot in Springfield, Illinois.* Southern Illinois University Press.
The Delegal riots in Georgia. (1899, September). *The Independent.*
Del Real, J. A. (2019, March 2). No charges in Sacramento police shooting of Stephon Clark. *The New York Times.* https://www.nytimes.com/2019/03/02/us/stephon-clark-police-shooting-sacramento.html
Demby, G. (2014, May 22). How to tell who hasn't read the new "Atlantic" cover story. Code Switch. National Public Radio. https://www.npr.org/sections/codeswitch/2014/05/22/314881767/how-to-tell-if-someones-actually-read-ta-nehisi-coates-essay
Demonstrations and political violence in America: New data for summer 2020. (2020, September 3). The Armed Conflict Location & Event Data Project. https://acleddata.com/2020/09/03/demonstrations-political-violence-in-america-new-data-for-summer-2020/
Detweiler, F. G. (1922). *The Negro press in the United States.* University of Chicago Press.
Deuze, M. (2009). The future of citizen journalism. In S. Allan & E. Thorsen (Eds.), *Citizen journalism: Global perspectives* (pp. 255–264). Peter Lang.
Dickinson, G., Blair, C., & Ott, B. L. (Eds.). (2010). *Places of public memory: The rhetoric of museums and memorials.* University of Alabama Press.
Dittmer, J. (1977). *Black Georgia in the progressive era, 1900–1920.* University of Illinois Press.
Dotson, K. (2014). Conceptualizing epistemic oppression. *Social Epistemology: A Journal of Knowledge, Culture and Policy, 28,* 115–138.

Dotson, K. (2017). Theorizing Jane Crow, theorizing unknowability. *Social Epistemology: A Journal of Knowledge, Culture and Policy, 31*, 417–430.

Douglass, F. (1857). West India emancipation speech. Black Past. https://www.blackpast.org/african-american-history/1857-frederick-douglass-if-there-no-struggle-there-no-progress/

Du Bois, W. E. B. (1899, May). The Negro and crime. *The Independent*.

Du Bois, W. E. B. (1903). The Talented Tenth. Teaching American History. https://teachingamericanhistory.org/library/document/the-talented-tenth/

Du Bois, W. E. B. (1903/1982). *The souls of black folk*. Penguin Books.

Du Bois, W. E. B. (1905, September). The Niagara Movement. *The Voice of the Negro*, 619–622.

Du Bois, W. E. B. (1910, October). Marrying of black folk. *The Independent*.

Duggan, L. (2000). *Sapphic slashers: Sex, violence, and American modernity*. Duke University Press.

Dunn, T. R. (2011). Remembering "a great fag": Visualizing public memory and the construction of queer space. *Quarterly Journal of Speech, 97*, 435–460.

Dutta, M. J. (2018). Culturally centering social change communication: Subaltern critiques of, resistance to, and re-imagination of development. *Journal of Multicultural Discourses, 13*, 87–104.

Dworkin, I. (Ed.). (2007). *Daughter of the revolution: The major nonfiction works of Pauline E. Hopkins*. Rutgers University Press.

Dyer, R. (1997). *White*. Routledge.

Dyson, M. E. (2003). *Open mic: Reflections on philosophy, race, sex, culture and religion*. Basic Civitas Books.

Editorial and publishers' announcements. (1900, May). *The Colored American Magazine*, 60–64.

Editorials. (1904, January). *The Voice of the Negro*, 33–36.

Editorials: Race purity and social equality. (1903, February). *The Independent*, 453–455.

Editor's note. (1903, March). *The Outlook*.

Editor's note: The Negro problem: How it appeals to a southern colored woman. (1902, September). *The Independent*, 2221.

Editor's note: A northern Negro's autobiography. (1904, July). *The Independent*.

Editor's note: The race problem—An autobiography. (1904, March). *The Independent*, 586.

Elliot, R. S. (1901, May). The story of our magazine. *The Colored American Magazine*, 43–44.

Enszer, J. R. (2015). "Fighting to create and maintain our own Black women's culture": Conditions magazine, 1977–1990. *American Periodicals, 25*, 160–176.

Entman, R. M. (1991). Framing U.S. coverage of international news: Contrasts in narratives of the KAL and Iran Air incidents. *Journal of Communication, 41*, 6–27.

Entman, R. M. (1993). Framing: Toward clarification of a fractured paradigm. *Journal of Communication, 43,* 51–58.

The epidemic of savagery. (1901, September). *The Outlook,* 9–10.

Ernest, J. (2002). Liberation historiography: African-American historians before the Civil War. *American Literary History, 14,* 413–443.

Ewen, S. (1996). *PR! A social history of spin.* Basic Books.

Experiences of the race problem. (1904, March). *The Independent,* 590–594.

Fabi, M. G. (2001). *Passing and the rise of the African American novel.* University of Illinois Press.

Fagan, B. (2016). *The Black newspaper and the chosen nation.* University of Georgia Press.

Farr, A. (2004). Whiteness visible: Enlightenment racism and the structure of racialized consciousness. In G. Yancy (Ed.), *What white looks like: African-American philosophers on the whiteness question* (pp. 143–158). Routledge.

Feagin, J. (2020). *The white racial frame: Centuries of racial framing and counter-framing* (3rd ed.). Routledge.

Fine, S. (1969). *Sit-down: The General Motors strike of 1936–37.* University of Michigan Press.

Finot, J. (1907). *Race prejudice.* Reprinted 2012. Forgotten Books.

Flores, L. A. (2016). Between abundance and marginalization: The imperative of racial rhetorical criticism. *Review of Communication, 16,* 4–24.

Florida's academic state standards—social studies. (2023). Florida Department of Education. https://www.fldoe.org/core/fileparse.php/20653/urlt/6-4.pdf

Foner, E. (1988). *Reconstruction: America's unfinished revolution, 1863–1877.* Harper & Row.

Foner, E. (2005). *Forever free: The story of emancipation and reconstruction.* Alfred A. Knopf.

Foner, E. (2019). *The second founding: How the Civil War and Reconstruction remade the Constitution.* W. W. Norton & Company.

Fordham, H. (2016). Subversive voices: George Seldes and mid twentieth century muckraking. *American Journalism, 33,* 424–441.

Foss, K. A., & Domenici, K. L. (2001). Haunting Argentina: Synecdoche in the protests of the mothers of the plaza de Mayo. *Quarterly Journal of Speech, 87,* 237–258.

Frances, B. G. (1906, February). The Colored Young Women's Christian Association of Washington. *The Colored American Magazine,* 126–129.

Franklin, V. P. (1985). *Living our stories, telling our truths: Autobiography and the making of the African-American intellectual tradition.* Scribner.

Franklin, V. P., & Collier-Thomas, B. (1996). Biography, race vindication and African-American intellectuals: Introductory essay. *The Journal of Negro History, 81,* 1–16.

Frederickson, G. (1997). White images of Black slaves (is what we see in others sometimes a reflection of what we find in ourselves?). In R. Delgado & J. Stefancic (Eds.), *Critical white studies: Looking behind the mirror* (pp. 38–45). Temple University Press.

Fricker, M. (1999). Epistemic oppression and epistemic privilege. *Canadian Journal of Philosophy, 29*, 191–210.

Fritze, J. (2019, August 8). Trump used words like "invasion" and "killer" to discuss immigrants at rallies 500 times: USA TODAY analysis. *USA TODAY*. https://www.usatoday.com/story/news/politics/elections/2019/08/08/trump-immigrants-rhetoric-criticized-el-paso-dayton-shootings/1936742001/

Gaines, K. (1996). *Uplifting the race: Black leadership, politics, and culture in the twentieth century*. University of North Carolina Press.

Gallon, K. (2012). Silences kept: The absence of gender and sexuality in Black press historiography. *History Compass, 10*, 207–218.

Gallon, K. (2013). "How much can you read about interracial love and sex without getting sore?": Readers' debate over interracial relationships in the Baltimore Afro-American. *Journalism History, 39*, 104–114.

Gallon, K. (2015). Mining images of race and gender in twentieth-century Black popular periodicals. *American Periodicals: A Journal of History, Criticism & Bibliography, 26*(1), 13–15.

Gallon, K. (2020). *Pleasure in the news: African American readership and sexuality in the Black press*. University of Illinois Press.

Gates, H. L., Jr. (1988a). Foreword: In her own write. In P. Hopkins, *The magazine novels of Pauline Hopkins*. Oxford University Press.

Gates, H. L., Jr. (1988b). The trope of the new Negro and the reconstruction of the image of the black. *Representations, 24*, 129–155.

Gates, H. L., Jr. (2019). *Stony the road: Reconstruction, white supremacy, and the rise of Jim Crow*. Penguin Press.

Giddings, P. (1985). *When and where I enter: The impact of Black women on race and sex in America*. Bantam Books.

Gilens, M. (1999). *Why Americans hate welfare: Race, media and the politics of antipoverty policy*. University of Chicago Press.

Gill, T. M. (2010). *Beauty shop politics: African American women's activism in the beauty industry*. University of Illinois Press.

Gillis, J. R. (1994). Memory and identity: The history of a relationship. In J. R. Gillis (Ed.), *Commemorations: The politics of national identity* (pp. 3–24). Princeton University Press.

Gillman, S., & Weinbaum A. E. (Eds.). (2007). *Next to the color line: Gender, sexuality, and W. E. B. Du Bois*. University of Minnesota Press.

Giroux, H. (2003). Spectacles of race and pedagogies of denial: Anti-black racist pedagogy under the reign of neoliberalism. *Communication Education, 52*, 191–211.

Gitlin, T. (1980). *The whole world is watching: Mass media in the making and unmaking of the New Left*. University of California Press.

Godshalk, D. F. (2005). *Veiled visions: The 1906 Atlanta race riot and the reshaping of American race relations*. University of North Carolina Press.

Goldberg, D. T. (2009). *The threat of race: Reflections on racial neoliberalism*. Blackwell Publishing.

Goodman, J. D., & Goldstein, J. (2014, August 20). Grand jury to take up death linked to police chokehold in Staten Island. *The New York Times*. https://www.nytimes.com/2014/08/20/nyregion/eric-garner-staten-island-police-chokehold-case-to-go-to-grand-jury.html

Gordon, L. R. (1995). *Bad faith and antiblack racism*. Humanities Press.

Gordon, L. R. (2000). *Existentia Africana: Understanding Africana existential thought*. Routledge.

Gould, S. J. (1981). *The mismeasure of man*. W. W. Norton & Company.

Grossman, J. (2016, August 3). James Baldwin on history. *Perspectives on History*. https://www.historians.org/publications-and-directories/perspectives-on-history/summer-2016/james-baldwin-on-history

Gruesser, J. C. (Ed.). (1996). *The unruly voice: Rediscovering Pauline Elizabeth Hopkins*. University of Illinois Press.

Guild, W. (1900, November). A plea from the south. *The Arena*.

Gunn, J. (2004). Mourning speech: Haunting and the spectral voices of nine-eleven. *Text and Performance Quarterly, 24*, 91–114.

Gunning, S. (1996). *Race, rape, and lynching: The red record of American literature, 1890–1912*. Oxford University Press.

Haiman, F. (1967). The rhetoric of the streets: Some legal and ethical considerations. *Quarterly Journal of Speech, 53*, 99–114.

Hall, R. S. (1906, November). Letter to the editor. *The Outlook*, 684–685.

Haller, J. S., Jr. (1971). *Outcasts from evolution: Scientific attitudes of racial inferiority, 1859–1900*. University of Illinois Press.

Hammerback, J. C. (1994). José Antonio's rhetoric of fascism. *Southern Communication Journal, 59*, 181–195.

Hammond, L. H. (1903, March). A southern view of the Negro. *The Outlook*, 14.

Hancock, A. M. (2004). *The politics of disgust: The public identity of the welfare queen*. New York University Press.

Hannah-Jones, N. (2019, August 14). The 1619 project. *The New York Times Magazine*. https://www.nytimes.com/interactive/2019/08/14/magazine/1619-america-slavery.html

Hannah-Jones, N. (2020, June 30). What is owed. *The New York Times Magazine*. https://www.nytimes.com/interactive/2020/06/24/magazine/reparations-slavery.html

Harding, S. (1993). Rethinking standpoint epistemology: "What is strong objectivity?" In L. Alcoff & E. Potter (Eds.), *Feminist epistemologies* (pp. 49–82). Routledge.
Hariman R., & Lucaites, J. L. (2003). Public identity and collective memory in U.S. iconic photography: The image of "accidental napalm." *Critical Studies in Media Communication*, *20*(1), 35–66.
Harlow, S. (2022). Journalism's change agents: Black Lives Matter, #BlackoutTuesday, and a shift toward activist doxa. *Journalism and Mass Communication Quarterly*, *99*, 742–762.
Harris, L. H. (1899a, May). A southern woman's view. *The Independent*.
Harris, L. H. (1899b, June). Negro womanhood. *The Independent*, 1687–1689.
Hart, A. B. (1905, May). Remedies for the southern problem. *The Independent*, 993–996.
Hartsock, N. (1983). *Money, sex, and power: Toward a feminist historical materialism*. Longman.
Hawley, W. L. (1900, November). Passing of the race problem. *The Arena*.
He defends lynch law. (1903, August 11). *The New York Times*.
Henry, K. (2014). "Slaves to a debt": Race, shame, and the anti-Obama jeremiad. *Quarterly Journal of Speech*, *100*, 303–322.
Here and there. (1900a, June). *The Colored American Magazine*, 123–126.
Here and there. (1900b, August). *The Colored American Magazine*, 185–190.
Here and there. (1900c, September). *The Colored American Magazine*, 257–261.
Here and there. (1900d, December). *The Colored American Magazine*, 134–144.
Here and there. (1901a, February). *The Colored American Magazine*, 274–284.
Here and there. (1901b, November). *The Colored American Magazine*, 54–58.
Higginbotham, E. B. (1992). African-American women's history and the metalanguage of race. *Signs: Journal of Women in Culture and Society*, *17*, 251–274.
Higginbotham, E. B. (1993). *Righteous discontent: The women's movement in the Black Baptist church, 1880–1920*. Harvard University Press.
Higgins, L. A., & Silver, B. R. (1991). *Rape and representation*. Columbia University Press.
Hill, K. K. (2016). *Beyond the rope: The impact of lynching on Black culture and memory*. Cambridge University Press.
Hill, K. K. (2020, June 19). Politics with Amy Walter: A national reckoning [Interview]. In *The takeaway*. WNYC Studios. https://www.wnycstudios.org/podcasts/takeaway/episodes/politics-amy-walter-national-reckoning
Hodes, M. (1997). *White women, black men: Illicit sex in the nineteenth-century south*. Yale University Press.
Hoerl, K. (2012). Selective amnesia and racial transcendence in news coverage of President Obama's inauguration. *Quarterly Journal of Speech*, *98*, 176–202.

Hoffman, F. L. (1896, August). Race traits and tendencies of the American Negro. American Economic Association.

Hollandsworth, J. G. (2008). *Portrait of a scientific racist: Alfred Holt Stone of Mississippi*. Louisiana State University Press.

Hopkins, P. (1900, June). Women's department. *The Colored American Magazine*, 118–123.

Hopkins, P. (1901, December). Sojourner Truth: A northern slave emancipated by the state of New York, 1828. *The Colored American Magazine*, 124–132.

Hopkins, P. (1901/1902). *Hagar's daughter*. In *The magazine novels of Pauline Hopkins* (pp. 3–284). Oxford University Press.

Hopkins, P. (1902a, February). Famous women of the Negro race, III: Harriet Tubman ("Moses"). *The Colored American Magazine*, 210–223. In I. Dworkin (Ed.), *Daughter of the revolution: The major nonfiction works of Pauline E. Hopkins* (pp. 132–139). Rutgers University Press, 2007.

Hopkins, P. (1902b, March). Famous women of the Negro race, IV: Some literary workers. *The Colored American Magazine*, 276–280.

Hopkins, P. (1902c, April). Literary workers, concluded. *The Colored American Magazine*, 366–371. In I. Dworkin (Ed.), *Daughter of the revolution: The major nonfiction works of Pauline E. Hopkins* (pp. 147–155). Rutgers University Press, 2007.

Hopkins, P. (1902d, May). Educators. *The Colored American Magazine*, 41–46. In I. Dworkin (Ed.), *Daughter of the revolution: The major nonfiction works of Pauline E. Hopkins* (pp. 156–162). Rutgers University Press, 2007.

Hopkins, P. (1902e, June). Educators, continued. *The Colored American Magazine*, 125–139. In I. Dworkin (Ed.), *Daughter of the revolution: The major nonfiction works of Pauline E. Hopkins* (pp. 163–170). Rutgers University Press, 2007.

Hopkins, P. (1902f, July). Educators, concluded. *The Colored American Magazine*, 206–213. In I. Dworkin (Ed.), *Daughter of the revolution: The major nonfiction works of Pauline E. Hopkins* (pp. 171–177). Rutgers University Press, 2007.

Hopkins, P. (1902g, August). Club life among colored women. *The Colored American Magazine*, 273–277.

Hopkins, P. (1902h, October). Higher education of colored women in white schools and colleges. *The Colored American Magazine*, 445–450.

Hopkins, P. (1903a, January). Heroes and heroines in black I. *The Colored American Magazine*, 206–211.

Hopkins, P. (1903b, October). Echoes from the annual convention of Northeastern Federation of Colored Women's Clubs. *The Colored American Magazine*, 709–713.

Hopkins, P. (1903c, November). As the Lord lives, he is one of our mother's children. *The Colored American Magazine*, 795–801.

Hopkins, P. D. (2011). Seduction or rape: Deconstructing the Black female body in Harriet Jacobs' *Incidents in the life of a slave girl*. *Making Connections: Interdisciplinary Approaches to Cultural Diversity, 13*, 4–20.
hooks, bell. (1981/2015). *Ain't I a woman: Black women and feminism*. Routledge.
hooks, bell. (1984). *Feminist theory from margin to center*. South End Press.
hooks, bell. (1989). *Talking back: Thinking feminist, thinking black*. South End Press.
Hunton, A. W. (1904, July). Negro womanhood defended. *The Voice of the Negro*, 280–282.
Hunton, A. W. (1905, December). The Southern Federation of Colored Women. *The Voice of the Negro*, 850–854.
Hunton, A. W. (1908, July). The National Association of Colored Women, its real significance. *The Colored American Magazine*, 417–424.
Hyde, W. D. W. (1904, May 21). A national platform on the race question. *The Outlook*.
Inskeep, S. (2020, July 15). President Trump issues divisive statement on race at Rose Garden address. National Public Radio. https://www.npr.org/2020/07/15/891290870/president-trump-issues-divisive-statement-on-race-at-rose-garden-address
Jackson, A. B. (1901, June). A retrospect. *The Colored American Magazine*.
Jackson, I. J. (1907). Do Negroes constitute a race of criminals? *The Colored American Magazine*, 352–355.
Jackson, R. L. (2006). *Scripting the black masculine body: Identity, discourse, and racial politics in popular media*. State University of New York Press.
Jacobs, H. (1861/2001). *Incidents in the life of a slave girl*. Dover Publications.
James, J. (1997). *Transcending the talented tenth: Black leaders and American intellectuals*. Routledge.
James, J. (2007). Profeminism and gender elites: W. E. B. Du Bois, Anna Julia Cooper, and Ida B. Wells-Barnett. In S. Gillman & A. E. Weinbaum (Eds.), *Next to the color line: Gender, sexuality, and W. E. B. Du Bois* (pp. 69–95). University of Minnesota Press.
Jensen, R. J., & Hammerback, J. (1998). "Your tools are really the people": The rhetoric of Robert Parris Moses. *Communication Monographs, 65*, 126–140.
Johnson, A., & Johnson, R. M. (1977). Away from accommodation: Radical editors and protest journalism, 1900–1910. *The Journal of Negro History, 62*, 325–338.
Jones, A. H. (1905a, September). A century's progress for the American colored woman. *The Voice of the Negro*, 631–633.
Jones, A. H. (1905b, October). The American colored woman. *The Voice of the Negro*, 692–694.

Jones, D. M. (1997). Darkness made visible: Law, metaphor, and the racial self. In R. Delgado & J. Stefancic (Eds.), *Critical white studies: Looking behind the mirror* (pp. 66–78). Temple University Press.

Jones, J. (1985). *Labor of love, labor of sorrow: Black women, work, and the family from slavery to the present.* Basic Books.

Jones-Rogers, S. E. (2019). *They were her property: White women as slave owners in the American South.* Yale University Press.

Kassanoff, J. A. (1996). "Fate has linked us together": Blood, gender, and the politics of representation in Pauline Hopkins's *Of One Blood*. In J. C. Gruesser (Ed.), *The unruly voice: Rediscovering Pauline Elizabeth Hopkins* (pp. 158–181). University of Illinois Press.

Kellner, D. (1995). *Media culture: Cultural studies, identity and politics between the modern and the postmodern.* Routledge.

Kelly, C. R. (2020). Donald J. Trump and the rhetoric of white ambivalence. *Rhetoric & Public Affairs, 23*, 195–224.

Key disputes in the Zimmerman trial. (n.d.). *The New York Times* archive. https://archive.nytimes.com/www.nytimes.com/interactive/2013/07/05/us/zimmerman-trial.html

King, C. (2019). *Gods of the upper air: How a circle of renegade anthropologists reinvented race, sex, and gender in the twentieth century.* Doubleday.

Kleniewski, N. (1984). From industrial to corporate city: The role of urban renewal. In W. K. Tabb & L. Sawers (Eds.), *Marxism and the metropolis: New perspectives in urban political economy* (pp. 205–222). Oxford University Press.

Knadler, S. P. (2002). *The fugitive race: Minority writers resisting whiteness.* University Press of Mississippi.

Knight, A. (2007). Furnace blasts for the Tuskegee wizard: Revisiting Pauline Elizabeth Hopkins, Booker T. Washington, and the *Colored American Magazine*. *American Periodicals, 17*, 41–64.

Lalami, L. (2019, December). "Bothsidesism" is poisoning America. *The Nation.* https://www.thenation.com/article/archive/trump-impeachment-journalism/

Langer, G. (2020, July 21). 63% support Black Lives Matter as recognition of discrimination jumps. ABC News. https://abcnews.go.com/Politics/63-support-black-lives-matter-recognition-discrimination-jumps/story?id=71779835

Levell, W. H. (1901, November). On lynching in the South. *The Outlook*, 731.

Lewis, F. G. (1906, December). The demand for race integrity. *The Voice of the Negro*, 564–574.

Lewis, S. C., Holton, A. E., & Coddington, M. (2014). Reciprocal journalism: A concept of mutual exchange between journalists and audiences. *Journalism Practice, 8*, 229–241.

Lindsey, T. B. (2017). *Colored no more: Reinventing black womanhood in Washington, D.C.* University of Illinois Press.

Lipsitz, G. (1998). *The possessive investment in whiteness: How white people profit from identity politics*. Temple University Press.

Livesey, A. H. (2018). Race, slavery, and the expression of sexual violence in *Louisa Picquet, the Octoroon*. *American Nineteenth Century History, 19*, 267–288.

Locke, A. (2017). *Bluebird, bluebird*. Mulholland Books.

Logan, R. (1965). *Betrayal of the Negro, from Rutherford B. Hayes to Woodrow Wilson*. Collier Books.

Lozano, N. M. (2019). *Not one more! Feminicidio on the border*. Ohio State University Press.

Lozano-Reich, N., & Cloud, D. (2009). The uncivil tongue: Invitational rhetoric and the problem of inequality. *Western Journal of Communication, 73*, 220–226.

Luckerson, V. (2020, October 3). What a Florida reparations case can teach us about justice in America. *Time*.

Lukács, G. (1968). *History and class consciousness: Studies in Marxist dialectics*. MIT Press.

Lynch, T. P. (2001). *Strike songs of the Depression*. University Press of Mississippi.

Lynch law and riot in Ohio. (1904, March). *The Independent*, 580.

Lynching. (1909, November). *The Outlook*, 637–638.

The lynching of Negroes. (1903a, July). *The Independent*, 1596.

The lynching of Negroes. (1903b, August). *The Independent*, 1834–1835.

The lynching of Negroes. (1906, December). *The Independent*, 1370.

Madhani, A. (2021, January 10). Trump legacy on race overshadowed by divisive rhetoric, actions. AP News. https://apnews.com/article/election-2020-donald-trump-race-and-ethnicity-chicago-coronavirus-pandemic-5d12485d162d56185799b3ff88b1df7a

Malik, K. (1996). *The meaning of race: Race, history and culture in Western society*. New York University Press.

Margo, R. A. (1990). *Race and schooling in the South, 1880–1950: An economic history*. University of Chicago Press.

Massey, D. S., & Denton, N. A. (1993). *American apartheid: Segregation and the making of the underclass*. Harvard University Press.

Matter-Seibel, S. (2003). Pauline Hopkins's portrayal of the African-American new woman in *Contending Forces* and the *Colored American Magazine*. In A. Heilmann (Ed.), *Feminist forerunners: New womanism and feminism in the early twentieth century* (pp. 76–86). Pandora.

Maxson, J. D. (2020). "Second line to bury white supremacy": Take 'em down Nola, monument removal, and residual memory. *Quarterly Journal of Speech, 106*, 48–71.

McAdoo, M. (1906, November). Opportunity for colored women in the business world. *The Colored American Magazine*, 303–305.

McCarthy, T. (2002). Vergangenheitsbewaltigung in the USA: On the politics of the memory of slavery. *Political Theory, 30*, 623–648.

McCarthy, T. (2004). Coming to terms with our past, part II: On the morality and the politics of reparations for slavery. *Political Theory, 32*, 750–772.

McClendon, J. H., III. (2004). On the nature of whiteness and the ontology of race: Toward a dialectical materialist analysis. In G. Yancy (Ed.), *What white looks like: African-American philosophers on the whiteness question* (pp. 211–225). Routledge.

McCurley, W. S. (1899, April). The impossibility of racial amalgamation. *The Arena*, 456–455.

McDonald, C., & Kurth, J. (2015, July 8). Foreclosures fuel Detroit blight, cost city $500 million. *Detroit News*. https://www.detroitnews.com/story/news/special-reports/2015/06/03/detroit-foreclosures-risky-mortgages-cost-taxpayers/27236605/

McEnery, S. D. (1903, February). The race problem in the South. *The Independent*, 424–430.

McKelway, A. J. (1906, November). The Atlanta riots: A southern white point of view. *The Outlook*, 557–562.

McNamarah, C. T. (2019). White caller crime: Racialized police communication and existing while black. *Michigan Journal of Race and Law, 24*, 335–415.

Mebane, G. A. (1900, November). The Negro vindicated. *The Arena*.

The medicine for the mob. (1907, February). *The Outlook*, 249.

Medina, J. (2011). The relevance of credibility excess in a proportional view of epistemic injustice: Differential epistemic authority and the social imaginary. *Social Epistemology, 25*, 15–35.

Meet the new black press. (2020, July 14). Nieman Reports. https://niemanreports.org/articles/meet-the-new-black-press/

Meier, A. (1953). Booker T. Washington and the Negro press: With special reference to the *Colored American Magazine*. *The Journal of Negro History, 38*, 67–90.

Merriam-Webster Incorporated. (2020). Secure. https://www.merriam-webster.com/dictionary/secure

Merritt, E. F. G. (1905, July). American prejudice: Its cause, effect and possibilities. *The Voice of the Negro*, 466–469.

Meyers, C. (2020). Partisan news, the myth of objectivity, and the standards of responsible journalism. *Journal of Media Ethics, 35*, 180–194.

Miller, K. (1904, January). The Negro as a political factor. *The Voice of the Negro*, 17–22.

Miller, K. (1905, August). A reply to Tom Watson: Is the Negro inherently inferior? *The Voice of the Negro*, 537–543.

Mills, C. W. (1997). *The racial contract*. Cornell University Press.

Mills, C. W. (1998). *Blackness visible: Essays on philosophy and race*. Cornell University Press.

Mills, C. W. (2007). White ignorance. In S. Sullivan & N. Tuana (Eds.), *Race and epistemologies of ignorance* (pp. 11–38). State University of New York Press.

Min, S. J. (2020). What the twenty first century engaged journalism can learn from the twentieth century public journalism. *Journalism Practice, 14*, 626–641.

Mob law. (1910, August). *The Outlook*, 808–809.

Mob violence, north and south. (1903, July). *The Independent*, 1769–1770.

Moensch, M. (2018, April 26). Newspaper apologizes for "shameful" coverage of lynchings. *The Washington Post*. https://www.washingtonpost.com/national/newspaper-apologizes-for-shameful-coverage-of-lynchings/2018/04/26/cc6bd7a8-499b-11e8-8082-105a446d19b8_story.html

Monthly review. (1906, November). *The Voice of the Negro*, 464–467.

Mossell, Mrs. N. F. (1901, August). The National Afro-American Council. *The Colored American Magazine*, 291–305.

Mott, F. L. (1938). *A history of American magazines: 1741–1930* (Vol. 3). Harvard University Press.

Mott, F. L. (1957). *A history of American magazines: 1741–1930* (Vol. 4). Harvard University Press.

Mott, F. L. (1958). *A history of American magazines, 1741–1930* (Vol. 2). https://hdl-handle-net.ezproxy.uakron.edu:2443/2027/heb.00678

Mrs. M. E. Murphy, president of the Colored Y. W. C. A., Baltimore, Md. (1908, September). *The Colored American Magazine*, 470–471.

Mrs. William Scott: The noted evangelist, the story of her life and work. (1902, July). *The Colored American Magazine*, 228–232.

Muhammad, K. G. (2010). *The condemnation of blackness: Race, crime, and the making of modern urban America*. Harvard University Press.

Munger, F. W., & Seron, C. (2017). Race, law, and inequality, 50 years after the civil rights era. *Annual Review of Law and Social Science, 13*, 331–350.

Mutnick, A. (2020, August 11). New GOP headache as candidate condemned for racist videos wins Republican primary. *Politico*. https://www.politico.com/news/2020/08/11/house-candidate-condemned-for-racist-videos-wins-republican-primary-394008?cid=apn

Myrdal, G. (1944). *An American dilemma: The Negro problem and modern democracy*. Harper and Brothers.

Nah, S., & Yamamoto, M. (2019). Communication and citizenship revisited: Theorizing communication and citizen journalism practice as civic participation. *Communication Theory, 29*, 24–45.

Nakayama, T. K., & Krizek, R. L. (1995). Whiteness: A strategic rhetoric. *Quarterly Journal of Speech, 81*, 291–309.

The National Association of Colored Women. (1904, July). *The Voice of the Negro*, 310–311.

The National Association of Colored Women. (1906, September). *The Colored American Magazine*, 193–197.
The National Association of Colored Women's Clubs. (1908, September). *The Colored American Magazine*, 497–504.
Nearing a solution. (1908, December). *The Outlook*, 859–860.
The Negro: A portrait. (1910, September). *The Outlook*, 77–80.
The Negro and justice. (1907, October). *The Independent*.
The Negro problem. (1903, April). *The Independent*, 937–939.
The Negro problem: How it appeals to a southern colored woman. (1902, September). *The Independent*, 2221–2224.
The Negro problem: How it appeals to a southern white woman. (1902, September). *The Independent*, 2224–2228.
The Negro question. (1903a, February). *The Independent*, 410.
The Negro question. (1903b, October). *The Independent*, 2308–2309.
Negroes burned at the stake. (1904, August). *The Independent*, 413.
Negroes lynched and burned. (1903, July). *The Independent*, 1536–1537.
Negroes lynched in Missouri. (1906, April). *The Independent*, 892.
Neubeck, K. J., & Cazenave, N. A. (2001). *Welfare racism: Playing the race card against America's poor*. Routledge.
The New York riot. (1900, August). *The Independent*.
Nixon, R. N. (1971). State of the Union message. *Vital Speeches of the Day*, 37, 226–230.
Observations of the southern race feeling. (1904, March). *The Independent*.
Ohmann, R. (1996). *Selling culture: Magazines, markets, and class at the turn of the century*. Verso.
Okker, P. (2003). *Social stories: The magazine novel in nineteenth-century America*. University of Virginia Press.
Omi, M., & Winant, H. (1994). *Racial formation in the United States from the 1960s to the 1990s* (2nd ed). Routledge.
O'Neill, C. (2017). *Weapons of math destruction: How big data increases inequality and threatens democracy*. Broadway Books.
Ornsby, G. F. (1903, October). The Negro war on white women and how to prevent lynching. *The American Lawyer*.
Otten, T. J. (1992). Pauline Hopkins and the hidden self of race. *ELH*, 59, 227–256.
"Our squad is big": Reps. Ocasio-Cortez, Omar, Tlaib and Pressley condemn Trump's racist attack. (2019, July 16). Democracy Now. https://www.democracynow.org/2019/7/16/trump_racist_attacks_congresswomen_of_color?utm_source=Democracy+Now%21&utm_campaign=c7bf0318b5-Daily_Digest_COPY_01&utm_medium=email&utm_term=0_fa2346a853-c7bf0318b5-190184841
Page, T. N. (1904a). *The Negro: The southerner's problem*. Charles Scribner's Sons.
Page, T. N. (1904b, March). The Negro: The southerner's problem. First paper: Slavery and the old relation between the southern whites and blacks. *McClure's*, 548–554.

Page, T. N. (1904c, May). The Negro: The southerner's problem. Third paper: Its present condition and aspect, as shown by statistics. *McClure's*, 96–102.

Page, T. N. (1907, May). The great American question: The special plea of a southerner. *McClure's*, 565–572.

Parris, L. T. (2015). *Being apart: Theoretical and existential resistance in Africana literature*. University of Virginia Press.

Patterson, C. L. (2020). Charlotte Perkins Gilman: A living in periodicals. *American Periodicals: A Journal of History & Criticism, 30*, 126–148.

Pendergast, T. (2000). *Creating the modern man: American magazines and consumer culture, 1900–1950*. University of Missouri Press.

Peterson, C. L. (1995). *"Doers of the word": African-American women speakers and writers in the north (1830–1880)*. Oxford University Press.

Peterson, T. (1964). *Magazines in the twentieth century*. University of Illinois Press.

Phillips, J. D., & Griffin, R. A. (2015). Chrystal Mangum as hypervisible object and invisible subject: Black feminist thought, sexual violence and the pedagogical repercussions of the Duke lacrosse rape case. *Women's Studies in Communication, 38*, 36–56.

Phillips, K. R. (2004). Introduction. In K. R. Phillips (Ed.), *Framing public memory* (pp. 1–14). University of Alabama Press.

Plessy v. Ferguson. (1896). Cornell Law School. https://www.law.cornell.edu/supremecourt/text/163/537

Pochmara, A. (2011). *The making of the new negro: Black authorship, masculinity and sexuality in the Harlem Renaissance*. Amsterdam University Press.

Poe, W. B. (1903, October). Negro life in two generations: The observations of a southern farmer. *The Outlook*, 493–498.

Pohlhaus, G, Jr. (2012). Relational knowing and epistemic injustice: Toward a theory of *willful hermeneutical ignorance*. *Hypatia, 27*, 715–735.

Powell, J. A. (2009). Reinterpreting metropolitan space as a strategy for social justice. In M. P. Pavel (Ed.), *Breakthrough communities: Sustainability and justice in the next American metropolis* (pp. 23–32). MIT Press.

The President's Advisory 1776 Commission. (2021). *The 1776 Report*. https://trumpwhitehouse.archives.gov/wp-content/uploads/2021/01/The-Presidents-Advisory-1776-Commission-Final-Report.pdf

Quadagno, J. (1994). *The color of welfare: How racism undermined the war on poverty*. Oxford University Press.

Quarles, B. (1979). Black history's antebellum origins. *American Antiquarian Society, 1*, 89–122.

Queen, H. E. (1906, September). Mrs. Mary Church Terrell at Cornell University. *The Voice of the Negro*, 637–640.

Race conflict in Louisiana. (1901, November). *The Independent*, 2615–2616.

Race prejudice. (1907, October). *The Outlook*, 452.

The race problem. (1903, March). *The Outlook*, 607–610.
The race problem: An autobiography. (1904, March). *The Independent*, 586–589.
Racial self-restraint. (1906, October). *The Outlook*, 308–310.
Rankine, C. (2014). *Citizen: An American lyric*. Graywolf Press.
Reeves, M. (2008). *Somebody scream! Rap music's rise to prominence in the aftershock of black power*. Faber and Faber.
The Rev. Quincy Ewing on lynching. (1901, August). *The Independent*, 2059.
Reyes, G. M. (2010). *Public memory, race, and ethnicity*. Cambridge Scholars.
Richardson, A. V. (2020). *Bearing witness while black: African Americans, smart phones, and the new protest #journalism*. Oxford University Press.
Richardson, M. (Ed.). (1987). *Maria W. Stewart: America's first black woman political writer—Essays and speeches*. Indiana University Press.
The riot at Springfield. (1908, August). *The Outlook*, 869–870.
Ritchie, A. J. (2017). *Invisible no more: Police violence against black women and women of color*. Beacon Press.
Ritchie, A. J. (2020, July 15). How to stop erasing black women from the conversation around police brutality. Interview with Ailsa Chang. National Public Radio. https://www.npr.org/2020/07/15/891433292/how-to-stop-erasing-black-women-from-the-conversation-around-police-brutality
Roessner, L. A. (2011). Coloring America's pastime: *Sporting Life*'s coverage of race & the emergence of baseball's color line, 1883–1889. *American Journalism, 28*, 85–114.
Roosevelt, T. (1905). Address at the Lincoln dinner. The American Presidency Project.
Roosevelt, T. (1910, January). The Negro in America. *The Outlook*, 241.
Ross, T. (1997a). The rhetorical tapestry of race. In R. Delgado and J. Stefancic (Eds.), *Critical white studies: Looking behind the mirror* (pp. 89–97). Temple University Press.
Ross, T. (1997b). White innocence, black abstraction. In R. Delgado and J. Stefancic (Eds.), *Critical white studies: Looking behind the mirror* (pp. 263–266). Temple University Press.
Rothstein, R. (2017). *The color of law: A forgotten history of how our government segregated America*. W. W. Norton & Company.
Routledge, Mrs. M. H. (1902, June). A hint to our women. *The Colored American Magazine*, 141–142.
Royster, J. (2000). *Traces of a stream: Literacy and social change among African American women*. University of Pittsburgh Press.
Russell, A. (2007). Digital communication networks and the journalistic field: The 2005 French riots. *Critical Studies in Media Communication, 24*, 285–302.
The safest of all crimes. (1903, January 29). *The Independent*, 277.

Santiago, L., & Shoichet, C. E. (2018, December 11). Trump says caravan migrants are turning back, Mexico says most are still at the border. CNN. https://www.cnn.com/2018/12/11/americas/mexico-caravan-trump/index.html

Savage, K. (1994). The politics of memory: Black emancipation and the Civil War monument. In J. R. Gillis (Ed.), *Commemorations: The politics of national identity* (pp. 127–149). Princeton University Press.

Schram, S. F. (2005). Putting a black face on welfare: The good and the bad. In A. L. Schneider & H. M. Ingram (Eds.), *Deserving and entitled: Social constructions and public policy* (pp. 261–286). State University of New York Press.

Schudson, M. (1978). *Discovering the news: A social history of American newspapers*. Basic Books.

Schudson, M. (2003). *The sociology of news*. Norton.

Schwartz, J. (1993). *The New York approach: Robert Moses, urban liberals, and redevelopment of the inner city*. Ohio State University Press.

Schwartz, S. (2021, April). 8 states debate bills to restrict how teachers discuss racism and sexism. *Education Week*. https://www.edweek.org/policy-politics/8-states-debate-bills-to-restrict-how-teachers-discuss-racism-sexism/2021/04

Seeing white. (2017). Scene on Radio [Podcast]. https://www.sceneonradio.org/seeing-white/

1776 Project PAC. (n.d.-a). About. Retrieved February 23, 2024. https://1776projectpac.com/about/

1776 Project PAC. (n.d.-b). Our endorsed candidates. Retrieved February 23, 2024. https://1776projectpac.com/endorsed-candidates/

1776 Project PAC. (n.d.-c). Promoting patriotism and pride in American history. Retrieved February 23, 2024. https://1776projectpac.com/

Shadrach, J. S. (1902a, September). Charles Winder Wood; Or, from bootblack to professor. *The Colored American Magazine*, 345–348.

Shadrach, J. S. (1902b, October). Rev. John Henry Dorsey. *The Colored American Magazine*, 411–417.

Shadrach, J. S. (1903a, February). The growth of the social evil among all classes and races in America. *The Colored America Magazine*, 259–263. In I. Dworkin (Ed.), *Daughter of the revolution: The major nonfiction works of Pauline E. Hopkins* (pp. 201–207). Rutgers University Press, 2007.

Shadrach, J. S. (1903b, March). Black or white: which should be the young Afro American's choice in marrying. *The Colored American Magazine*, 348–352. In I. Dworkin (Ed.), *Daughter of the revolution: The major nonfiction works of Pauline E. Hopkins* (pp. 208–214). Rutgers University Press, 2007.

Shaffer, C. (2014, November 24). Tamir Rice's neighborhood has history of gangs, violence. Cleveland.com. https://www.cleveland.com/metro/2014/11/cleveland_neighborhood_where_t.html

Shapiro, H. (1970). The muckrakers and Negroes. *Phylon, 31*, 76–88.

Shapiro, H. (1988). *White violence and black response: From Reconstruction to Montgomery*. University of Massachusetts Press.

Sheldon, W. D. (1906, September). Shall lynching be suppressed, and how? *The Arena*, 225–233.

Sherrard-Johnson, C. M. (2007). *Portraits of the new Negro woman: Visual and literary culture in the Harlem Renaissance*. Rutgers University Press.

Shockley, A. A. (1972). Pauline Elizabeth Hopkins: A biographical excursion into obscurity. *Phylon, 33*, 22–26.

Simons, H. (1972). Persuasion in social conflicts: A critique of prevailing conceptions and a framework for future research. *Speech Monographs, 39*, 227–247.

Simpson, M. C. (1903, October). Response to the address of welcome to the Northeastern Federation. *The Colored American Magazine*, 707–708.

Sinha, M. (2019, December 1). Donald Trump, meet your precursor. *The New York Times*, Sunday Review, 2.

Slide, A. (2004). *American racist: The life and films of Thomas Dixon*. University Press of Kentucky.

Smith, A. M. (1901a, February). Chicago notes. *The Colored American Magazine*, 285–291.

Smith, A. M. (1901b, April). Chicago notes. *The Colored American Magazine*, 465–469.

Smith, A. M. (1902a, March). Woman's development in business. *The Colored American Magazine*, 323–326.

Smith, A. M. (1902b, May). A few essential business qualities. *The Colored American Magazine*, 26–28.

Smith, A. M. (1903, July). Noted business women of Chicago: Mrs. Hattie M. Hicks. *The Colored American Magazine*, 507–509.

Smith, B. (1983). Introduction. In B. Smith (Ed.), *Home girls: A Black feminist anthology* (pp. xix–lvi). Kitchen Table, Women of Color Press.

Smith, J. D. (1993). General introduction. In J. D. Smith (Ed.), *Anti-black thought 1863–1925: Racial determinism and the fear of miscegenation* (Vol. 8, pp. xi–xvii). Garland Publishing.

Smith, M. M. (2006). *How race is made: Slavery, segregation, and the sense*. University of North Carolina Press.

Smith, W. B. (1905). The color line: A brief in behalf of the unborn. In J. D. Smith (Ed.), *Anti-black thought 1863–1925: Racial determinism and the fear of miscegenation* (Vol. 8, pp. 45–316). Garland Publishing.

Smith-Rosenberg, C. (1985). *Disorderly conduct: Visions of gender in Victorian America*. Oxford University Press.

Solinger, R. (2000). *Wake up little Susie: Single pregnancy and race before Roe v. Wade*. Routledge.

Southern points of view. (1906, May). *The Outlook*, 87–90.

Spelman, E. V. (2007). Managing ignorance. In S. Sullivan & N. Tuana (Eds.), *Race and epistemologies of ignorance* (pp. 119–131). State University of New York Press.

Spetalnick, M., Shalal, A., Mason, J., & Holland, S. (2021, January 20). Analysis: Trump's legacy—A more divided America, a more unsettled world. Reuters. https://www.reuters.com/article/usa-trump-legacy-analysis-int/analysis-trumps-legacy-a-more-divided-america-a-more-unsettled-world-idUSKBN29P0EX

Stover, J. (2003). *Rhetoric and resistance in black women's autobiography.* University Press of Florida.

A study of the race question. (1906, September). *The Outlook*, 87–89.

Sturken, M. (1997). *Tangled memories: The Vietnam War, the AIDS epidemic, and the politics of remembering.* University of California Press.

Sugrue, T. J. (1996). *The origins of the urban crisis: Race and inequality in postwar Detroit.* Princeton University Press.

Summers, J. (2021, November 12). A bill to study reparations for slavery had momentum in Congress but still no vote. National Public Radio. https://www.npr.org/2021/11/12/1054889820/a-bill-to-study-reparations-for-slavery-had-momentum-in-congress-but-still-no-vo

Sumner, D. E. (2010). *The magazine century: American magazines since 1900.* Peter Lang.

Sweeney, B. (2019). Throwing stones across the Potomac: The *Colored American Magazine*, the *Atlantic Monthly*, and the cultural politics of national reunion. *American Periodicals, 29,* 135–162.

Tate, C. (1992). *Domestic allegories of political desire: The black heroine's text at the turn of the century.* Oxford University Press.

Tayleur, E. (1904, January). The Negro woman: Social and moral decadence. *The Outlook*, 266–271.

Taylor, E. B. (1904). A view of the Negro from a northerner resident in the South. *The Outlook*, 670.

Taylor, K.-Y. (Ed.). (2017). *How we get free: Black feminism and the Combahee River Collective.* Haymarket Books.

Tebbel, J., & Zuckerman, M. E. (1991). *The magazine in America, 1741–1990.* Oxford University Press.

Terkel, S. (1992). *Race: How blacks and whites think and feel about the American obsession.* The New Press.

Terrell, M. C. (1901, March). Negro women. *The Independent*, 633.

Terrell, M. C. (1904a, June). Lynching from a Negro's point of view. *North American Review, 178,* 853–868.

Terrell, M. C. (1904b, July). The progress of colored women. *The Voice of the Negro*, 291–294.

Terrell, M. C. (1904c, October). The International Congress of Women. *The Voice of the Negro*, 454–461.

Terrell, M. C. (1905, March). Service which should be rendered the South. *The Voice of the Negro*, 182–186.

Terrell, M. C. (1906, September). Race prejudice and southern progress. *The Colored American Magazine*.

Thomas, D. (2015, September 9). Why everyone's saying "black girls are magic." *Los Angeles Times*. https://www.latimes.com/nation/nationnow/la-na-nn-everyones-saying-black-girls-are-magic-20150909-htmlstory.html

Thompson, G. (2018). The seriality dividend of American magazines. *American Periodicals, 28*, 2–20.

Tillman, B. R. (1900). Their own hotheadedness. History Matters. http://historymatters.gmu.edu/d/55/

Tillman, B. R. (1903). The race problem. Speech given to Senate of the United States. Digitally archived. https://www.loc.gov/item/91898597/

Tillman, S., Bryant-Davis, T., Smith, K., & Marks, A. (2010). Shattering silence: Exploring barriers to disclosure for African American sexual assault survivors. *Trauma, Violence, & Abuse, 11*, 59–70.

Tinson, C. (2017). *Radical intellect: Liberator magazine and black activism in the 1960s*. University of North Carolina Press.

Todd, R. D. (1902a, March). The octoroon's revenge. *The Colored American Magazine*, 291–295.

Todd, R. D. (1902b, October). Florence Grey, Part 3. *The Colored American Magazine*, 469–477.

Tolnay S., & Beck, E. M. (1995). *A festival of violence: An analysis of southern lynchings, 1882–1930*. University of Illinois Press.

Torture and lynching. (1902, June). *The Outlook*, 533–534.

Triece, M. E. (2001). *Protest and popular culture: Women in the U.S. labor movement, 1894–1917*. Westview Press.

Triece, M. E. (2007). *On the picket line: Strategies of working-class women during the Depression*. University of Illinois Press.

Triece, M. E. (2013). *"Tell it like it is": Women in the national welfare rights movement*. University of South Carolina Press.

Triece, M. E. (2016). *Urban renewal and resistance: Race, space, and the city in the late twentieth to the early twenty-first century*. Lexington Books.

Triece, M. E. (2017). Whitewashing city spaces: Personalization and strategic forgetting in news accounts of urban crisis and renewal. *Journal of Communication Inquiry, 41*, 250–267.

Triece, Mary E. (forthcoming, 2025). *Radical advocate: Ida B. Wells and the road to race and gender justice*. University of Alabama Press.

Trump, D. (2017, August 15). Trump's comments on white supremacists, "alt-left" in Charlottesville. *Politico.* https://www.politico.com/story/2017/08/15/full-text-trump-comments-white-supremacists-alt-left-transcript-241662

Trump, D. (2018, November 9). Presidential proclamation addressing mass migration through the southern border of the United States. National Archives. https://trumpwhitehouse.archives.gov/presidential-actions/presidential-proclamation-addressing-mass-migration-southern-border-united-states/

Trump, D. (2019, January 8). President Donald J. Trump's address to the nation on the crisis at the border. National Archives. https://trumpwhitehouse.archives.gov/briefings-statements/president-donald-j-trumps-address-nation-crisis-border/

Tuchman, G. (1972). Objectivity as strategic ritual: An examination of newsmen's notions of objectivity. *American Journal of Sociology, 77,* 660–679.

Twohey, M. (2016, July 10). Rudolph Giuliani lashes out at Black Lives Matter. *The New York Times.* https://www.nytimes.com/2016/07/11/us/politics/rudy-giuliani-black-lives-matter.html

Ugwu, R. (2018, July 29). Is America ready for Terrance Nance? *The New York Times,* 12.

Ugwu, R. (2020, September 9). The hashtag that changed the Oscars: An oral history. *The New York Times.* https://www.nytimes.com/2020/02/06/movies/oscarssowhite-history.html

Van Tassell, E. F. (1997). "Only the law would rule between us": Antimiscegenation, the moral economy of dependency, and the debate over rights after the Civil War. In R. Delgado & J. Stefancic (Eds.), *Critical white studies: Looking behind the mirror* (pp. 152–156). Temple University Press.

Vardaman, J. K. (1904, February 4). A governor bitterly opposes Negro education. Teaching American History. https://teachingamericanhistory.org/library/document/a-governor-bitterly-opposes-negro-education/

Vera, A. (2020, May 26). White woman who called police on a black man birdwatching in Central Park has been fired. CNN. https://www.cnn.com/2020/05/26/us/central-park-video-dog-video-african-american-trnd/index.html

Victor, D. (2016). What have nonwhites done for civilization? *The New York Times.* https://www.nytimes.com/2016/07/19/us/politics/steve-king-nonwhite-subgroups.html?action=click&module=RelatedCoverage&pgtype=Article&region=Footer

Wallace, L. R. (2019). *The view from somewhere.* University of Chicago Press.

Walling, W. E. (1908, September). The race war in the North. *The Independent.*

Walters, A. (1901, March). Negro progress. *The Independent,* 651–652.

Washington, M. (2007). "From motives of delicacy": Sexuality and morality in the narratives of Sojourner Truth and Harriet Jacobs. *The Journal of African American History, 92,* 57–73.

Washington, M. M. (1905, April). The advancement of colored women. *The Colored American Magazine*, 183–189.

Washington, Mrs. B. T. (1904, July). Social improvement of the plantation woman. *The Voice of the Negro*, 288–290.

Watson, M. (1999). *Lives of their own: Rhetorical dimensions in autobiographies of women activists*. University of South Carolina Press.

Waxman, O. B. (2021, July 16). "Critical race theory is simply the latest bogeyman": Inside the fight over what kids learn about America's history. *Time*. https://time.com/magazine/us/6075407/july-5th-2021-vol-198-no-1-u-s/

The way out. (1903, December). *The Outlook*, 984.

Webster, Y. O. (1992). *The racialization of America*. St. Martin's Press.

Weisenfeld, J. (1997). *African American and Christian activism: New York's black YWCA, 1905–1945*. Harvard University Press.

Wells, I. B. (1892). *Southern horrors: Lynch law in all its phases*. The Project Gutenberg EBook. https://www.gutenberg.org/files/14975/14975-h/14975-h.htm#PREFACE

Wells, I. B. (1893). "The Requirements of Southern Journalism." *A.M.E. Zion Church Quarterly*. In M. Bay (Ed.), *The light of truth: Writings of an anti-lynching crusader* (pp. 88–95). Penguin Books, 2014.

Wells, I. B. (1895). *The red record: Tabulated statistics and alleged causes of lynching in the United States*. The Project Gutenberg EBook. https://www.gutenberg.org/files/14977/14977-h/14977-h.htm

Wells, I. B. (1900a, January). Lynch law in America. *The Arena*, 15–24.

Wells, I. B. (1900b, April). The Negro's case in equity. *The Independent*.

West, E. (2018). Reflections on the history and historians of the black woman's role in the community of slaves: Enslaved women and intimate partner sexual violence. *American Nineteenth Century History*, *19*, 1–21.

What we believe. (n.d.). Black Lives Matter. Page removed as of September 2020.

Whedbee, K. (2001). Perspective by incongruity in Norman Thomas's "Some wrong roads to peace." *Western Journal of Communication*, *65*, 45–64.

Which states passed laws restricting school curriculum? (2023, March 30). USA FACTS. https://usafacts.org/articles/which-states-passed-laws-restricting-school-curriculum/

White justice and Black. (1900, April). *The Independent*, 961.

White, M. (1992). Ideological analysis and television. In R. Allen (Ed.), *Channels of discourse, reassembled* (pp. 161–202). University of North Carolina Press.

"Why don't y'all let that die?": Telling the Emmett Till story in Mississippi. (2019, August 28). Debbie Elliott, reporter [Transcript]. National Public Radio. https://www.npr.org/templates/transcript/transcript.php?storyId=755024458

Wiegman, R. (1993). The anatomy of lynching. *Journal of the History of Sexuality*, *3*, 445–467.

Williams, A. N. (2017). Recovering Black women writers in periodicals archives. *American Periodicals, 27,* 25–28.

Williams, F. B. (1902, December). After many days: A Christmas story. *The Colored American Magazine,* 140–153.

Williams, F. B. (1904, July). A northern Negro's autobiography. *The Independent.*

Williams, F. B. (1905, June). The colored girl. *The Voice of the Negro,* 400–403.

Williams, F. B. (1906, March). Refining influence of art. *The Voice of the Negro,* 211–214.

Williams, F. B. (1908, May). Work attempted and missed in organized club work. *The Colored American Magazine,* 281–285.

Williams, S. (2015). Digital defense: Black feminists resist violence with hashtag activism. *Feminist Media Studies, 15,* 341–344.

Williams, S. F. (1904, July). The social status of the Negro woman. *The Voice of the Negro,* 298–300.

Winter, L. P. (1906, December). The Negro question again, II. *The Outlook,* 845.

Wolseley, R. E. (1971). *The black press, U.S.A.* Iowa State University Press.

Wood, A. L. (2009). *Lynching and spectacle: Witnessing racial violence in America, 1890–1940.* University of North Carolina Press.

Wood, J. (2005). Feminist standpoint and muted group theory: Commonalities and divergences. *Women and Language, 28,* 61–64.

Wood, J. P. (1971). *Magazines in the United States* (3rd ed.). Ronald Press.

Yates, J. S. (1904, July). The National Association of Colored Women. *The Voice of the Negro,* 283–287.

Yates, J. S. (1905, June). Kindergartens and mothers' clubs. *The Voice of the Negro,* 304–311.

Yates, J. S. (1907, February). Woman as a factor in the solution of race problems. *The Colored American Magazine,* 43–52.

Yellesetty, L. (2013). The racist face of the housing crisis. *The Socialist Worker.* https://socialistworker.org/2013/03/12/racist-face-of-the-housing-crisis

Young, R., & McMahon, S. (2020, June 16). #SayHerName puts spotlight on black women killed by police. Here and Now. WBUR. https://www.wbur.org/hereandnow/2020/06/16/black-women-deaths-protests

Zackodnik, T. (2015). Memory, illustration, and Black periodicals: Recasting the disappearing act of the fugitive slave in the "new negro" woman. *American Periodicals, 25,* 139–159.

Zelizer, B. (1992). *Covering the body: The Kennedy assassination, the media, and the shaping of collective memory.* University of Chicago Press.

ZORA. (n.d.) Website. https://zora.medium.com/

Zucchino, D. (2020). *Wilmington's lie: The murderous coup of 1898 and the rise of white supremacy.* Atlantic Monthly Press.

INDEX

Abbott, Ernest Hamlin, 79–80
advertisements, 28
African American New Woman, 30, 107–9
African American Policy Forum, 167
Afro-American Women's League, 99
Alabama State Colored Women's Federated Clubs, 99
Alexander, Hooper, 52
alternative journalism, 2
amalgamation, 67, 80–81, 83
Anthony, Susan B., 94
Archer, William, 82
Arena, The, 10, 22, 35, 45, 148–49; and Black writers, 11; circulation, 23; and cult of white purity, 67–87; and fictive white civilization, 54–60; and forum, 78–79; and race question, 9, 64–65; and scientific racism, 153; strategies used in, 41; and symposium, 81
Atlanta Massacre, 50, 67, 72

Baker, Ray Stannard, 36–37, 49–50, 152
Baldwin, James, 3, 38, 163
Barber, Jesse Max, 26, 73
Birth of a Nation, The, 72
Black abstraction, 10, 41, 60–64

Black Codes, 43, 164
Black critical memory, 11, 83, 158. *See also* countermemory
Black feminism, 8, 10
#BlackGirlMagic, 168
#BlackInThe Ivory, 169
Black Lives Matter, 38, 167, 169–70; and Strike for Black Lives, 172
Bland, Sandra, 167
Boas, Franz, 124–25, 131
bothsidesism, 52. *See also* leveling
Bowen, Cornelia, 99
Boyd, Rekia, 167
Brinton, Daniel Garrison, and scientific racism, 70
Brown, Gertrude Dorsey, 31, 33, 122, 145, 173; and fiction writing of, 137–39; and mulatta iconography, 132; and trope of passing, 126
Burgess-Ware, Louise, 31, 34, 87, 145, 173; and fiction writing of, 133–35, 143; and mulatta iconography, 132; and trope of passing, 126
Burroughs, Nannie Helen, 121, 130
Bush, Olivia Ward, 100

Center for Intersectionality and Social Policy, 167

Central Park Five, 17
Chinn, Shellonnee, 166
citizen journalism, 166
Citizens Protective League, 64
Clansmen, The, 72
Cleveland, Grover, 179n12
Clifford, Carrie, 26, 31, 105, 145, 173; and debate with A. J. McKelway, 51–52; and debate with Thomas Nelson Page, 73; and jeremiad, 128–29; and trope of passing, 132
club work, 97, 99–104
Coates, Ta-Nehisi, 163–64
Colored American Magazine, The, 6, 64, 149, 166; and Black women's contributions to, 11, 27, 31, 93; circulation, 32; and countertestimony, 104–17; editors of, 33, 88–89; and haunting, 117–23; journalistic practices of, 24; and literary context, 10; and Pauline Hopkins, 34–35; and recalibration, 18; and reconstitution, 96–104; and white magazines, 19, 26, 29
Combahee River Collective, 92, 101, 161, 162
Conditions, 94
Cooper, Anna Julia, 5, 30, 31–32, 91, 94, 96, 98, 105, 107, 162, 173
Councill, W. H., 81
countermemory, 7, 44, 86–87, 88–123, 149, 161; and narrative inversion, 145
countertestimony, 104–16
Crenshaw, Kimberlé, 38, 161, 162, 170, 173
Crisis, The, 34
critical race theory, 17, 155–56, 162, 184n3, 185n6
Cullors, Patrisse, 38, 161, 166, 169, 173

cult of white purity, 9, 10, 66–87, 130, 149
Cunningham Packnett, Brittany, 166

Darwin, Charles, 70
Davis, Angela, 161
Davis, Shantel, 167
DEI (diversity, equity, inclusion), 11
DeSantis, Ron, 41
digital media, 165–66, 170
documentation, 11, 90, 95, 96–116
double consciousness, 90
double jeopardy, 91, 182n4
Douglass, Frederick, 94, 116, 173
Du Bois, W. E. B., 11, 20–21, 34, 41, 73, 87, 178n9; and interracial marriage, 83; on role of Black magazines, 29–30; and talented tenth, 95, 98

e-carceration, 150
engaged journalism, 24
epistemic advantage, 14
epistemic closure, 63
epistemic oppression, 15–16, 66
epistemic resources, 4, 16, 18, 157
epistemology, 8
"epistemology of ignorance," 8
Evans, Iesha, 166
Ewing, Eve, 166
extra-discursive actions, 171–73

Facebook, 18
false balance, 52. *See also* leveling
Ferrell, Brittany, 166
fictive white civilization, 25, 41, 54–60, 153
Flint, Michigan, sit-down strike, 171–72
Florida Board of Education, 41
Floyd, George, 159
#FreeCeCe, 169

Garner, Eric, 45, 167
Garza, Alicia, 38, 161, 166, 169, 173
General Federation of Women's Clubs, 107
Gray, Freddie, 167
Great Replacement, 37
Greene, Marjorie Taylor, as racist, 38
Guild, Walter, 78–79

Hagar's Daughter, 34, 93, 139–44. See also Hopkins, Pauline
Hall, G. Stanley, and scientific racism, 70
Hannah-Jones, Nikole, 154, 161, 164
Harper, Frances Ellen Watkins, 30, 96, 107, 109, 121, 162
Harris, Mrs. H. L., 81, 84
Hart, Albert Bushnell, 50
hashtag activism, 166–70. See also digital media
haunting, 11, 90, 96, 116–23
Hawley, Walter, 78–79
Hegel, G. W. F., 43
High, Birdie, 110–11
Hoffman, Frederick, and scientific racism, 70
Hopkins, Pauline, 30, 37, 75, 87, 90, 96, 145, 159, 162, 173; and biographical series, 34, 94, 106–8; and *Contending Forces*, 27, 31; and fiction writing of, 139–44; and haunting, 120–21; and importance to Black press, 93; and interracial marriage, 128; and mulatta iconography, 132; and one-drop policy, 131–32; and trope of passing, 126; and Women's Department, 101–2
Hume, David, 43
Hunton, Addie Waites, 31, 33, 100, 121, 173

Incidents in the Life of a Slave Girl, 53, 117
Independent, The, 10, 22, 36, 45, 73, 148–49, 152; and Black abstraction, 60–64; and Black women, 6, 11, 25–26; circulation, 23; and cult of white purity, 67–87; and fictive white civilization, 54–60; and leveling, 48–54; and race question, 9, 64–65; and scientific racism, 11, 153; strategies used in, 41
interracial marriage, 26, 50, 52, 60, 77, 82–83, 128
interracial mixing, 25–26, 67–68, 78–79, 81–82, 87, 120
intersectionality, 15, 91, 107, 162, 170
intertextual networks, 9
inverted epistemology, 89. See also racial contract

Jackson, Ida Joyce, 145
Jacobs, Harriet, 53, 117
Jane Crow, 16
Jefferson, Thomas, 43
jeremiad, 94, 128–29
Jim Crow, 9, 19, 24, 42, 59, 97, 151
Johnson, Marissa, 166
Jones, Anna H., 99

Kansas City Colored Women's League, 99
Ku Klux Klan, 75, 177n4

Leopard's Spots, The, 72
leveling, 10, 41, 47–54
liberation historiography, 11, 89, 161
Liberator, The, 31, 94
literacy, 93
Lorde, Audre, 161
Lost Cause, 10, 23, 25; and contemporary uses, 37; in magazines, 47–48, 149; and monuments, 156

Lyles, Charleena, 167
lynching, 9, 22, 46–40, 53, 55–64; as state sanctioned terrorism, 62; stoked by white press, 71–72

Make America Great Again, and fictive past, 11, 37
Martin, Trayvon, 169
McAdoo, Maybelle, 31, 33, 101, 173
McClure's, 10, 22, 35, 45, 73, 148–49, 152; circulation, 23; and cult of white purity, 67–87; and fictive white civilization, 54–60; and leveling, 47–54; and race question, 9, 64–65; and scientific racism, 11, 153; strategies used in, 41; as ten-cent monthly, 36
McCurley, W. S., 81
McEnery, Samuel Douglas, 77, 81
McKelway, A. J., 51–53, 73
Mebane, George Allen, 78–79
media culture, 27
media frames, 24
Merritt, Emma F. G., 29, 31, 33, 145, 173; and jeremiad, 128–29
miscegenation, 76, 78
Morrison, Toni, 161
Mossell, Gertrude E. H. Bustill, 105
mother tongue, 170
muckrakers, 22, 36, 41
mulatta iconography, 132
#MuteRKelly, 169
myth of Black rape, 9, 17, 53, 67

narrative inversion, 124–25; and racial hierarchies, 128–31; as strategy, 125–27; and unfixing race, 131–45
National Association for the Advancement of Colored People, 47
National Association of Colored Women, 32, 99–100
National Emergency Committee Against Mob Violence, 47

native reporting, 24
new Jim Code, 150
new Jim Crow, 150
New Negro, 97–98
New Negro Woman, 98
Niagara Movement, 47
Northeastern Federation of Colored Women's Clubs, 100, 129

objectivity, 22–24
Of One Blood, 34
Ohio Federation of Colored Women's Clubs, 51
Omar, Ilhan, 38
omission, 44
one-drop rule, 80, 131
ontological integrity, 38
#OscarsSoWhite, 169
Outlook, The, 10, 22, 35, 45, 148–49; and Black enfranchisement, 6; and Black writers, 11; circulation, 23; and cult of white purity, 67–87; and editorials, 82–83; and fictive white civilization, 54–60; and leveling, 48–54; and race question, 9, 64–65; strategies used in, 41; and scientific racism, 153
outsider within, 13–14, 160

Page, Thomas Nelson, 37, 40, 48, 131; and cult of white purity, 71, 82, 86; and debate with Carrie Clifford, 26, 75
participatory journalism, 24
passing, 77, 121–22
perspective by incongruity, 125–27, 130
photographs, 22, 30, 105, 98; as magazine covers, 109–10, 111–15, 116
Plessy, Homer, 180n8
Plessy v. Ferguson, 9, 24, 42, 80
Poe, William Baxter, 79
politics of respectability, 96, 118–19, 123, 183n22

INDEX

profiles, 105–9
Public Enemy, 78
public safety assessment, 150–51

Queen, Hallie E., 105, 107, 109

race problem, 5, 75. *See also* race question
race question: debates over, 6, 148; in magazines, 5, 9, 19, 90, 149
race vindication, 127
racial contract, 177n2
racial profiling, 151–52, 162
radical embodied advocacy, 24
Radical Reconstruction, 42
Rankine, Claudia, 161, 165, 173
reader identity, 27–30
readership, of magazines, 27–32, 92–93
reality gap, 14, 157
recalibration/recalibrate, 8, 15, 18, 29, 157, 161
reconstitution, 11, 96–104, 110, 161
Reconstruction, 8, 44, 59, 74, 101–2, 177n4; and terrorism against Black people, 67
redemption rhetoric, 152–57
Reddit, 18
regulated latitude, 68
#RememberRenisha, 169
reparations, 163–64
resistive memory, 76, 87, 149, 154. *See also* countermemory
rhetoric of contamination, 74–80
rhetoric of shame, 128
Rice, Tamir, 45; press coverage of, 181n12
Roosevelt, Theodore, 48, 53, 65, 180n12; and cult of white purity, 71

Say Her Name, 38, 101, 145, 167, 170
Scarborough, W. S., 78
scientific racism, 11, 37, 42–43, 70–71, 150, 153

selective amnesia, 44, 47
seriality dividend, 94
1776 Commission, 155
1776 Project PAC, 155
sexual violence against Black women, 10, 17, 66, 74–75, 79, 85–86, 116–23; by police, 167
Simpson, M. Cravatt, 31, 34, 145, 173; and jeremiad, 129
1619 Project, 154–55, 164
Smith, Albreta Moore, 31, 34, 90, 104, 173; and importance to Black press, 93
Smith, Hoke, 46
Smith, William Benjamin, and cult of white purity, 71
social imaginary, 8, 16–17, 90, 147
Springfield, Illinois, 55–56
standpoint, 13–18, 157, 160, 166, 182n8
#StandWithJada, 169
Stanton, Elizabeth Cady, 94
Stewart, Maria, 17, 94, 129
Stone, Alfred Hart, and scientific racism, 71
strategic forgetting, 28, 44, 49

talented tenth, 31, 95, 98, 145. *See also* Du Bois, W. E. B.
Tayleur, Eleanor, 84
Taylor, Breonna, 167
Taylor, Susie King, 105
ten-cent monthlies, 21
Terrell, Mary Church, 7, 31, 33, 57, 83, 105, 145, 162, 173; and haunting, 119; and irony, 130; profile of, 109
Till, Emmett, 3, 4, 17, 147, 177n1
Tillman, Benjamin, 46, 61, 73, 153
Tlaib, Rashida, 38
Todd, Ruth D., 31, 34, 87, 126, 145, 173; and fiction writing of, 135–36, 143; and mulatta iconography, 132
Tometi, Opal, 38, 161, 169, 173

Trump, Donald: as racist, 38, 153; and redemption rhetoric, 154–55
Truth, Sojourner, 106, 162, 183n21
Tubman, Harriet, 106, 109, 162
Twitter (X), 8, 18, 167; Black Twitter, 169

uncivil tongue, 170

Voice of the Negro, The, 64, 149, 166; and Black women's contributions to, 11, 27, 31, 93; circulation, 32; and countertestimony, 104–17; editors of, 33, 89; and haunting, 117–23; journalistic practices of, 24; and literary context, 10; and Pauline Hopkins, 34–35; and race question, 29; and recalibration, 18; and reconstitution, 96–104; and white magazines, 6, 19, 26, 29

Walker, Alice, 161
Walling, William English, 56
Walters, Bishop Alexander, 83
Washington, Booker T., 11, 25, 41, 65, 73, 87, 95, 107
Washington, Margaret Murray, 11, 27, 130, 145
Wells, Ida B., 11, 21, 25, 27, 95, 96, 162
Wheatley, Phillis, 116
white ambivalence, 41
white anxiety, 9, 25, 37, 38, 43, 162; and cult of white purity, 68–74; and fictive white civilization, 55; over teaching history, 184n3
white caller crime, 151
whiteness, 28, 44, 59–60, 68, 128
white racial frame, 184n2
whitesplaining, 4
white terrorism, 3, 4, 11, 12, 19; 24–25, 69, 147; and Atlanta Massacre, 50; and memory, 45–47; during Reconstruction, 67; and scientific racism, 43; in Springfield, Illinois, 55–56; in Springfield, Missouri, 62; white magazine contributions to, 28–29. *See also* lynching
white violence. *See* white terrorism
white women, and racism, 84–85
willful white ignorance, 7, 11, 16–17, 40, 65, 91, 147, 158, 161; as gaslighting, 165
Williams, Fannie Barrier, 31, 33, 76–77, 80, 87, 90, 92, 107, 132, 145, 173; and club work, 101; and fiction writing of, 136–37, 143
Williams, Sylvanie Francoz, 25, 31, 34, 130, 145, 173; and haunting, 119
Wilmington, North Carolina, massacre, 46
Winona, 34
Winter, Lovick P., 85

X (formerly known as Twitter), 8, 18, 167; Black Twitter, 169

Yates, Josephine Silone, 31, 32, 33, 90, 99–100, 166, 173

ABOUT THE AUTHOR

Photo by Adam Jaenke

Mary E. Triece is a professor in the School of Communication and the director of the Women's Studies Program at The University of Akron, where she has taught since 1998. Triece's areas of research and teaching include social movement rhetorics, rhetorical theories, and feminist criticisms. Her books include *Protest and Popular Culture* (Westview Press, 2001), *On the Picket Line* (University of Illinois Press, 2007), *"Tell It Like It Is"* (University of South Carolina Press, 2013), and *Urban Renewal and Resistance* (Lexington Books, 2016), which was awarded the 2017 Diamond Anniversary Book Award from the National Communication Association. Triece's work has also appeared in *Critical Studies in Mass Communication*; *Women's Studies in Communication*; *Communication Studies*; *Western Journal of Communication*; *Journal of Communication Inquiry*; *communication + 1*; and *Rhetoric Society Quarterly*.

www.ingramcontent.com/pod-product-compliance
Lightning Source LLC
Chambersburg PA
CBHW022017220426
43663CB00007B/1115